WELL FROGGED OUT

WELL FROGGED OUT

The Fans' True Story of **France '98**

COLIN WARD

Best-selling author of *Steaming In* and
All Quiet on the Hooligan Front

MAINSTREAM
PUBLISHING

EDINBURGH AND LONDON

First published in Great Britain in 1998 by
MAINSTREAM PUBLISHING COMPANY (EDINBURGH) LTD
7 Albany Street
Edinburgh EH1 3UG

ISBN 1 85158 981 3

A catalogue record for this book is available from the British Library

Typeset in Sabon
Printed and bound in Great Britain by Butler & Tanner Ltd

Contents

Prologue

The curtain came down on arguably the biggest ever World Cup. USA '94 had been contested in the richest country on earth, the matches played in front of the largest ever aggregate of live spectators.

The final had been contested by two of the most successful countries in World Cup terms, Italy and Brazil. Brazil's triumph meant that they could now be called the greatest football nation in the world, something all football fans knew in any case, but it also meant that Americans would be able to say they saw it come about in their country. Not that it seemed to matter much to them: over 60 per cent of the American public didn't even know the World Cup was being staged. When O.J. Simpson, wanted for murder, tried to escape from the LA Police Department, all US television networks tuned in and forgot the World Cup. Soccer, as the US like to call it, was, after all, just a kick in the grass, while O.J. was a black man who'd become a sporting icon playing football – American football, a TV pantomime that bore no resemblance to real football. No contest really, in a country where 12-year-olds blast each other with Uzi sub-machine guns because it's written in the constitution that they can.

England, the nation which had invented football, and then taken its wonderful passion and given it to the rest of the world including Brazil, had not competed. For some it was heinous, for others it was retribution because England fans were the dregs of the earth. The sad fact of the matter was that England had not competed in three out of the past six World Cups. No government fell, nobody was sacked, yet everybody professed to care.

Now the political decision to give the World Cup to the US had been carried out, the World Cup could be returned to the continent which had invented and refined the game: Europe. Sure, the South Americans were skilful but they were also dirty players. The World Cup of 1998 was going to be played in France and football fans everywhere cheered loud and heartily.

Introduction

Terry Venables, England's revered football manager and shortly to coach England in the finals of the European championships (as host, so there was no qualifying), stood facing the cameras. His nervous smile and pensive manner told the whole story. Terry always looked and sounded confident, but now there was caution in his voice. Had Terry not been a successful football manager, he could have been a confidence trickster – his one-liners and quick-fire patter, combined with a snow-white smile made him everybody's favourite rogue. But today his demeanour spoke volumes of the World Cup qualifying draw that he had just witnessed.

Certainly England had got their easy games, if there *was* such a thing nowadays (every manager covered his arse by stating there are no easy games in world football) in Moldova and Georgia. But now, staring them in the face, was England's nemesis in 1974 against Poland, and then in 1978 against Italy (so nearly the champions in the US), when England were prevented from qualifying.

No red-blooded Englishman will ever forget the damage done to their masculine psyche by Poland in 1973 or forget the name Jan Tomasczewski. Plucky little Poland had come to Wembley to be fed to the slaughter while England marched on. But the English sporting press which wrote this forgot that a country which had spent its entire existence being squeezed by Russia and Germany and had fought for its survival as a country, only to be shackled by the Soviet empire in 1945, wouldn't come to Wembley to lie down and die. Poland ended the careers of Sir Alf Ramsey and Bobby Moore, England's greatest ever manager and captain, respectively.

Poland and Italy were now giant obstacles in England's mission to finish top of their group to gain automatic qualification and, as Terry Venables well knew, that had never happened in the past. Sure, there was another chance, as the political animals in FIFA had once again expanded the size of the World Cup, but sudden-death knockouts for the second place were too agonising to bear thinking about.

The prospect of this was too frightening for mere mortals and the stuttered bursts from Terry about aiming for that top slot betrayed his fear. Playing in the World Cup finals wasn't a worry, as England might simply be no good at winning old Jules Rimets' trophy on foreign soil, but they always gave a good account of themselves. Qualification, on the other hand, was a nightmare. In '74 and '78 England were second in the group and only the top teams qualified: Poland and Italy. When they changed the rules for the '82 World Cup, England did everything possible and finished third, yet qualified in the end because the other team battling it out with them were more incompetent. After the finals in '82, where England went home undefeated, Bobby Robson took charge. Here was a man who seemed to understand that qualification and competing in the finals were two different propositions, but that unless you qualified, you couldn't grace the finals. It was rather like the great actor who was continually being refused film parts because he fluffed his lines at the casting audition, so preventing his participation on the big stage.

Bobby took England to two consecutive final stages to be denied by the 'Hand of God' (a cheating bastard called Maradona) and German stoicism at penalty kicks. But England's ability to live up to the adage, 'Lions led by Donkeys', was well borne out by the fact that England's administrators allowed Bobby to leave after finishing fourth in Italia '90. In fact, they told him they would not be renewing his contract, so Bobby went on his way to more success and fame as an English coach abroad.

Then came the appointment of Graham Taylor, a man well suited to the hurly-burly of football in the English lower leagues. Armed with his statement that he saw no difference in the football being played at all levels, he had transformed Watford and taken them through all four divisions of the football league. Once in the top league he never actually *won* anything, although being a good runner-up plus a nice chap is a skill well admired by the English administrative classes – so Graham was given a chance. At stake was England's participation in the upper echelons of world football. Throughout football there is one claim: that there is a world of difference between club football and international football. This was a claim made by those with a proven track record of winning at the highest level. Graham Taylor set out to prove them wrong. The fact that he was an ignominious failure made no England fan feel good, fans who often trekked to places so inhospitable that even the locals were trying to escape. Perhaps Graham's greatest claim to fame was the fact that his stern words stopped Elton John drinking. I myself joined the thousands of other England fans and turned to drink every time his England selections took to the field: it was the only way to watch his pathetic tactical formations run ragged by a succession of foreign teams.

It all came to pass when Graham Taylor picked a centre-back to play left-back because the Norwegians had a tall winger. The players were confused, so it's no wonder the fans were. On a fateful Oslo evening England lost to Norway and the dreadful realisation hit England that they would be staying at home while Norway would be at USA '94 playing in front of full-house, 70,000 capacity stadiums. The only way that they should have been allowed to go to America was on the balsa-log raft, Kon-Tiki, with Thor Heyerdahl. England had one last chance with a make-or-break match in Holland. When fate intervened, once again, Graham Taylor lost his cool and blamed the referee and linesman. His shout of 'DO I NOT LIKE THAT' became a clarion call for nervous incompetents. The fact that Graham subsequently earned thousands in advertising campaigns said it all for a nation of professional losers. When I picked up the paper and read that we would be better off not subjecting our young footballing athletes to 90°F heat and 70 per cent humidity to satisfy the advertising needs of prime-time TV, I went out and got drunk to forget.

So USA '94 went on without England. The Irish fans enjoyed the craic (banter), the Brazilians samba-partied and the Germans ate their way around a country where culinary excess is encouraged with single meals bigger than the entire food consumption of an African peasant for a week. The Norwegians came home without winning a match.

England looked on glumly, pretending not to care, yet the fans cared more than anything. Players like Tony Adams, who had been overlooked for Italia '90, felt sick. 'One World Cup would be nice,' was his comment. Time is never on a footballer's side, however, so the slogan that there's always another chance in four years' time sticks in their throat. When the '94 final was settled on penalties after 120 minutes of stagnant football, we all had a good belly laugh. In order to satisfy TV requirements, players had been subjected to sickening heat and were so tired that they barely had the strength to kick the ball – just walking up the steps to the seats exhausted the spectators. By the time Roberto Baggio's wild penalty came back to earth we were almost patting ourselves on the back for failing to qualify, whilst at the same time cursing the people who had allowed England not to qualify by refusing to change procedures to help our players.

Now, to get to France '98, England would have to finish above Italy to be sure of qualifying or face the dire prospect of seeing the biggest show on earth played out less than 25 miles from the White Cliffs of Dover. Stuff Vera Lynn; there'll be crocodile tears over the White Cliffs if we fail this time. Yet at the time of the draw, the English donkeys had no idea who would be following 'Lucky' Terry.

The hardest task facing England since Oliver Cromwell had to wrestle with his conscience and invite Charles II to return to the throne was that of finishing above Italy. And there was nobody at the helm. Italy, a team which England hadn't beaten in over 20 years and the team which had prevented us qualifying in 1978; Italy, where football was religion, where governments fall every other month yet disaster is looked upon as being when their beloved football team (Azzurri) is beaten.

Standing in front of these leaderless, rudderless lions were the combination of Italy and Poland that made every England fan wince. Fate had to be on our side. We couldn't fail again. The prize was so great that no stone should have been left unturned to ensure success. Only a ferry journey across the straits of Dover, then a train to the venue. Only a three-hour train journey from London to Paris through the tunnel for the final. The prize of a place in the World Cup Finals starting in France in June '98 was so great that this time we had to rise to it.

1

Nervous Moments

As I drove around the Paris inner ring road, the new Stade de France loomed up in the suburbs of St Denis. With its futuristic, shiny silver metallic roof glinting in the early evening Paris sunshine, it looked like the design for a spaceship in the latest *Star Trek* movie. Seeing the half-finished roof, stationary diggers and building equipment made me realise that England's crucial match with Poland was less than one week away and the prize they were playing for was the chance to perform in the final proper, in this glorious stadium before 80,000 cheering fans. It was a prize that England needed to grasp with such a grip that the very thought of failing would be banished forever. But now, standing outside the unfinished stadium the dream seemed as far away as ever. It was late May 1997. I dreamt that in just over one year's time, I would be walking these steps to watch England in the World Cup final.

The inner ring road of Paris is a nightmare. A friend of mine once negotiated it in the rush hour. It has three lanes of traffic which, when not snarled up, have lunatic Frenchmen coming in at all points east every 150 yards. My friend, who had served two tours on the mean streets of Northern Ireland and one in war-torn Bosnia, literally shit his pants at the mad French drivers and vowed never to do it again. Now as we were stuck in yet another traffic jam, we marvelled at the the new stadium, but wondered how long the traffic jam would last when everybody poured out of it. This wasn't the St Denis of Rue fame where ladies of the night plied their trade, but the shiny suburb of commuter Paris. Not far from here, as the jets roar overhead from Orly, were the no-go estates of French Africa where police patrol with bullet-proof armour, automatic weapons and tear gas. Yes, the England fans would feel at home here.

We were off to see Bobby Robson, England's most successful manager in foreign tournaments, now working as Barcelona's football coach. As we sat in the traffic, we had plenty of time to reflect on the chances of qualifying, let alone playing in the final itself.

It had all started so brightly for the fans. England beat Moldova 3–0 in Moldova, which Italy followed up a couple of weeks later, winning 3–1. The fans saw this as an omen. We were one goal ahead of Italy. Perhaps we had delivered a psychological blow. Poland came to Wembley and it was almost like a trip to the office. The Press had decided very early on that Poland were only there to make up the numbers and that they would graciously step aside while England and Italy fought it out for the right to automatic qualification. Even then, there was the chance of solitary automatic qualification for the best runner-up slot in each of the six qualification groups.

Strange people, the English press corps. They have a collective mentality; when they speak it seems to be as one voice. It is almost as if they think collectively, like the Midwich Cuckoos, able to read each other's thoughts. Only the select few seem able to stand out and have a differing view of life and football. Usually, the day before a match England are marvellous, unbeatable, strong, resilient athletes, and the next day, if they lose, they are prosaic, predictable, second best. What a difference a day makes! At least they're consistent when describing the fans, though. We have no right to be anywhere, least of all on foreign soil watching our players, our country. If they had their way, fans would pay their money, cheer into a karaoke box transmitted to the pitch and then go home early, so the players wouldn't be distracted by such mundane things as the fans applauding.

Since Poland's momentous win in 1973, they had never won against England. Mr Nice Guy, Gary Lineker, had made his reputation against Poland. He always seemed to score against them. One warm evening in Mexico, Gary scored a beauty against Poland, went on to score two more, got his reputation and projected England forward when they were so close to going home from the 1986 World Cup as nobodies.

Poland were not the team of 1973, which Franz Beckenbauer had described as the best in the world, but while their football had long since gone into decline, they still had enough good players to frighten England. One of their best players, Juskowiak, who played for Borussia Moenchengladbach, would not be playing as he had fallen out with the manager. Nice to see the Polish stubborn streak was still alive and kicking.

On a warm September evening, with the England fans still singing and dancing to the songs of Euro '96, Poland scored first through Citko. Alan Shearer, however, nearly broke the net just before half-time, then scored the customary winner in the second half, taking up where he had left off in the European Championships, when he finished as top scorer and cemented his reputation as the best striker in Europe – a fact which made Newcastle United pay £18 million for his services. England had not played well, but had conjured a result from their memory. That is how most teams qualify to the finals. Nevertheless, it is not something the English Press like to dwell on. Everything England do must be done with the panache and style which had been declared the previous day – anything less is treason, punishable by a lousy review and a witty one liner from an incompetent sub-editor. Poland had been beaten – just.

In Italy's first home match, they scored a late goal to scrape home against Georgia, but the Press did not make the same song and dance about it, describing Italy's stifling defences home and away with such adjectives as professional and disciplined. England would shortly be travelling to the capital of Georgia, Tbilisi, a tricky place to go to, as the Italians described it, and if they rated it difficult then it must have been. One of the Georgian players was the mercurial Kinkladze, who had lit up the Manchester City midfield in a club which was so gloomy, light didn't emanate from it at all, so he must have been good.

Harry, known as 'Arry to his mates and pronounced 'Arrriee, with the extension on the end of his name, wanted France '98 more than anything else. The bungled failure of Graham Taylor's team to qualify for USA '94 had been the final straw in his rocky marriage.

'The only reason I stayed with her was because she was a stewardess with British Airways and it meant £10 flights to the US to watch England.'

With England's failure came recrimination.

'Christ, I was there in Oslo in '93 when that mis-hit shot, come cross rebound, bounced back and that Norwegian fired it in. Our players were all over the shop – didn't know whether they were coming or going. I was gutted. The trouble was that the Norwegians were so friendly and apologetic for beating us, that you couldn't get worked up enough to chin them. They couldn't believe they had beaten the mighty England.'

Harry travelled to Rotterdam for the final winner-takes-all match against Holland. Deep down the Dutch were frightened of the power and passion of English football. Harry, like many England fans, had no ticket; just a bellyful of hope. Ticketless and milling around the ground, he was picked up along with 50 others. The Dutch police said they would take them to watch the match on TV somewhere nearby. They drove them 40 miles into the countryside and threw them off the coach in the middle of nowhere. By the time they reached civilisation England had lost 2–0.

'Sure, they were unlucky,' said Harry, 'but good teams make their own luck. How did it come down to luck anyway?' England were out of the World Cup without even kicking a ball in anger in the US.

Harry came home to an earful of grief from his father-in-law about how the hooligan trash had disgraced England in Holland. All Harry had was mud on his shoes and sore feet after walking five miles back to civilisation; so he chinned him. He lived with his in-laws and this was the last straw; Harry left. His last act was to leave his wife pregnant. Harry was a crazy man when he got back. He would stare at people, get drunk and get into fights. It was out of character as Harry had a kind-looking face that lit up when he smiled, but that was what England meant to the Harrys of this world. Fun and humour often got lost in the worries about football, especially England. His demeanour was that of all fans following England – eternally cheerful with no idea of history. England good, foreigners and English Press bad. One dared to beat England, while the other wrote calumnies about him and English footballers, creating doubt where there should be harmony.

Harry was born and bred in Worthing and, like a large number of people in that area, supported a London team: QPR in his case. His logic was that it was easier to get to London than either Southampton or Portsmouth, and anyway both of those are crap and never win anything. Harry drank in a little bar called the Frog Pond, run by his mate, Barry. It was a lads' haven with football talk till 9 p.m. then girls on parade. Barry had a policy of employing girls who had passed the Barry test: '. . . if I fancy them they get the job!' One of Barry's head-turning barmaids had a friend, and that is how Harry met Sally, even if her name was Rachel.

With his marriage now over, though, Harry was on a mission to follow England right through the qualification matches and on to France. Harry had once drunk Moldovan Pils lager, but that was as close as he wanted to get to Moldova. In any case, nobody in the Frog Pond actually knew where Moldova was on the new rearranged map of Europe. It looked like a long slog for nothing. There'd be nothing to do except watch 90 minutes of football. But Georgia was a different matter. Now, in early August, he was trying to convince the rest of the lads what a great idea it would be to travel to Tbilisi.

'I'm telling you that Georgia is one hell of a place. Stalin was born there and the people really like a drink,' said Harry.

'Stalin. He was a boring communist who killed people by the million,' replied Barry.

'Look,' pleaded Harry, 'I've read it in the travel magazines. There's geezers out there whose party trick is to drink a bottle of wine in one hit. They make Geordie Alf look like a teetotaller.'

That made the lads take note, but Barry added reasoning to the argument by pointing out to Harry some home truths about travel to countries which, although not behind the Iron Curtain any longer were certainly a hard grind for England fans.

'You know what these trips are like with the FA. Long hours spent travelling, waiting at departure lounges, transfers on to a plane where the pilot comes out with an eye patch and a wooden leg; then at some regional airport you get transferred into cramped rickety coaches where the drivers smile at you showing their two remaining olive-stained broken teeth on their top lip then they drive like loonies trying to impress you, shouting "Welcome English Hooligans", then drop you in the back end of some God-forsaken car park where the FA commissar tells you it's best to sit and wait on the coach. And some bunch of English anoraks are playing football Trivial Pursuit and reading travel brochures about a city they will never see.'

Barry was in full flow now as the whole bar hung on his every word: 'When they let you near the ground you sit there for an hour before kick-off and the locals shout and sing at you in some incomprehensible gibberish. Half-time, and some idiot sells you a salmonella kebab-style sandwich which tastes like shit, then you get bricked and bottled by hostile locals. Before you know it you're sitting around an airport again for hours – you arrive back in England completely exhausted, just in time to collect a paper which proclaims to everybody you are rabble.'

'So you're not that keen on Tbilisi,' someone remarked. The bar erupted in laughter. Whilst the general consensus was Stuff It, Harry was undeterred.

He looked at the terms for the FA Travel Club, a wonderful English institution founded on the principles of maximum revenue, minimum service. With no guarantees other than the honour of having one's photo on a membership card, the cost of joining was £18. The only certainty was that you'd be treated equally alongside the dumb cattle and sheep which were also being exported from the British Isles, and that you would have to adopt the same IQ to stop you going mad amidst the absolute boredom.

Harry went to Georgia, a place once described as God's own country, but a country where you don't hear any other British voices. In 1997, they were expecting 25 UK tourists. People there often live to be over 100, but all Harry and the others on the FA excursion saw was a language that has no connection to any other they had encountered before. Place names seemed like a hieroglyphic mess; welcome was *mohrzandit* and good morning, *dila mshwidobisa*. It was frightening to the good English boys who liked nothing better than to order more lovely lager from people who spoke English, wherever they went. Get a MacDonald's? You'd have a better chance of snogging a surviving Soviet relative of the Romanovs.

But the football was brilliant as England played their socks off from the first minute. Teddy Sheringham, who scored one and made the other goal in a 2–0 win, described it as the most professional performance he had ever been involved in. Harry felt safe, even if he was tired, to be with the England Travel Club, but when he and three of his friends met some guys at half-time who not only ate the kebab but said it tasted great, before going on to state that Georgian women were some of the most beautiful they had ever seen, with olive skin and passionate brown eyes, they looked at them as though they were from another planet.

'Yeah mate, planet anorak football.'

'Did you know that Joseph Stalin killed over six million of his own people?'

'What are they on?'

And the anoraks trundled happily over to the fence to admire yet another view or look at some local culture.

'Look at that lot. They're fuckin' scary. That's the same lot who went to Albania with T-shirts written in Albanian: "English football fans are pleased to be in the Republic of Albania".'

'Shit, that *is* scary.'

'Fuckin' Albania,' stated one of them with a quiet resonance while shaking his head. The others all agreed.

As they walked away someone made a comment which got nods of approval.

'Yeah, but what's the point in having beautiful women if you can't pull them because they can't understand a thing you say?'

Harry arrived back in England, agreed with his three travelling companions not to mention the anoraks, felt exhausted and slept for 16 hours.

'What a trip,' he proclaimed to the Frog Pond whilst all the regulars smirked. When he told the story about beautiful girls they almost laughed him out. Despite his ribbing, Harry felt good and was ready for the big one against Italy at home in February.

Bobby Robson stood on the steps overlooking the magnificent Nou Camp stadium.

'Look at this, boys. What a fantastic sight.'

Bobby stood there surveying his kingdom. I had to agree it looked awe-inspiring and magnificent, even though it was empty. Bobby was 24 hours away from the biggest game of his career in Spain. Barcelona had to beat Deportivo La Corruna who were third in the table, and hope that their nearest rivals, Real Madrid, would lose if the Spanish League title were to be his to savour. Even though the pressure that this football-mad city put on its managers was almost intolerable, Bobby had time to meet and talk with us, three football fans.

It reminded me that Bobby could take pressure and was, after all, the past master of negotiating tricky World Cup qualifying tournaments. If Bobby had been in charge, I doubted whether it would have come to the sudden-death gunfight at the Katowice corral.

Bobby wanted to talk about football, but he was guarded on England's fate in Poland. He knew the pitfalls. No team of Bobby's, during his long reign, had ever won in Poland so he knew the score. Now, in the cavernous expanse of the empty Nou Camp, he talked about Wembley and how it compared unfavourably with Barcelona. Suddenly, he realised he was sounding unpatriotic. Bobby was a patriot. He loved England. Despite his terrible mauling at the hands of the English Press, Bobby had been the most successful England manager ever in foreign World Cups, so he added this rider:

'Wembley is a ground with great atmosphere. I was there a few weeks ago to see the match against Georgia. Great atmosphere, but only 60,000 people. Tomorrow in here there will be 112,000 cheering Catalans.'

Yet for all his love of Barcelona, one sensed that he'd pack it all in tomorrow for the chance to be there as England manager in Poland and beyond, if there was to be a beyond. But all football fans knew that Wembley was a carsy. It wasn't fit to host international football any longer, but Bobby couldn't say that.

Bobby was just a fan at heart, shown clearly when he started to imitate one of the Real Madrid players who had dived to get a penalty the weekend before. Wiggling his hips while giving a running commentary and throwing in the odd Spanish swear-word, he loved football as much as he loved life itself. Even though that penalty award could have cost him his job, he still laughed ironically, just as fans learn to do.

His final shot spoke volumes about his thoughts for England and Glenn Hoddle, the new England manager.

'Poland will be a night for men, for people with stout hearts, with strength and belief.'

A night for men and for footballers. A night to be English once again. I could almost picture Bobby sitting at home singing along to *Last Night at the Proms* and directing the orchestra when *Pomp and Circumstance* comes on.

'Can we do it?' I asked.

Bobby smiled that wry 'don't ask me that question' smile which meant that even if he doubted, he wouldn't say, just in case I was a journalist or any expression of doubt would put a jinx on England's chances.

'I'll be there,' I said, but Bobby didn't hear because he was already away with his thoughts. Bobby had managed some of the players who would be facing Poland, so he had an insight that we could never approach. Yet in ten days' time, when Bobby, like us, would live every kick of the match versus Poland, he wouldn't know any more than the rest of us. From his lofty position he was now just a fan and, like us, powerless to do anything except hope and cheer.

2

Despair

Italy had not been playing well. In Euro '96 they had not even reached the quarter-finals of the European championships and their new coach didn't seem to have the right tactics for his players. Then came the worst result possible for England. Italy sacked their coach and in came Cesare Maldini, father of their most accomplished defender, Paulo. His first statement was that he would return to Italy's main strength, defence: denial of space in midfield and lightning-fast counter-attacks. It was a system which England had been unable to defeat for over 20 years.

Harry sat in the bar feeling terrible. Seeing England lose at football presented him with a serious problem, upsetting his breathing and bringing him out in cold sweats. For three long nights afterwards he lay there reliving every kick and missed opportunity. The Press were slating England, and justifiably so. His mate relayed him a story which had been told to him by his brother who played for Chelsea reserves, and this had been mockingly communicated to Graeme le Saux by Roberto di Matteo who had starred for Italy at Wembley. Just before the kick-off, Cesare Maldini went into the Italian dressing-room with the England team sheet. His son Paulo, the Italian captain, snatched it from him, read it, then reread it again and again, shaking his head.

'Where's Ian Wright?' he asked. 'Is he injured? Surely this must be a mistake!' Wright wasn't injured and it wasn't a mistake. Instead of Ian Wright was it Matthew le Tissier, the Southampton player with a big box of tricks but no pace.

Paulo Maldini started to laugh. Le Tissier was a box of tricks but he didn't frighten Italian defenders. They played against his sort every week in *Serie A*, all twists and turns but lacking the pace to get the extra time needed at this level to make a telling shot where it really counted.

But Wright was a different kettle of fish from Italian defenders. Wright made Paulo shit himself. He'd played against him last season, and although Wright finished on the losing side, he'd given Paulo his most uncomfortable 90 minutes in a long time. Coming in from all the wrong angles; attacking the space behind the defenders at every opportunity; never saying die to any bouncing ball; looking at every shot as his chance to score. *Mamma mia*, Wright was so unpredictable, he had to be playing. When Paulo realised that in fact he wasn't, he started to laugh and relax. He sat back, put his feet up on the lap of another player and pretended to be smoking a cigar, saying that all his defence would be having an easy afternoon now that his greatest worry was out of the way. All the attack needed to do was score once and they could enjoy their cigar-and-armchair existence.

It had been a rather stale, negative sort of match. Neither team seemed to have the upper hand. Suddenly a ball was hoisted forward by the Italians from the back. It seemed to be in the air forever. Pearce, England's stout-hearted full-back – Mr Dependable – didn't react as fast as he should have, but little Zola, once of Parma, now at Chelsea, did. Cutting back on himself, Zola intercepted and found the angle. Campbell hesitated just for a fraction of a second, but that was all it took. In a flash, Zola fired in the shot and a nation collectively held its breath. Campbell lurched across, the ball deflected and shot past the lunging dive of the goalkeeper. The BBC used to have a commentator called David Coleman. He used to announce the first goal as if it had been some sort of evangelical certainty. His shout of 1–0 in BBC clipped tones now rang in everybody's ears; a ghostly echo of commentaries past. A nation sat stunned. England didn't come back from a 1–0 deficit against the Italians, and 70 minutes later our worst fears were confirmed as Italy gleefully danced across the turf as though they had already qualified for the tournament proper in France.

The best chance of the evening fell to Matthew le Tissier, but he headed it wide with the goalie flailing. England fans accused Glenn Hoddle of picking le Tissier because he had wanted to give him the chance that he had never had. England felt cheated and betrayed – even more so when Glenn tried to tell everybody that Matthew had been a success.

'So why did you substitute him, Glenn?'

Even though England beat Moldova 3–0 at home a few weeks later, the sense of despair had set in. Now England would have to battle to get that second slot. Unless England were the best runners up in the eight qualifying groups, they would have to be in a play-off to get to France. Perhaps the jock twit Harry had met the previous week on a day trip to Calais had been correct when he said that this was the closest he would get to France for the World Cup Final.

'Thank God for the French Army,' said Winston Churchill in 1938 when war with Germany looked inevitable. Thank God for the Polish football team, hoped Harry and the rest of England. Someone else had to beat Italy or at least take points off them if England were to have a chance. In Poland it almost became a reality as Poland pushed Italy to the limit, hit the post and gave Italy a hard time. But they still came away with a 0–0 draw. When England beat Georgia at home, the crowd sang as if it were still possible to qualify because Poland were next in Italy and there was still hope. Italy, however, swatted Poland 3–0 like an annoying insect. England's clash in Poland was looming. Once more England's fate would be inexorably entwined with that of Poland.

3

Press and Poles
Together

'We all know Poland is the game,' said Sol Campbell, the England defender. He had been blamed for the mistake at Wembley. Now Sol would get the chance which Bobby Moore never had in 1973.

The Polish FA had decided to play the match in Katowice, Silesia, a region so blighted by dirty, burning coal that its air had been declared a health hazard by the World Health Organisation. To any full-blooded Englishman, dirty air didn't matter as the only thing worth contemplating was being there. England were travelling to a place in which they had never won, to a stadium that had finished Bobby Moore and shattered the aura of invincibility that surrounded Sir Alf Ramsey. An area of tough men, of proud people. Mining communities don't breed just miners, they breed men. France '98 hung on England's ability to be something better than they were in February against Italy.

I first saw Harry in the departure lounge at Heathrow Airport as we waited for the early evening flight to Warsaw. England was sweltering in an 80°F heatwave, and Harry was talking to three England fans who were resplendent in their shorts and red England away shirts. They were providing early-evening entertainment for the travelling businessmen. I was travelling on the Lot Airlines flight to Warsaw, then on to Krakow.

Harry was amused by our three friends who lived and worked in Bermuda and had flown all the way back, via Heathrow ('You mean flights don't go to Poland from Bermuda?'), for this big match. The plane was full of Polish people travelling back to their country. Only a few years ago their faces would have been full of trepidation, but the Polish had once again proved their indomitable spirit by revitalising their economy. English people love their country, but I have never seen or heard people talk about their country the way Poles do. To my right was the compulsory ignorant English person, in this case a fat woman, who informed our Bermudan exiles that they had better be prepared to enjoy cabbage. She also hoped they'd kept their wills updated, as this was Lot Airlines and they were renowned for crashing. To those who were nervous flyers, it was disconcerting; to those who observed this fat trollop insulting the Poles, it was just pathetic. Quite why she was travelling to Poland is beyond me.

'Piss off to Calais on a booze cruise,' shouted Harry later in the flight when her loud, rude comments could be heard ten rows back to where we were.

'Well you don't think I'm here for the effing sightseeing,' would be her comment as she loaded on yet more beer to her trolley. How else do you think she got so fat?

We were looking forward to following our country. Here we were being football ambassadors, while the femme fatale curse of the *Daily Mail*-reading English embarrassed us. When the aircraft taxied down the runway on time, our fat megaphone was still at it, shouting to the Bermudan beer bellies who were happy bothering nobody: 'Prepare to crash, boys!' Her behaviour was worse than any football hooligan's drunken excesses. Thankfully the Polish people ignored her.

I first spoke to Harry on the flight when I walked to the back of the plane and he offered me one of the numerous beers he had cadged from the stewardess. It was, he smilingly informed me, a trick he had learned from his air hostess wife. Harry was travelling on his own to meet his other two pals from Worthing: Barry, mine host of the Frog Pond, and Alan. Harry was skint but Barry had decided that he needed a seasoned East European traveller and had booked him on the Warsaw flight. At one point in the flight, a young Pole approached us to ask whether we were English footballers. In our dreams we were, but the closest we would ever get would be to cheer our heroes like mad in two days' time. We would dream of being Alan Shearer in our Sunday leagues, or we'd take our children proudly along to their Saturday football leagues and tell other dads how good our little boy was, and go home as proud as punch. We could dream while we watched. Football gives you dreams which nobody can ever take away. Not even in Poland do footballers travel economy class, consuming the entire contents of the beer trolley before the biggest match in decades, but we both admired their simple philosophy. Watching the Poles on the flight, one couldn't help notice how thoughtful they seemed without appearing miserable.

When the flight landed, the Poles erupted in a spontaneous burst of cheering and clapping. I had seen this before on an internal flight in the US, but that was cheering to celebrate that the flight had landed safely. This was because they were returning to their Polish homeland. This was the passion England would be facing tomorrow evening.

Entering the terminal at Warsaw Airport, Barry and Alan (known as Tids) were waiting. Following football is all about choosing one's fellow companions: choose badly and the trip can be a nightmare. The knack is to find like-minded fellows who aren't racist or bigoted with a malevolent streak. Generally you have a couple of hours to tell whether they are dodgy, violent or good fun. I had only been with Harry for the best part of two hours, yet I instinctively knew that his descriptions of his friends augured well for a fun trip.

Barry was already performing to the crowd. Slightly balding, with the self-confidence that comes with being a successful self-made businessman, he lived his life with a permanent smile. His mate Tids, looked like a throwback to the swinging '60s with his long hair. Barry changed his cash into zlotys, a currency which only a few years ago was worthless. Now English people were queueing up to get the country's money. The man at the desk told Barry to be careful as he was now zloty rich. Barry quickly established himself as the leader and invited me to join his little team, but I was off on a flight to Krakow.

Vince, Gareth and Mark laughed at me when I pulled out a fistful of dollars at the kiosk.

'Who do you think you are: Clint Eastwood?'

'I thought that the dollar was the main currency in this country,' I replied, trying not to look embarrassed.

'That was years ago; things have moved on. When we first came here, things were a bit of a mess but now the economy is really booming. Best thing you can do is change them when you get to Krakow.'

These three were expats with a difference. They had come out here in the first wave of English firms which were investing in the country when Poland was really struggling. There was no food in the shops or beer in the bars, but they stayed to watch Poland rebuild its economy.

They were living up in Gdansk, spoke Polish, all had Polish girlfriends and really loved the place.

Vince and Gareth both had failed marriages behind them. On my travels, watching England, I meet so many fans who have failed marriages that I sometimes think following football should be cited as grounds for divorce.

Upon arrival at Krakow, they offered to share a taxi with me as we were staying in hotels next door to each other. They were in the Continental Orbis while I was 50 yards away in the Wanda Orbis. We all agreed to meet in the Continental bar then go to the casino.

It was a Thursday, yet the Polish people were gambling away quite merrily. It could have been anywhere, but the fact that we were allowed in with jeans made it different from English casinos. After a successful evening, Mark decided to check out a local night-club. The Blue Lamp club was nothing exceptional from the outside, but it was named after the colour of the light which was swinging gently in the wind. Back in England it had been scorching, yet here in Krakow it was drizzling and cold, the type that gets into your bones and sets off the rheumatism.

As we walked through the door, the light was dim, but it was basically a bar with a dancefloor. I immediately sensed an atmosphere. Standing in the corner at the far end of the bar was a group of around five to seven Polish men. As we walked towards the bar, they stared long and hard at us. I took one look then kept my eyes focused straight ahead towards the bar. Mark looked at me as if to say 'Christ, they're looking for it.'

As we approached the bar, the barman was happily serving pints to some English lads who were propped up against the bar and the worse for drink. Mark ordered a drink in Polish.

'Fuckin' Polak are you?' asked our English friends in a Bristol accent.

'No mate, we're more English than you, we're from London,' I replied.

That was my first mistake, the second was allowing Mark to order in Polish – they needed a translator for the misdeeds they were planning.

One of the lads pointed towards the Poles who were staring at us. Looking over, and now that my eyes were becoming more accustomed to the light, I noticed how big the Poles were. With their short hair and fit torsos they looked like Polish marines.

'See that lot. We're gonna have it with them any second now. They're standing there giving it the bigun like they own the place.'

'Well they do, sort of, don't they? They live here,' I pointed out.

'Yeah, but they're looking for it.'

I saw the folly of trying to hold a conversation with our friends.

'Are you with us?' one of them asked.

'Leave it out – they look awesome,' I replied, thinking that I could add some rationality to the proceedings.

I laughed thinking it was all bravado, but our entrance must have spurred the Bristol lads into action because no sooner had I moved away from the bar than a chair was hurled across the divide into the Polish lads.

I swore I saw one of the Poles smile as they charged across the gap and both sets of protagonists got stuck in.

The only punch I threw was at anybody who tried to get in my way as I went for the exit. Bursting out into the drizzle, Mark and I ran across the road and jumped into a waiting taxi.

I turned round just as something came through the front window of the club. I was halfway up the road before turning round again, and I never did see whether it was a chair or a person. In the warmth of the taxi both Mark and I laughed at the Bristol guys fighting such gorillas. In a few months' time, Andy Golota made something happen that had never happened before: he caused a riot at Madison Square Garden when he beat up Riddick Bowe, arguably the best heavyweight in the world, then got disqualified for fouling. His fans rioted; his nationality: Polish. That was what the England fans would be up against the following night.

I awoke on Friday morning and went down for breakfast. There were one or two other England fans in the breakfast room and we exchanged hellos. I sat down to a meal of cold meats and was joined by a shifty-looking character named Phil, from Stoke. He looked like he hadn't slept all night, a fact which was about to be borne out by the most incredible story.

After the introductions he started on the stories. His mates were staying here, but there was no way he could afford the cost of a room here.

'So how much did you pay?' he asked me.

'It's £69 for a room on my own.'

'Cor, you must be loaded,' he exclaimed, which caused all the other England fans in the room to look round.

'Ask me how much I paid.'

So I did. He then smiled the most exaggerated smile I have ever seen and produced a business card from his top pocket. On it was written CLAP Club.

He laughed so uproariously that it was infectious. One of the other England fans walked over and shouted.

'Oy, lads! There's a CLAP Club here in Krakow.'

That business card caused uproar in the breakfast room. One of the other England lads wanted to buy it off him for £5 to take back to England to produce at one of his stuffy suppliers.

My new friend Phil couldn't wait to tell me that he'd come out of a nightclub at around 2.30 a.m., caught a taxi to the whorehouse, then paid only £30 to stay there until 6.15 a.m. with a lovely blonde thing.

'Legs up to her armpits, mate, and half the price you paid. And I'm in here this morning eating your breakfast for nothing.'

If nothing else he was certainly a fine ambassador for England. I have often since wondered what CLAP translates to in Polish. It might mean friendly or helpful, but nobody thought long enough about that to worry. For the time being it was producing plenty of laughs.

Whatever else is in and around Katowice, the lasting monument to man's inhumanity to man and especially the Nazi inhumanity to both Poles and Jews, is Auschwitz. Some Polish people are embarrassed that so many come to a historic city like Krakow then travel to this ghoulish reminder and get so distressed that they see or talk about nothing else when they return home.

Phil and his four Stoke mates were all visiting Auschwitz on Friday morning, then going on to Katowice to see the England Under-21 match. I tagged along with them. As it was part of an organised tour from the Continental, we were to pick up an English-speaking guide upon arrival. One of the group had a guide book and I started to read it. The coach had a hole in the window above where I was sitting, the weather was freezing and the draught was giving me a stiff neck. All the England fans on the trip had come dressed for summer, so anybody with any warm clothes had their bag raided. Some of the guys had a mixed bag of colours.

As the coach pulled in to the car park, the jokes started from the back. There was no malice in them, but only English football fans would have cracked these.

'You better do something about them showers or someone will die in there.'

'Dead good this place, innit?'

'Hurry up mate, we're dying to get in here.'

A dark-haired woman got on and welcomed us to Auschwitz. She would be our guide and went through our itinerary.

We filed off not knowing what to expect. We had all read about it and seen it on the TV, yet somehow nothing could prepare us for what we were about to see. As we pulled in, I read in my guide book that the Jews and Poles had indulged in an argument as to who had the most rights to be represented. Two hours later I would find that part of it hard to believe.

We sat in the cinema and watched the film. Even walking through the gates, everybody was a little blasé as they had seen it all before. The notorious *Arbeit Macht Frei* (Work Means Freedom) inscription above the entrance gate has bred a contempt from familiarity, because nobody seems to give it a second glance. But as the tour continued, the jokes turned sour as the faces on the wall blurred into one striped pyjama. People spoke in whispers, frightened they would insult their memory by looking happy. When people did speak, it was stilted, the words 'Why' and 'How' were repeatedly heard. When we entered the room with the spectacles and hair, and then saw the children's clothes, there was a collective, sharp intake of breath.

Phil came up to me. 'I thought I was hard, but this is painful.'

I never saw anybody break down and cry because the simple fact is that it was so horrific that it is almost impossible to comprehend: everybody is in a state of numbness which shuts out emotion. It is no wonder that the people who say it never happened can always find a willing listener.

By the time we got to the punishment cells, where the Germans crammed people in to stand up and suffocate and starve to death, we were beyond shock. Everybody wanted out, but were all afraid to be seen as cissies. When we got to the cell where the Polish saint, Maximilian Kolbe, took the place of a condemned man who went on to live a full life after surviving this horror, we all looked at each other as if to say: 'See, even amid evil there is always something good.'

By the time I got to the first experimental gas chambers where they practised killing on Russian soldiers, I was totally numb with a sick feeling inside my whole body. Only recently, a Nazi war criminal had been discovered living in the leafy Surrey lanes of Dorking. Before this visit I had argued that he should be left alone since he was old and what had happened was a long time ago. As I left, I thought to myself,

'Hunt them down, hunt down every last one of them and bring them back here and hang them, just like they brought back the camp commandant, Rudolph Hess, and hanged him after the war.'

However, the horror of Auschwitz was only just unfolding. About a mile down the road, the true horror of the mass extermination becomes apparent as Birkenau looms ahead. The train line runs through an arch. It used to bring cargos of human misery; now it is just a relic but the architecture of the arch still chills the blood. Together we climbed the steps above the arch and looked out across the hundreds of chimneys which were once huts full of humans waiting to die, where skin and bone tried to hang on to life. The gas chambers may have been long gone, but the railway line retains a historical poignancy and the sheer size of the camp left me speechless. Added to this were the photos showing frightened women and children walking to their deaths.

Our Polish guide spoke in a monotone voice, almost matter-of-fact, but everybody felt something. I walked along the railway line alone. The wind chill made the temperature just above freezing. I tried to imagine the most terrible thing that had ever happened to me then realised it was nothing. Standing next to this line, I imagined the millions of people who had walked along this road. Despite being in an open space, I suddenly felt very uneasy and panicky. The Polish lady asked us if we had seen enough and if we wished to walk up to where the gas chambers stood, but nobody wanted to stay there a minute longer than necessary.

The coach dropped us at the station. The ones who had cracked the sick jokes going in looked worse than the rest of us who were just about hanging in there. For a short while we sat at Oswiecim station buffet, drinking piping-hot coffee to warm our frozen bones and saying nothing, but after sitting on the train for five minutes, struggling to understand what we had just seen, we remembered why we were in Poland in the first place – that we were football fans and our destiny was to look forward towards the evening's England Under-21 match and greater glory the following evening.

The lads went off to find a bar while I was heading off to my hotel, the Hotel Warsawa. I had booked in here because I knew it was where the England Press corps would be staying. I wanted to observe them at close quarters because if England lost, their worst excesses would be meted out to Glenn Hoddle. Glenn knew the score and had established the first team squad in a country club hotel about 20 minutes' drive from Katowice, away from the prying gaze of the Press and any other distractions.

The Hotel Warsawa is a white, modern building with a wide open lobby and black marble floor, giving it a light, airy feel. Rooms were clean and spacious at £70 per night. It had a revolving door but was too modern to feel Polish. It was more like something out of the new resorts of Torremolinos. With all the Englishmen present it could well have been but for the freezing cold weather which hit you as you walked the 20 yards from the taxi rank to the revolving front doors.

I had booked in here to observe the Press at close quarters and perhaps do a couple of interviews for my book. I had already had some conversations with Patrick Barclay and had arranged to have a drink with him on Friday evening. I also knew that the Press would not venture too far away from this hotel as there was nothing much to do in Katowice, so I would have a captive audience. I had jokingly asked for access to the press conference, but I think the Polish National Manager had more of a chance of being invited. Writers were no longer welcome around England after one had been given access at Italia '90 and had done the most savage hatchet job ever seen. I was to find out the full legacy of Pete Davies and the scars he had left over the next 48 hours.

As I checked in, I spied my first real journalist, Rob Shepherd of the *Daily Express*, a young man with a love of the dessert trolley by the looks of his paunch and double chin, a man who can only be described as cynical when you read his reports. Thirty going on seventy would be apt. He had placed his laptop on the reception counter when he informed another journalist that he was struggling to write a story about Paul Gascoigne's knee. He looked at me nervously.

I needed to know the kick-off time of the Under-21 match, but just as I was about to ask Rob my mobile went off. It was Mark, who arranged to meet me on Saturday along with Barry and the lads. I informed Mark that I had a real journalist next to me and asked Rob what time the match kicked off.

He carried on as if to ignore me, but before he could, I was in his face and didn't give him the chance.

'Any idea, Mr Famous Writer?'

'7.30,' stuttered Rob.

'Well done, Mr Shepherd.' I glanced down at his laptop.

'Written anything defamatory or scurrilous today Rob? How's Gazza?'

'Gazza's fifty-fifty.'

Fifty-fifty. What the hell is fifty-fifty and how could he know? Like all the other press, he was stuck here with a lager and a laptop and absolutely no information.

'What are the odds this time of a pressman getting a smack in the teeth in Poland, Rob?'

I looked at him with the look that people give when they know someone is bullshitting. I raised my eyebrows, but Rob hurried away before I could utter another word, pleased to have survived.

I got the impression that he would like to have said something witty, but my presence at the counter made him uneasy.

Two young guys had obviously noticed how I turned the Press man into a nervous wreck, and came over.

Andy and Dave, QPR fans from west London, had just booked into the hotel and were thinking of going to the Under-21 match. By now the lobby was a hotbed of activity with people scurrying everywhere. While watching the activity, which was like the first day of primary school with everybody standing around undecided or frantically going nowhere very quickly, we made small talk about our surroundings. The Press corps and the Under-21 team's officials were dropping kit bags here or calling out to somebody there. The female Press officer, looking very smart in her blue England two-piece business suit, was walking around with a clipboard informing journalists that they could go on an early coach or make their own way, trying to get a definite answer as to how many seats she should allocate on the coach. It was a frantic round of questions and answers. Despite the fact that many of the journalists had been here previously, they were still humming and hawing about whether they wanted to go on the coach, or even attend the match at all.

A couple of fit young men in sporty track suits came up to the counter. I didn't recognise them, but from their demeanour I assumed they were Under-21 footballers. Immediately the Press officer was telling them what they had to do. They nodded, glanced at me, I nodded to them, then they turned away. I didn't recognise them, but they thought I was going to try and talk to them. If only they knew. As far as I was concerned they were Englishmen abroad, somebody to say hello to. All that hero worship – gosh, you're a footballer – had long since passed me by. Dave saw their actions and took offence.

'Oy, you tossers, you're nobody. We don't even recognise you,' he laughed.

More footballers came into the lobby, and I didn't recognise any of them. There were some leather armchairs in the lobby, the kind you sink into forever when you sit down. Sitting in one of them and watching us intently was Ian Stott, Chairman of Oldham and a member of the England Management Committee. With his white hair and arrogant air of aloofness, he looked the part. Had he been born 100 years earlier, he could have sat around on a committee and ordered young men to run to their deaths across the shell-marked fields of northern France. Now he could satisfy himself with being a member of the committee that had incompetently allowed England to fail in World Cup qualifiers on too many occasions. We were making him nervous, (why, I don't know), but there was the fun of it. Football is a multi-million pound business, yet here were three fans standing in the same lobby as the players seen as a threat to England.

Also sitting in the chair next to Ian was the lovely Jill. I have known Jill for years and have seen her on away trips for both Arsenal and England. She is employed at the Football Association headquarters at Lancaster Gate as some sort of administrator, but if she wasn't here in an official capacity she would be here as a fan. Jill does not have a ring on her finger, but she is in love with football and married to the life of being a fan. I have never met a fan who doesn't see Jill as their surrogate sister: whatever happens, she dishes out tickets and advice with her trademark smile. Ask Jill a question and she either gives you an answer or points you in the direction of someone who might be able to provide one. In fact, she is in direct contrast to the FA hierarchy who seem to thrive on disinformation, as though they have been on training courses with MI6.

I walked over to speak to Ian but saw a man looking pensive. His dilemma was the momentous decision of whether to board a coach for the Under-21 game or share a taxi. Unable to decide, he stood talking to all and sundry. He was obviously quite popular as many journalists made comments to him.

I introduced myself and explained that I was a freelance writer. Turning, he assessed my threat without giving too much away. He was in his early 40s with hair that was starting to grey at the edges and he told me he was from the Press Association. I didn't have a clue what he meant, so I asked if that made him a proper journalist. He roared with laughter at my ignorance and this broke the ice.

'What was the press conference like today?' I asked.

'That's the problem here today. Everybody's got the right hump.

Glenn would only give one press conference, and that was yesterday. In the past, the manager has held the press conference at the journalists' hotel and given the boys an update on the Friday, but Glenn bussed us all into the middle of nowhere and gave us a series of one-liners which told us everything he felt we needed to know but actually told us nothing.'

I was intrigued. I sensed that all was not well between Glenn and the Press.

'What do the Press think of Glenn, then?'

'He's okay, in so much as he answers their questions, but he won't give much away. There is always something else. He holds back and that unnerves some of the boys because they haven't got an angle to build a story. I have never seen so many Press men at one match before either. Every paper has three journalists, some four, and today they have got nothing to write, yet are having to file stories all day because every one they file is not deemed good enough by the editors. It's raising the temperature. Some of the boys feel under too much pressure.'

I remarked on how many journalists were present. My Press Association man laughed.

'Plenty for weddings, christenings and funerals. They aren't here necessarily to praise Caesar, but to bury him. Glenn has a lot to prove, especially after the débâcle against Italy in February. He just will not bring himself to admit that he was wrong to play le Tissier. Some of the boys are sitting in the press conference muttering under their breath, "Shout it out, Glenn. I was wrong. Le Tissier was a bad move, I was wrong," but he won't do it. That sort of thing unnerves the Press boys. They like their England managers to be like them, to be indecisive, change their minds and show weakness. It would help them to warm to him because they feel that if Glenn shows weakness, they can turn the knife in him more easily. Glenn makes some of the boys tread warily.'

So Glenn made them nervous. What the Press Association man did not mention was Glenn's faith, his belief in God. A number of Press men mocked it. However, what Glenn had, I had seen in others before. Glenn was looked upon as a bit of a poseur, but that was a lie. To those who knew Glenn or knew of him, he was hard and opinionated with a self-belief which he never lost despite being misunderstood by a series of England managers and journalists when he was a player. To add to that, he discovered an inner strength and belief in God which frightened those who had no faith or morals. I remember my father-in-law telling me how he had been invited to a party of some born-again Christians and had come away impressed by their strength of purpose. In just over 24 hours, England would need that strength of purpose, yet if any doubt existed, they would not find it in Glenn. There were thousands of Englishmen travelling with the same belief in the Almighty. God was on our side – it was just a question of the interpretation and around £1 million in readies that separated Glenn from the fans.

While we were talking, another journalist approached us. Paul Hayward was the star young writer at the *Daily Telegraph* where he had recently been voted the Sports Writer of the Year. He was blond with a baby face, but did not seem imbued with the cynicism which appeared all-pervasive amongst the assembled Press. He asked about Auschwitz, as he wanted to pay a visit. I informed him that it shut at 6 p.m. but insisted that he pay a visit, especially Birkenau as it was awesome. He thanked me and asked me what I did. When I said that I was a freelance writer, here to write an objective piece about the Press scene, he lifted his eyebrows a touch as if to say: 'Interesting', then moved on.

Patrick Barclay (Paddy to those who know him), working in Poland for the *Daily Telegraph*, is one of the select band of writers who are looked upon as heavyweights. Able to command huge salaries because of their writing ability, they are also well respected by their peers. Barclay is Scottish, which often makes him better at writing about England than some of his English counterparts, since he writes without prejudice or patriotism but with a cynical Scots view of all things English. Not that he is *totally* in love with his job. He once described his best World Cup as one where England didn't qualify and all he had to write was 100 words a day which left him free to enjoy the football. Perhaps that is what makes him stand out amongst his fellow writers, that he is a man who actually writes about something he loves. The way some of them write, you couldn't even imagine them crossing the road to watch a game unless they were guaranteed a free pass for the press box. I had been involved in a series of practical jokes with Patrick over a character called Bootsy Egan. I didn't know what he looked like except that he was balding. I was looking forward to meeting him.

I moved around the lobby, asking the assembled Press where Paddy was. Terry Butcher was in the lobby along with other ex-England internationals, all of them there to do expert summing up, which is basically a gravy train for players to earn money for what is a fancy marketing ploy by TV companies to differentiate their product.

Terry was a big man who would have relished the battle which awaited England the following day. Terry had been a centre-half colossus for Bobby Robson for many years, but he too seemed nervous when I approached him to ask if he had seen Paddy Barclay.

'He was here a minute ago,' then desperately averted his gaze lest I spoke to him.

Finally, Paddy came into the foyer. He was smartly dressed with a well-cut sports blazer, designer logo rollneck and beige slacks with smart brown shiny shoes. He looked every inch the professional, unlike some of the journalists who were scruffy and unkempt.

Paddy laughed at my practical joke and agreed to meet me in the bar later. Paddy also knew I was there to cover the Press corps. Within four hours, this fact would be known by the whole hotel.

The Under-21 game was being played at the ground of GKS Katowice, whose fans were reckoned to be some of the fiercest in Poland. Crowd trouble in Poland was pretty lively. Almost every week there were some outbursts of trouble at some ground. Even Gdansk, who played in the Polish third division, had water cannons at their matches. In the match versus Italy, played in Rome, the Italian police had been shocked when the Polish fans laid into each other. Andy, Dave and I set off by taxi with some trepidation. As we alighted from the taxi on to open scrubland in front of a small ground, the taxi driver informed us that he would be waiting for us here after the match. We didn't believe him, but we tipped him up front. (The extra £5 seemed worth it, especially when we saw a gang of Polish skinheads eyeing us up.)

'Walk purposefully, lads,' said Dave. Great advice, but where to? We had no tickets, and the only ticket office we could find was surrounded by Polish skinheads. We walked past them and heard a few comments which we ignored. As we started to walk around the ground, they started to follow us. It looked dodgy, so we back-tracked past them once again with the police still in view.

We smiled at them nervously as we walked past. Nothing for it but to walk up to the ticket office and purchase a ticket.

Whenever you travel to watch England in a foreign country, there are usually some restrictions as to where and how you can buy tickets, thanks to the excesses of previous travelling England fans. I always feel good when I actually have the ticket in my hand and get to my allotted seat. Every moment before that is in constant danger of being spoiled by some over-zealous policeman who believes all he reads about England football fans. No problem in Poland – our money was good. Tonight the biggest enemy for everybody would be the cold and rain.

Coming on to the forecourt, I spotted Jill sheltering under a concrete staircase. We joined her and had a convivial conversation about Arsenal and football generally. I expected her to go into the VIP or press section. Instead she joined us as we set off for the English section, she moving to the seats near the rear of the stand while we sat near the section which separated the Polish and English fans.

Under-21 matches are strange affairs. Played by wannabe footballers in front of almost empty provincial stadiums, they often merit only two or three lines in the papers the next day. England fans attend because they are either bored with doing anything else or feel that they have to support their country. It was raining, piercingly cold and the ground looked tatty. Opposite us was a small stand where all the Polish people gathered, including our belligerent skinheads surrounded by a contingent of riot police. Behind the goals were open terraces where nobody stood. Many of the England fans had come dressed for summer, only to be cruelly caught out by the cold. A fan walked into the stadium proudly wearing his T-shirt which said. *Born in England . . . Live in England . . . Die in England.* I never cease to be amazed by the unadulterated ambition some English people show the world.

The players ran out onto the pitch which had large puddles of surface water on the opposite wing and at other points. The first thing that struck me was the fact that I didn't recognise any of the players except Emile Heskey, the muscular, black, centre-forward for Leicester. Looking at the blank faces of the other fans I realised that they didn't recognise them either. That itself told a tale: due to the large influx of foreign players and the influence of Sky in televising only Premiership football, most of these young players did not represent the well-known Premiership teams. Our best young talent were now learning their trade in the lower divisions.

By kick-off time, the riot police equalled the number of English fans. Mark recognised the young QPR player, Danny Murray, who was playing in midfield. The match became a farce when the ball kept getting stuck in the puddles. Players would run past the ball when it stopped dead in standing water then charge in to kick up the water, as though they were a Sunday pub team. Outstanding for England was the young right-back Des Hamilton, but nobody had a clue who he played for. When he received the ball, the Polish fans chanted monkey noises at him while the English cheered. While players all around him struggled on the greasy surface, Des had a speed and sureness of touch that set him apart from the rest. When I found out later that he was in Newcastle's reserves, I could hardly believe it. It seemed as if Newcastle had a bottomless pool of talent.

In the first half came two of the three main defining moments of the match. After 10 minutes, a group of about 20 fans came in. They announced their entrance theatrically.

Standing with their right arms raised, palm open, they started a chant.

God Save our Queen
God Save our Queen

Other fans stood up and joined them.

No surrender
No surrender to the IRA
Fuck the Pope
Up the UDA

The Polish fans immediately counter-chanted, so nearly 90 per cent of the England fans stood up to give a rendition of 'God Save the Queen'. Personally I feel this song is a relic of our status as subjects, not citizens, and should be consigned to the dustbin along with all inherited privilege. So I declined. I looked around and saw the undercover police. No England away match would be complete without the presence of undercovers from the police Criminal Intelligence Unit, nor a compulsory UK police press release stating that known hooligans were travelling abroad. Before the Poland match, I read a small piece in the *Daily Mail*, which reassured me that the finest police minds in England would be putting their resources to use in Poland.

It was Dave who first noticed the undercover sitting just to our left. He pretended to watch the match, but every two seconds averted his gaze furtively to look at the guys who had come in and started the chanting. He even made eye contact with his colleague who was sitting further back and moving his head as if to point out to his mate that he should keep an eye on them. It was so pathetic it was funny.

The second event took place midway through the first half. The game was drifting along with neither team showing any penetration. Suddenly there was a through ball and Heskey accelerated after it. With the speed of an Olympic sprinter he put ten yards between him and the defenders. His second touch was terrible, however, and the keeper came out, forcing Heskey to pull the ball wide while getting it under control. As Heskey drifted to the right, the goalkeeper gave himself a wry smile which said 'you've overrun it'. But in a split second the smile was replaced by open-mouthed incredulity as Heskey fired a shot with such power that the keeper never moved. From a tight angle, Heskey nearly broke the net.

It raised a cheer from the English fans in a stadium that was now so cold, that everybody was rubbing their arms against their bodies and stamping their feet while looking at their watches. Only another hour of this. At half-time, the sheer folly of the security surrounding England fans was exposed. Fans trying to get to the toilet (and in this cold that meant everybody) were told that they could only go two at a time under escort. When the first two returned after five minutes and two more were let out, someone pointed out that at the rate they were going, it would take eight hours.

'Have a word, plod,' Mark said to the undercover.

'Why me?' replied the undercover, feigning surprise.

'Half-wit to half-wit. They might listen to you.'

Our undercover looked embarrassed but two minutes later, everybody was allowed down to the concourse to go to the toilet or get something to eat. The fans who went to the toilet were met by young Polish fans who wanted to swap club badges, Chelsea and Leeds being the most sought after.

The second half was the longest 45 minutes I have ever endured. Up front for England was a young player with the worst first touch I have ever seen. In football parlance, he played a 'mare and couldn't trap a bag of cement'. Nobody knew at the time who he played for, but later we discovered his name was Lee Bradbury (he was soon to move from Portsmouth to Manchester City for £3.5 million). The lads from Stoke were busy asking the undercover police the names of all the players and generally teasing them – it was pure boredom which was only enlivened when the Polish equalised. The final defining moment was when Darren Huckerby started warming up on the touchline in front of us. People started applauding him, not because he was a good player but because we actually recognised somebody who was playing for England. Never before had the power of TV and the changes in football been more starkly demonstrated.

After the final whistle, everybody was kept in for around ten minutes then allowed to leave. Jill sat in her seat at the back along with everybody else. I was surprised that, being an FA official, she should be sitting with the fans, but I suppose she has to know her place. Fans sit with fans, Press with Press while Committee sit in the VIP section. In England one must know one's place! 'God save the Queen . . . ' As we were leaving, a huge lad from Leeds decided he'd inform me of events in Poland so far.

' . . . group of lads got chased out of bar up road with machetes. Did you hear about Geordie boys getting slashed up by Turks in Berlin? Ay, fast as fuck them Turks with the blades. It's gonna be naughty. They don't like gingers here.' Then he disappeared down the steps.

There is always a story about somebody who has been slashed or cut, and the lad telling the story is nearly always overweight. Perhaps all that eating makes them worry too much?

We were escorted to the gates by Polish paramilitary forces and then left to our own devices. Everybody's breath was visible as we breathed out into the freezing night air. We were blue with cold and the forecast for tomorrow was even colder. All three of us prayed for our Polish taxi driver and sure enough there he was, greeting us like long-lost friends.

Back at the Warsawa, we settled down in the restaurant. Within ten minutes, the Press started filing in, giving our table funny looks – but we thought nothing of it.

It was only when we went into the bar that their constant curiosity started to puzzle us. Mark returned from the toilet where he had bumped into Neil Webb, who was here working for Channel 5 as an expert summariser. Neil had enjoyed a wonderful career in football until it was cruelly cut short by injury, and even though he still looked fit enough to play, he had recently been unable to get a game for non-league Aldershot – a painful reminder of how harsh football can be and how easy it is for footballers to slip down the ladder. Mark had bumped into Neil and struck up a conversation with him. At the end of it, Neil spoke to him in confidence.

'I shouldn't really be talking to you. All the Press have got together and told each other to be careful because there is a writer here in the hotel doing a book on the World Cup and everybody has to watch what they say.'

'That's our mate, the guy who's drinking with us at the bar. The big guy with the ginger hair.'

Neil was horrified that he had consorted with the enemy and beat a hasty retreat.

Meanwhile Mark returned to the bar laughing. Around 20 minutes later a bearded, middle-aged, tubby man wearing a red jumper walked in. With a glass of red wine in his hand, he strode over to the three of us purposefully until he was about three feet from me.

'So you're the fuckin' wise guy, are you?'

Before I could say a word he started again.

'So you're the new fuckin' Pete Davies, are you? You're gonna write a fuckin' book on the World Cup, are you? Who the fuck do you think you are, eh?'

I was about to remark that his conversation would be empty without the word 'fuck', but humour wasn't on the menu. I could sense the anger, tinged with fear, in his voice.

'I'm not Pete Davies, but I am a writer.'

'Fuckin' writer? You're a fuckin' wanker.'

'I'd stick to pig's ear [cockney rhyming slang for beer] if I were you mate – the vino is rotting your brain,' I said pointing to his glass of wine and trying to add a little bit of humour to the proceedings.

'Cor blimey, this tosser thinks he's an Eastender now,' he exclaimed sarcastically, turning to the bar. 'Whereabouts in London are you from, then?'

'Leatherhead actually.'

'Leatherhead! Real fuckin' east end that is, you fuckin' fraud.'

He turned to leave, but Dave hadn't finished.

'What's your problem? First you come in here and insult us then you're so full of bile that you'll probably slag off England. Why do you do it?'

Our bearded friend was shell-shocked by this attack of logic, and he hadn't finished either, but he was in an argument where reason was against him so he hurled one final insult before turning and walking out.

'I tell you what. If you think we say terrible things about you lot, then you want to hear what the players say. They think you're shit.'

It was a nasty remark designed to hurt us. While we might have contempt for the Press, the thought of players having contempt for us after the hardships we endure to cheer them up is too big a burden to carry. I meant to ask him exactly which players he was talking about, but by the time I thought of that, I was back in England. As he stormed out another fan made a statement to the hushed bar which brought the house down.

'I don't think he rates you,' he said, pointing to me.

'I'll drink to that.'

For about ten minutes I brooded because I felt I needed to redress the balance. I discovered that the verbal attack had come from the *Times* correspondent, Joe Lovejoy, so I walked up to the table in the restaurant where his group was sitting.

As I walked towards them Alex Montgomery of the *Sunday People* turned to the others.

'Here we go,' he said, as though there were going to be a verbal attack, perhaps even a physical attack. Joe Melling, a squat, dumpy little man of the *Mail on Sunday*, sat next to Joe Lovejoy.

I ignored the comment from Alex and addressed my comments to Lovejoy.

'Do you have a problem with me? Because I found your performance in the bar a little over the top.'

'Don't talk to him. Ignore him,' snarled Melling at Lovejoy.

I looked at the dumpy man. 'Oy, chill out, let Uncle Joe here speak for himself.'

Lovejoy was taken aback because usually all the Press get is a mouthful of abuse – not unlike that which he had dished out in the bar.

'You're here to stitch us up, to do a number on us.'

'Shut up Joe. Fuckin' ignore him. You don't have to talk to him,' implored Melling.

'Why don't you rest your jaw and give Joe's brain a chance,' I said to Melling.

I turned back to Joe.

'If you've got a problem with me, then the correct way to settle it is over a conversation at the bar. Your performance in there earlier was absolutely disgraceful. Perhaps we could talk about it. I actually feel insulted that you think that I'm going to do a Davies. That man sat at your table, took your hospitality, then stabbed you in the back. If you want to chat, I'll be in the bar.'

'Don't hold your breath,' said one as I turned my back.

'Fuck off, wanker,' said another.

I turned again to look at this pathetic group.

'Only when I turn my back, eh lads?' I sighed. 'You're the worst kind of England fan. Abusive and intolerant. You should be ashamed of yourselves.'

Despite the abuse which they continued to hurl at me, I just grinned at them, giving them a little wave, the way the villain waved at Gene Hackman in *French Connection* because he knew he'd won. I walked back to the bar feeling very proud that the cream of English sports writers had been humiliated by a humble England fan using the English language, while they had resorted to Anglo-Saxon profanities because they were incapable of anything else.

Five minutes later, the relative peace and calm we were enjoying was interrupted by someone barging in between us. A man of average height in his early 50s stood there snarling at me. It was Kevin Moseley of the *Daily Express*.

'Right you wanker. Outside.'

He walked out and I followed him. He had been drinking, so there was no threat. He perched himself on one of the comfy, leather, lobby armchairs.

'Don't sit down; you're going to buy me a drink then I'm going to tell you a few things.'

'Leave it out! You're the one with an expense account,' I replied.

'Fuckin' expense account; you know nothing, wanker. Do you want to fuckin' learn or not?' he said.

I did, and the man's modus operandi intrigued me, so I went to the bar. Returning with a gin and tonic for him I sat down opposite. Before I could settle down he was across the table snarling at me, close enough for me to smell his breath, which stank as if he'd been heavily dosing himself with two-star petrol. In his open mouth I could see his gold tooth.

He started his vitriolic diatribe by asking me what I thought I was doing. My attempts to answer him were in vain. This went on for a few minutes: he'd ask a question then interrupt me when I tried to answer. It was a poor display, but one or two things he said revealed a lot to me about the life he was living.

' . . . do you think I *want* to be here?'

'Well, I would have thought so. Why else are you here?' I asked, perplexed.

'You stupid bastard. You know fuck all. Of course I don't want to be here, nor do I want to be flying out to France on Monday for Le Tournoi. I want to be at home with my family, just like you. Look at you – a fucking amateur having a laugh. We're professionals. Joe

Lovejoy is a professional and you and your mates take the piss out of him. You should kiss his feet and beg him to teach you.'

Suddenly, because I started to laugh at the thought of kissing Joe's feet as though he were some kind of guru, Kevin attempted to throw a punch. It was the punch of a drunk and it came at me at about 2 m.p.h. I caught his fist and warned him that he was too old, but not old enough to exempt him from taking a livener slap up the ribs. This incensed Kevin.

'You're not hard. I could have you done. I know hard men, real fuckin' hard nuts from the East End who would eat you for breakfast.'

Just then Roy Collins of *The People* walked up.

'Don't talk to him, Kevin. He'll turn you over.'

'He hasn't got the bottle,' said Kevin masterfully.

Then he stood up and followed Roy towards the bar. Thinking the conversation was over, I followed too.

'Sit still, I never told you to move. I'll get you a beer.'

Kevin returned with two drinks.

Having calmed down as quickly as he flared up, he then started to talk eloquently about the job he was involved in. What he said was fascinating. Every football fan thinks they can do a journalist's job and all they see is the continental trips and life of glamour, but I learned that for men like Kevin, the constant writing had long since paled into a dreary day at the office and foreign trips, a long, boring chore.

'You amateur writers think we live the life of Riley, with expense accounts and surrounded by friends, but there aren't many good people here you can rely on. Joe Lovejoy however *is* one of the good guys. Then there are older guys like me who have worked their way up from the bottom – we haven't got any qualifications or natural writing talent, so these young blokes like you come along with their fancy fuckin' degrees and threaten our existence. What we do have, though, is our contacts. I can count on players and managers out there who are my friends. They give us inside information and tips because they like us. We're not in to this career building; we're just hanging on to pay our mortgages. We're shitting our pants. Look at me, I'm getting too old for all this shit then some fucking writer – a wanker like you – comes along to tell the truth about us. The truth – don't make me laugh. The truth is boring. Ours is a hard life, doing things we don't like, writing things we don't agree with. Don't think you're above all that – if you had the bottle to sit where I sit, you'd find out. Anybody who says different is a liar. Then you lot, the fans, have a pop at us. Now stop being so fucking aggressive and get in that bar and learn something about real journalism.'

Everything he did reinforced the stereotype of the hard-working and drinking Pressman. This man was an icon, and the more he threatened, swore and spat at me, the more I liked Kevin. He was the comic book hero, an Avenger, Scoop Molesey, a writer with attitude who had the courage to stand up for his mate Joe on a one-to-one with the whipper-snapper young writer. Kevin wasn't afraid of me (at that moment it was hard to see Kevin being frightened of anything). He was a fan who happened to work in newspapers.

Kevin had blown the lid on the tensions that were eating away at the Press. Undoubtedly, Glenn Hoddle had learned from his predecessors: footballers would no longer be giving interviews to the friendly journalists – every time they wanted to say something, they would have to go through the Press liaison officer who made sure no questions overstepped the FA mark. Minders would sit there vetting the replies. The only player who was beyond this was Ian Wright who just said what he thought. Once upon a time, not that long ago, players on these foreign trips would sit on the luggage carousel alongside journalists. Now the Press and players were segregated, and their only contact was at official press conferences where players of Glenn's choice would be wheeled out to answer a series of banal questions. Alternatively, questions were answered through furtive phone calls with the players' agents, which usually involved some exchange of payment. No wonder the guys from the old school, brought up in the days when exclusive actually meant something, were worried. How could they develop a story from the tripe they were being fed?

In the old days, Press and players alike used to chew the cud over a beer, then really tie one on together after the match. After one tour of South America, the players invited the Press along and the next morning the players were staggering around, still drunk. One England player, John 'Budgie' Byrne, would often consume more 'sherbert' than the whole Press combined – *before* the match. Now the players were isolated from Press and fans alike, in a sort of military operation, only taking time to call their agents or other hangers on, while the Press had to sit around and wait for crumbs to be thrown at them. The greatest irony was that ex-footballer Trevor Brooking, with smiles and conversation for everyone, was one of the most popular guys in the Press entourage. Perhaps it is because Trevor comes from an era when footballers were not as well paid.

The Press have only themselves to blame since they consistently invented stories which were at best half-truths. Now they are paying the price and most of them are longing for the good old days. Nevertheless, when star England players earn over £1 million a year, it is no wonder that their every move is scrutinised. These guys are the new pop stars. The game has moved on, and while the Press might hanker for the good old days, deep down they know they have gone forever. As long as the hungry public demand a report of every false move – a lager-induced bruise or a dalliance with a pretty barmaid – they are on a hiding from editors, players and fans alike.

The hotel bar at the Warsawa would have been more at home in the pages of a John le Carré novel with its dark, claustrophobic atmosphere. For a hotel with over 200 rooms, the bar was disproportionately small and held around 50 people at a push. Now, on the eve of England's date with the Poles, it was packed to the gunnels. I stood there, fresh from my tongue-lashing from Kevin Moseley, with the eyes of the Press on me. I walked past Roy Collins of *The People*, who said something about me stitching people up. I turned on him.

'What is your name, Roy?'

'Why do you want to know? I'm not telling you. I've met your sort before.'

'Oh yeah, Roy, and what is my sort, then? Too honest for you, am I?' I said, mockingly.

Roy obviously thought it best to keep quiet, and looked worried. There were so many things I wanted to say to him, but just then he overheard a snippet of conversation. The silly twit was so paranoid that he didn't even see the stupidity of refusing to tell me his name when I was calling him by it.

At that point, Nigel Clarke announced to the bar that he'd resigned from *The Mirror* and was off to be number two at the *Daily Mail*. Roy raised his glass then paid another Pressman the ultimate compliment: he sent him a drink. It was comical.

I moved further down the bar to where Rob Shepherd was standing and I asked him about Gazza and what formation Glenn Hoddle would be adopting tomorrow should Gazza not be considered fit to play.

Rob, seeing something in the questions, looked at me suspiciously.

'This is hardly the time or place to be discussing tomorrow's match.'

'When is the time and place to talk football, Rob? Over breakfast tomorrow?' I asked.

'Okay,' he stammered, then he slunk away like a frightened cat.

Brian Woolnough, a gorilla of a man, from *The Sun*, stood there looking impassive. We exchanged a few words, but he seemed unsure as to whether he was allowed to talk to me. I was then approached by Steve Curry, another man in love with the dessert trolley, his belly coming into the bar at least two minutes before he did.

'We're just fans with typewriters,' Steve said. But he might have said it with some feeling because the other fans in the bar didn't get that impression at all. In the far corner, meanwhile, a gaggle of fans were having the time of their life. It only served to show the massive inequality which existed in this bar. The Press, despite their sense of purpose, seemed hopelessly barren compared to fans: they could never match our fun and esprit de corps however much they tried.

Paddy Barclay called me over and we had some small talk before he cut to the chase.

'You must understand what these chaps are operating under, and why your presence here is upsetting them so much. Look at these guys. They're intimate with each other.'

I must have given him a strange look because he laughed suddenly.

'Not that sort of intimate. They are intimate with each other in that they live off each other and discuss their marriages and share their insecurities. You are threatening that, daring to show them up as being overgrown boy scouts.'

Paddy then told me a story which went some way in explaining why they felt so threatened.

'Pete Davies got accreditation to write a book on the World Cup. No writer had ever been given the access he had. At the first press conference, he upset the pecking order of all the old hacks like Joe and Kevin by asking a smart question which interrupted the proceedings. A lot of the guys didn't like him, wouldn't have anything to do with him but one or two took pity on him when he seemed to be struggling. After all, they had expense accounts while he had a small advance to work with. Some of the senior guys with the big expense accounts took him to dinner, and invited him in to their little circle. When writers in the lower echelons saw him being accepted it seemed okay to allow him some leeway so others chipped in with favours. Jane Nottage was asked to help him since his clothes were ponging, so she got his shirts put in the laundry with the other FA laundry. It was off the record and done on an "FA don't need to know" basis. When his book, *All Played Out*, was published, he boasted of stitching up the FA by getting his laundry done. It could have cost Jane her job. He even rounded on the people who helped him: the guys who had fed him and shown him the ropes were slaughtered in print, accused, among other things, of being drunks and sleeping with prostitutes. It was a terrible blow to these guys, you know, to this intimate macho men thing. He bit the hand that fed him and betrayed the basic trust of people who had put themselves on the line to defend him. What he did caused a break in the camaraderie. When these guys argue it's as though they were husband and wife, they are that close. In fact, some of this lot love their colleagues and their typewriter more than they love their wives. That's why they're making sure they all stick together now.'

I started to understand a little more about the sports Press. In their own way they were the same as the fans. Some of them probably did care about England (not like our obsessional caring), but even still they would never gain the fans' complete respect. Were England to lose tomorrow, the 'For God's Sake' or 'In the Name of God Go' headlines would be out for Glenn Hoddle, and it would be their names under the report and headline, even if they didn't write some of the really cutting, horrible stuff. When the Press really want to do a number on someone in football they use a pseudonym so that nobody takes the flak or gets the blame, so now I always check out the name at the end of a slush story. Years earlier I had been offered a pseudonym if I wanted to write about England fans.

As Harry said of journalists: 'When Murdoch sacked the print workers he did so in the complete knowledge that the NUJ would be at their desks the next day for their 30 pieces of silver.'

My conversation with Paddy meant I was more accepted by the Press. One even bought me a drink. Joe, with his ubiquitous glass of red wine, came into the bar with Kevin and both said hello. Whilst I would never be unconditionally accepted, I was okay now I had been sorted out.

I walked past the restaurant. The tables had been laid up end to end and all the Under-21 players were sitting down. Here were young men with the world at their feet if they had the talent and dedication to grasp it. They had the chance to earn millions just for being able to kick a football. Many things have been written about young footballers, but this team must have been the best behaved I had ever encountered. They kept themselves to themselves, didn't drink, just sat at the table chatting, laughing and joking. When English players join foreign teams they are encouraged to sit down as much as possible to rest their legs, so they get used to sitting around. Any foreign agent would have been impressed by the demeanour of these players. English players have a reputation as being heavy drinkers, but there was no evidence of that here in the Warsawa hotel.

Peter Taylor gained his reputation as a footballer with a spring in his step and a smile on his face. Now that he was the England Under-21 manager he seemed to be transforming misery into an art form. Mona Lisa Taylor. For the two days I saw him in Poland he walked around with a permanent hangdog, worried look about him. After the match I heard him moaning to a journalist about the state of the pitch and how he was going to put in an official complaint. He also spent the entire time walking around in a pair of shorts. It got so bad, that on the day of the match, one England fan called after Peter: 'Oy, mate! Don't they pay you enough to afford a decent suit?' Peter didn't even look over; he just stared at the floor while moaning about something else.

4

Hojoff Boys

I staggered down to the hotel lobby at around 11 o'clock the next morning realising that I had been drinking with real men. Jill was sitting in one of the armchairs waiting to distribute match tickets to England fans. I asked her for a ticket, even though I knew she was not allowed to sell me one as I hadn't joined the FA Travel Club. (Jill, I don't want to become a member of any club that wants to have me as a member.) Seeing the state I was in, she offered me an aspirin. Sitting next to her in the lobby was Neil Webb, still giving me funny looks. At around midday, one of the Press tried the door of the bar, swore when he couldn't gain entry, then shuffled away when the England fans mockingly shouted 'Mine's a lager, drunky.'

I was off to the ground for a ticket. The match was being played in Chorzow, pronounced Hojov, but trying to explain that to the taxi driver was not helping my hangover.

'Football stadium. Goal. England, World Cup, Hojov.' The taxi driver looked at me blankly then walked across to his colleagues. I went through the routine again.

'Football stadium. Goal. England, World Cup, Hojov.'

Now I had three taxi drivers looking at me as though I'd landed from Mars. Just as I was about to give up, a spark of recognition flickered in the eyes of one of the taxi drivers and after gibbering something in Polish, he opened the door. The ground is in the suburbs of Katowice, set behind a row of tall trees. As we pulled on to the road surrounding the ground, there were already riot police in place and a large number of Polish fans milling around the ground. It was freezing cold, there were no shops, restaurants or bars in the vicinity and yet there were over a hundred Polish fans waiting. It was eight hours to kick-off. Surely they would be frozen to death by that time. My taxi driver had now become my friend and he was out of the taxi asking around to see where I could get a ticket. He sped off on a mission, chattering animatedly, insistent that I would get my ticket. He stopped outside a ticket booth, where there were around 40 or 50 Polish fans waiting. The taxi driver announced to everybody that I was English and looking for a ticket, or at least that's what it seemed, since within seconds they were all around me asking questions I didn't understand.

'Ne comprendo,' was my pathetic reply, but I just wanted to get my ticket and get the hell out of there with my new Polish guide. A man came forward who spoke English.

'I have a ticket amongst the English fans – 50 zlotys.' I didn't doubt for a minute that I'd be right in the middle of the Poles, but it didn't matter as long as I was inside the ground.

That's £10, I thought. I stuffed the 50 into his hand and jumped back into the cab.

'Take me to Cuba,' I said, feeling smug.

The taxi driver chattered away all the way back to the Warsawa. I smiled a lot and hoped that he wouldn't mention any Polish goalkeepers.

By the time I returned, the bar was open and some English fans were in there. Other English fans just sat around the lobby. On the counter was a noticeboard which stated what time the Press bus was leaving and other flight details. I also noticed that the Under-21 footballers were being taken on an organised trip to Auschwitz.

Barry, Harry and Tids had travelled down to Krakow, where Barry decided to hire a car and visit the death camps. At the car hire office, he asked the lady what Auschwitz was like.

'I have never been; my parents died there.'

Barry, oblivious to her answer, asked again. It was only when Harry gave him a dig in the ribs that he stopped. Only Barry could have done that.

The Worthing trio along with the English lads living in Poland had all decided to meet mid-afternoon in the Warsawa.

Barry and the boys arrived at Auschwitz just as the Under-21 team got there and they tagged along. Barry asked the boys about the result and who scored. In answer, they all looked towards Heskey like clever schoolboys.

'Me,' said Heskey.

'Good goal, was it?' asked Barry.

Heskey looked at his team mates, afraid to say too much in case he took some stick. When one of his team nodded, Heskey replied.

'Not bad, not bad.' Then the rest started laughing.

'It was a corker,' said one of his team mates.

The lads walked around Auschwitz with the England players. Barry got on well with them, but in his game he was used to meeting footballers. All the players were respectful and well behaved except one: Stephen Hughes, the Arsenal player, was surly, arrogant and generally acted the idiot. One or two of his mates were embarrassed by his tantrums. It seemed as if he was angered by the fact that fans were tagging along, which was rather strange. If anybody had reason to be conceited it was Emile Heskey, a goalscorer with the pace and power which will always be in demand in football, yet he was modest enough to play down his goal.

The Barry tour arrived at the Warsawa around 3 p.m., the Gdansk lads ten minutes later. Barry had a great wheeze: he wanted to go for a tour of the ground then on to a restaurant. On the way to the ground there was a big wheel. Polish riot police were stationed near it, although had anyone requested a ride in that cold they could have been sectioned under the Polish mental health act.

Once at the ground, the Polish riot police were everywhere. Barry had a theory that we were invisible as everybody seemed to ignore us. To prove his theory, he stopped the car in the middle of the main forecourt which had around 30 riot vans full of police. Then he stopped the engine and started giggling. We all sat there; four men approaching middle age, giggling like little schoolboys, humouring Barry that we were indeed invisible. As we drove around, they parted and waved cheerily at us. I couldn't help noticing their huge white riot sticks. I didn't fancy getting whacked across the head with one of them in this cold. I imagined myself shattering like an ice cube. Eventually we were stopped by a policeman. We sat there grinning at him, saying football, Bobby Moore, Glenn Hoddle. When Harry mentioned Gazza, the policeman smiled and put his finger up to his head to signify 'nutter', then sent us on our way, laughing raucously at our stupid pranks as though we were naughty schoolboys who had played a silly prank on the teacher.

We headed back to the town and drove around, looking to see what was going on. We spotted a bar surrounded by riot police. By the time we got there, all that was left on the pavement were broken bottles. The England fans were inside the bar, the riot police outside and the Polish fans were nowhere to be seen. All along the road were groups of England fans inside bars and outside, all making the same basic conversation about punch ups. Some fans obviously never tire of the bellicose attitude which brings them notoriety.

Then the chants from inside the bars could be heard:

God save the gracious queen
God save the queen.
No surrender
No surrender to the IRA

Ingerland, Ingerland, Ingerland, was sung so brutally that any feelings of gentleness or humour promptly vanished

A time to sing, a time to drink, but for now, a time to move on – a Chinese restaurant beckoned. As we entered we were greeted by two beautiful Brigitte Neilson look-alikes. They were the kind of stunning girls that made you look twice to be sure you had really seen them.

'Cor blimey,' exclaimed Harry, 'I thought they were all shot-putters.'

'What would you like to eat?' asked our blonde waitress.

'You choose,' said Barry smiling, hoping they would return the compliment. We were in no fit state to talk as we all had sore jaws where they had hit the table as we sat down and the blonde lovelies walked over. After our delicious meal we drove around the city again. Barry, who had now been nicknamed 'Dirty Den' after his sickly performance with the gorgeous waitresses, kept stopping the car near large groups of Polish skinheads to see if the riot police would come over.

'I reckon we really *are* invisible.'

It got to the stage where he almost started to believe it, and that was without a drink inside him.

'What is he on?'

All looked quiet, although the Polish riot police were taking no chances: four armoured water cannons were trundling their way along to the ground. Anybody foolish enough to start trouble and risk being sprayed with cold water in those temperatures must have escaped from the lunatic asylum.

We arrived back at the Warsawa ready to meet the English

expatriates. By now the bar was heaving. It was around three hours to kick-off, and in the corner a group of middle-aged English fans were already the worse for wear. Not for these people the songs of brutishness but the decision to drink until they dropped. By the time we left for kick-off, two of them were face down at the bar while the others never made the front door. Our little group of Barry the chancer, Harry the plumber, Tids the retired Bee Gee and the English expatriates settled into the bar. We set the stools across the bar and declared it a Press-free zone to the assembled Pressmen who were there. As we drank and talked about football, Rob Shepherd came in. I had told the lads that he had been composing stories about Gazza for two days. There was some doubt about England's most charismatic player after he had been injured in an inconsequential friendly at Wembley against South Africa the previous Saturday. Because of his marital, drinking and general social problems, the Press were always harping on about Gazza's fitness to represent England, but as Rob went to leave the bar Harry had this to say.

'Oy, Rob – if Gazza is fit, he plays. If Gazza's half fit, he starts. If Gazza has a broken leg and raging syphilis then we imply that Gazza will have some part to play in the game. Because, Mr Newsman, he is the best we have and other players are frightened of him. See? I could have done your job this week. Come to think of it, if you'd written that you could have saved yourself a lot of heartache and joined us in the Chinese restaurant with the Polish lovelies.' Harry then made a silly face and Rob walked out. All through the afternoon three Pressmen stood at the bar. Every so often, they turned around and looked at our little group and when we caught their eye we raised our bottles to them.

In the meantime, Mark kept us entertained with stories about Polish crowd trouble.

'These Poles think they're English hooligans and are living in a '70s time warp. If England get in front here tonight, they'll all start fighting each other. There are the Warsaw boys and the Gdansk lads who really go for it. Then you have the Chorzow gang who will want to put on a show as it's on their patch, and the GKS who are reckoned to be the nastiest.'

It was fascinating stuff. He went on to mention the riot police who love nothing better than belting everybody. Mind you, so would I if I had been standing around for eight hours, as some of those guys had.

By now, more and more people were arriving and everybody was spilling out into the lobby area. It was pure chaos, like a Laurel and Hardy film. The England fans were laughing and joking, full of hope and beer while the Press looked sombre and studious. It was an interesting contrast. Trevor Brooking came into the lobby with a word for everybody. The only way to describe it was that it was like a Hollywood première where the fans and stars mingled together, but without the hero worship. Many of the fans were in their late 20s and 30s and veterans of many foreign matches, so ex-footballers and young Under-21 players held no awe for them. No hero worship here, lads. You've got your job to do and we've got ours. Ours is to cheer, inspire and get back to work the following week to save up for the next trip. The man who said that top-level sport is 90 per cent inspiration, 10 per cent perspiration could well have been talking about us lot. When England players have been under the cosh for the first ten minutes, they only have to look behind the goal to feel the power again, because we will not flag, whatever the odds.

With one last toast of pure Polish vodka, one last shout of 'Prost', and one last shout of 'Super Alan Shearer' into the cold early evening, we left the hotel about 40 minutes before kick-off and parked near the ground. On the way to the ground, there was a huge mob of riot police near the big wheel in the amusement park. Nobody was riding it. We parked on the verge and agreed to meet in a Krakow disco sometime later as Barry, Harry and Tids would be kept in after the match.

As we approached the ground, some Warsaw skinheads and some local Hojoff lads met and started fighting. It was not a vicious fight – just lads being lads and posturing while they punched. The Polish riot police had their big white sticks and just whacked everything that moved. Whether the parties involved were guilty or innocent was immaterial; they were all subject to the same thrashing. Afterwards the police walked back to their positions and took up their statuesque mode with blank expressions, as though it were another day at the office.

Not far behind was a group of England fans shouting and chanting, fuelled by their belief in their own invincibility. When they saw the fight and its consequences they looked frightened, as well they might. One Polish fan picked himself up, shouted 'English' to his mates and they all surrounded them. The English fans were petrified, but all the Polish fans wanted to do was get their photo taken. It was like a Christmas pantomime scene. The English fans scurried away after the photo shoot lest the Poles decided to go from pictures to punching. As we entered the ground we were all searched, and I headed for my seat while my expatriate friends headed for theirs. My hunch that I would be among the Polish supporters was borne out. I had a theory that if I sat in my seat and said nothing I would be okay, but ten seconds after I sat down my Polish friend next to me started chatting. I tried to do my best Mr Bean act and smile ridiculously, but this boy was no fool. Within 20 seconds he had announced that an England supporter was in their midst, gesturing to me to stand up and take a bow. I hoped that the natives would not get too restless and that after that night I would be able to father some more children.

The atmosphere in the stadium was boisterous and noisy even though the stadium was only about half full. The stadium was a cavernous bowl without any roofing to make the noise stay in. Large banks of terracing were left empty as the fans were all in the main section which ran the length of the pitch. The England fans were to my left, behind the goal. Opposite was the largest Press area I have ever seen at any football match. With only five minutes to go before kick-off, the noise started.

POLSKA POLSKA POLSKA. This wasn't the brutal chant which I had heard earlier from the England fans, but rather the sound of passion from a people who were expressing their love. It was rhythmic and powerful enough to warm the bones of the Poles. When the players emerged, the shouts intermingled with crimson flares which were going off all around. As kick-off finally came, all around me were standing and the POLSKA cheers were frenzied, but the start of the match was being played in a reddish brown smoke screen due to the cold air which stopped the smoke rising away. It became comical. All it needed was for a troupe of dancing girls to dance on and it could have been the Katowice Palladium. From my vantage point, I could barely pick out the players.

For the first couple of minutes, every kick and tackle by the Poles was cheered wildly as the Poles pushed forward. My heart is always in my mouth when watching football abroad. To concede now means a mountain to climb later. Five minutes into the match, the Polish got a corner. The Poles rose from their seats in anticipation, their hearts swelling, ready to explode if it went in. Suddenly England broke through: it was Robert Lee, with the lightning speed of the American general in another continent over a hundred years previously; a pass, and Ince carried the ball forward before releasing a stunning crossfield pass. Running on to it at an angle directly in front of me was Alan

Shearer. Like a cheetah catching a gazelle, he homed in then struck the ball. All my thoughts of keeping a low profile were forgotten and I was out of my seat.

It was then that I shouted as the ball left his boot and just for one single second, time stood still. In the still photographs, people's faces behind the goal are captured in their moment of realisation of the magic moment. *Super – Super Al – Super Alan Shearer!*

I forgot where I was and leapt out of my seat, my fists punching the air as though nobody else existed. They could beat me, but nobody could stop me cheering for that one moment. It isn't bravado – it's just something that takes over in the moment like a form of madness and passion rolled into one. I stood and shouted myself hoarse just like every other Englishman in the ground. The Polish fans and players now had their mountain to climb but try as they might, they could not. Just before half-time it should have been all over. First the defender clawed Shearer to the ground. Penalty, I screamed. The second time the defender clawed Shearer to the ground like an all-in wrestler, the referee heard me. Up stepped Super Al, but the Shearer penalty hit the post and stayed out.

In the second half, England played a masterful game of controlled football. Gazza had long since departed on a stretcher after another brutal challenge. His replacement, Batty, who looks like an England fan who has been on a pre-match bender, tackled everything that moved. Along from me in the next Polish section were the Sheffield Wednesday band – a group of fans who have taken upon themselves the task of following England with their assorted instruments and drum up support to a musical accompaniment. Their favourite tirade is to play the theme music to *The Great Escape*. While they tried it in the second half, they were too far away from the England fans to be noticed.

When it became obvious that Poland were going to have a blank day the fighting started. It was at the far end from me, but even from a distance of 60 yards it looked terrifying. One fan, wielding the martial arts weapon of a rice flail, led the charge into the next section. No police intervened as they were all watching the England fans. For a full ten minutes, the battle raged, while the Sheffield Wednesday band struck up another tune, oblivious to the violence going on in the next section. I dreaded the Poles turning their thoughts to the English in the stand. Then the Hojoff lads walked down the front, climbed up the metal fencing, let off crimson flares and chanted their defiance at all rival supporters. Fairly soon, this macho display was being repeated all around the ground as the protagonists beat their chests like gorillas in Africa. To a lone Englishman in amongst the Hojoff boys, it was pretty alarming. I tried to concentrate on the match as more scuffles broke out.

With five minutes to go, there was an incident of the kind that has football managers' careers hanging in the balance. Southgate missed a crossed ball. The Polish player didn't anticipate the ball coming through and the chance was lost with the empty net gaping. Almost immediately England shot up the other end and scored through Sheringham, making it 2–0. The Poles continued to stream towards the exits as the final whistle went.

Standing at the back of a football stadium can be the loneliest place in the world, even when surrounded by 30,000 other football fans. Perched on the top of the steps, I had to get back to my friends without breaking the age-old cliché of being seen to be lost. Setting off to find them, I wondered if this time my luck would run out, if this time I'd made the worst mistake of my life in not sticking to the other England fans. But no. I spotted my friends and we strode purposefully back to the car, and as we drove away, the massed gangs of Polish skinheads gathered for their little soirée.

Back we sped to the Krakow Continental with the heater on full blast. Now, as conquering heroes, the cold was forgotten. In the small bar of the Continental, groups of England fans were gathering. Many of them had hired taxis for the day and one group were treating the taxi driver to champagne. Sitting at the bar was a stunning example of Polish hospitality: Mark explained to me that she was a house prostitute, and that the hotel knew her and allowed her to ply her trade in the bar. England fans, who knew no better, made small talk and when she reciprocated they thought that they were impressing her with their charm. Seeing her with a tight-fitting, one-piece black-and-white-striped dress on, which showed off her shapely curves, most fans would like to have impressed her. Quietly in the background, the in-house music had been drifting out across the bar when suddenly, opening chords familiar to everybody pierced the smoky electric atmosphere. It was an anthem, created for us by the sound of Oasis, 1997.

As the first words were picked up, people got out of their chairs and started singing along.

And maybe Alan Shearer's gonna save us. Cos after all he was the

Wonderwall. All around, Poles were giving us affectionate nods of approval. Oasis were the sound of England. Englishmen were having the time of their lives and singing in harmony to celebrate. Good-time songs came over the stereo. 'Things could only get better'. A few days earlier, Labour had sung along to this tune to celebrate the end of Tory rule. That night I doubted England *could* get any better, but already my thoughts were drifting ahead to Rome in October.

Barry looked the part in the throbbing disco with his designer shirt. Harry was eulogising about Alan Shearer to a young Polish lady who didn't understand a word he was saying. The fact that the music was garbage didn't prevent everybody from enjoying themselves. By the time I got back to the hotel sunrise was nearly upon me. I booked a taxi back to the airport then fell asleep in a lobby chair.

My taxi driver shook me from my slumber, barking 'Taxi aerporto,' and after I had cleared my room, which I had wasted £60 on, he drove me to the airport. Booking an 8.30 a.m. flight the day after a match always seems a good idea at the time. When we arrived at the airport, the taxi driver told me that the fare was double the 40 zlotys it showed on the meter. Nice to see that Polish taxi drivers are alive to the main chance. I thrust my last 55 zlotys into his hand and got out of the taxi. The driver jumped out and ranted as only taxi drivers do when their passengers decline the rip-off. I thrust my jaw forward.

'Take it out of that,' I said pointing to my jaw. The Polish cultural attaché sped off shouting Polish obscenities.

In the departure lounge, my Stoke-on-Trent friend Pat arrived singing the praises of Polish women. One of his mates summed it all up: 'Best trip I've ever been on, and I've been on a few.'

Also in the departure lounge were Joe Melling and Alex Montgomery who were flying back economy class. I asked them what Glenn Hoddle said at the press conference. Joe was forced to be a little more civil now that he was sitting amongst 20 laughing England fans.

'We don't go to that: someone else does.' Of course, I should have known. They just write the match report. One of the other journalists writes a report on the after-match conference while another writes about the repercussions and another looks at every other angle.

Barry and Harry, who were due to travel back on Monday afternoon, were sharing a room at a large hotel in Warsaw. In the lifts were a number of calling cards of prostitutes with their pictures and telephone numbers. Harry got back to his room and decided to celebrate with some female company. Within two minutes the bang on the door was loud enough to make him jump. As Harry opened the door, a larger blonde woman bounced in taking Harry by surprise.

'My name is Olga,' she said, as she proceeded to lay out her charges by the hour.

'Sounds reasonable to me,' said Harry.

'Are you English?' asked Olga.

'And proud,' said Harry.

With that, Olga, who had started to undress, pulled her top back on.

'I am Ukrainian. I love to come to England with you and have your children. I make you good wife, cook you lots of meals and bear you good children. Ukrainian women very strong and hardworking.' And she whacked the flat of her hand on her strong sturdy hips. Harry looked at her in shock.

'Many good children.'

'No, I just want some naughty sex,' protested Harry.

'No, I cannot love with you until I have cooked you a meal to show you how good I will be for you as a wife.'

Harry bundled her out of the door while she was still telling him what a wonderful wife she would make for him. Her last desperate shout as he slammed the door on her was,

'English men are gentlemen, make good husbands, not like Ukrainians.'

At Warsaw airport, the doors to the airport swung open and a noisy group of England fans bearing cuts and bruises from a confrontation with the Gdansk boys burst through the door. *We're coming home, we're coming home, England's coming home*, and to the perplexed Poles they chanted, 'We took a licking but keep on ticking'.

On the plane from Krakow I was allocated a seat next to a charming, effervescent Polish lady. Although she was around 35, she had a clear, fresh complexion with ice-blue eyes. She was an interior designer who was making a fortune in England. I regaled her with stories about England, while she told me about interior design. By chance, sitting behind me were Alex and Joe, the economy journalists. I got the feeling they were earwigging my conversation so I threw in a story about the unscrupulous English Press. What really brought a smile to her face was when I told her that the two men behind me were famous for indulging in the Polish hotel bar hospitality, and as I winked at her, I flashed the card that Pat had given me with a picture of a shapely, half-dressed lady under the name Salon Masazu. The card could hardly have left anybody in any doubt as to the sort of club in question. I added that the two Pressmen behind had given me it at the airport and recommended I visit it. She turned around and looked at them smiling, as people do when they perceive others have done something risqué.

'They are very naughty boys,' I said in my best Kenneth Williams voice, which made her roar.

When she offered me her business card I turned round and asked Joe and Alex if it was all right to offer her Salon Masazu's calling card. Joe and Alex never said a word, but looked at me with disgust – without the rest of their journalist colleagues present now they didn't dare hurl any abusive language at me. As we disembarked I bade my Polish lady friend farewell and turned to Joe and Alex.

'It's like the movies, isn't it? The good guys always get the girls,' and I strode purposefully into the terminal where my wife and family were waiting.

5

Countdown to Truth

The victory in Poland brought a change in the general mood. England had come to Poland and played with a verve and self-belief which many had not thought possible. On Monday England flew out to France for Le Tournoi – a four-team tournament including France, Italy and Brazil. Now the meeting with Italy in just over a week's time would take on a new significance. Glenn Hoddle started to talk about beating Italy in Rome's Olympic stadium, something that would have got someone laughed out or committed to the loony bin, had it been mentioned before the match in Poland.

England met Italy in Le Tournoi and played them off the park. The worries of Paulo Maldini in February when he was shitting himself about playing against Wright came true as Wrighty covered every inch of the pitch and scored an impressive goal, striking the ball on the rise from a superb long ball from Paul Scholes. Suddenly the siege mentality was lifted as players talked amicably with travelling England fans and journalists alike. Glenn Hoddle started to warm to his job as England went on to win the trophy. The psychological blow to Italy was a great one. Playing a friendly in France would not be the furnace that the Stadio Olympico would be in October but England played with a one-touch sureness of foot that made Italy's players look pedestrian. They began to believe they had the armoury to win big matches and beat the likes of Italy with some style and panache. Even the French Press heaped praise on England.

L'équipe chic, ces Anglais. Being called chic by the French was praise of the highest order.

In August, with the new season only two weeks away and the match against Italy in ten weeks' time, Shearer went for a ball in an inconsequential pre-season friendly. It didn't look serious, but it wasn't until his team mates frantically called for the stretcher that everybody feared the worst. The next day the whole country realised the enormity of the injury. England would be without the most feared striker in Europe. The gravity of the situation was not lost on Harry who smashed his wrench into a copper tank when he heard the news.

Every England fan was focused on the match in Rome, but first they would have to contend with the Wembley match against group whipping boys, Moldova. On the same day, Italy would be travelling to Georgia. Should Italy slip up, the stakes would be even higher in Rome.

Barry, Harry, Tids and Barry's partner, Motty decided to travel in style. They hired a stretch limo complete with full bar to travel the 50 miles to Wembley. As they approached the ground, they got caught up in the early evening rush of traffic that always surrounds Wembley for midweek matches. While they were at a standstill, people peered in through the dark glass windows, as the lads inside drank like film stars. Eventually someone opened one of the back doors.

'Who's in there?' asked a northern voice.

Barry, with his balding head, looks like Grant Mitchell from Eastenders. One of the lads said: 'It's Grant Mitchell,' from the inside of the car.

'Shut it,' said Barry, in inimitable style.

The fans outside were really impressed and the word travelled the length of the street.

As the limo pulled up outside the pub, the drinkers waiting outside watched to see who would emerge. When the lads tumbled out, the words 'Who are they?' echoed all across the forecourt.

Motty pushed Harry forward. 'Step aside lads; this man has just won the Lottery.'

The crowd parted like the Red Sea and Harry walked into the pub. By the time he got to the bar, the whole pub stood looking at him awaiting their free drink. Motty moved forward.

'Sorry, lads. We can't let our mate buy the whole pub a drink now that he's a multi-millionaire. It's the least we can do for him.'

On the previous Saturday, Lady Diana had been buried while the nation stopped. The match in Rome had paled into insignificance as the nation stopped to mourn, but afterwards, the crowd sang *God Save the Queen* with a fervour unsurpassed in living memory – the crowd reacted as only football fans can, and cheered.

Just before kick-off, the game took on a new meaning as news of an Italian draw from Georgia drifted through: people who had lit candles in remembrance of Diana suddenly realised that life would go on with a new hope regarding thoughts of Rome.

At the end of an evening which saw Gazza back at his best, showing off his full repertoire of tricks and mazy dribbles, culminating with his scoring a goal in a 4–0 win, England sat at the top of the group looking down on Italy. A year on from the start of the tournament England stood one match away from achieving their goal. Now the calculators could be thrown away. If England drew in Rome they would qualify as group winners. If we lost, it would come to play-offs. The war of nerves started in the press conference with the first question. Glenn spoke for the first time about the self-belief that would be necessary in Rome.

Steve Hickmott (Hickey to those who knew him really well) sat in his air-conditioned bar in southern Thailand. Hickey was going back to the Eternal City, to the country in which he'd been maligned and libelled by the English establishment, and taken a licking by the Italian police in the last World Cup England had competed in. Hickey, a man who'd been called an Evil Thug by the *Daily Mail*; a man who had been told by the trial judge that he had seriously considered giving him a life sentence – the same judiciary which only a few weeks previously had freed a brutal violent rapist because the girl had dared to dress provocatively.

Now Hickey could contemplate flying to Rome and staying in the best hotel at the expense of the British taxpayer because he was richer to the tune of £200K, thanks to modern electronic analysis of the police evidence which had proved it was all a fabrication and led to his being compensated him accordingly. Hickey would be joining the many other football fans who had come a long way since the dark pre-Heysel and Hillsborough days.

6

Lions and Christians

Odd things happen when a match of momentous consequence comes along. This was a match which every man, woman and child started talking about, and not just the football fans who'd marked it down on their calendar the day the draw was made, those who, even before the venue and date were set, were preparing to go to Italy. In the heads of England fans it was unnecessary to tell anybody that you were going to Rome because it was already tacitly understood – the same way people say Friday is lads' night down the pub or Saturday is rave music night. No, this would be an event which would attract people who had never been to a match before, especially as many of these new spectators had come into the game over the past couple of seasons and had not been around football when England last played in a World Cup.

On the Tuesday before the match, the English police put out their usual Press release, but this time they really put the cat among the pigeons. Under the banner headline, '700 Hooligans Heading For Rome' they talked about how the most feared hooligans would be descending on Rome. Not since Rome burned while Nero fiddled would such a fearsome army be invading. It was an ill-advised ploy which seemed to be designed to give the British police some jurisdiction outwith these shores. As a strategy it backfired because the Italian police suddenly started talking tough when the words were printed verbatim in the Roman and national Italian dailies. The Italian police were on the TV almost immediately saying that England football fans would certainly be welcome, but that they would come down hard on anybody who broke the law. To ensure everybody enjoyed themselves, they would find it necessary to remove people's belts upon entering the stadium. David Mellor, ex-politician and head of the government-appointed task force, saw the writing on the wall and sought assurances that football fans would be treated as human beings. He got his assurances, but it seemed to me to be the same assurances Chamberlain got from Hitler: a verbal assurance not worth the paper it wasn't written on.

One evening, Carl Gallagher informed me, very matter-of-factly, that he was going to Rome. He did that once before many years previously when he told me he was going to Poland. Laughing, I informed him that I, too, was going to Poland. In hindsight, the joke was a bad idea. It wasn't until he turned up on my doorstep with £300 for his flight and hotel in brand new £20 notes that I suddenly realised he was serious. But now Carl was getting the nods in the pub because everybody knew he was serious.

Carl lived his life with a permanent smile on his face even if he was yet another hard pressed Chelsea fan. He was barely old enough to comprehend Chelsea's previous Cup Final win in 1970. He had enjoyed the 1997 FA Cup win against Middlesbrough so much that his feelings about the two Italians playing for Chelsea, who would be competing against England, made you suspicious that he might not be fully committed. It was a sentiment expressed by Tony Banks, the New Labour Sports Minister, who stupidly stated that if Zola scored against England he would feel like jumping up and celebrating. It was a ridiculous, thoughtless remark which won him no friends. Tony had already been booed before the Moldova game when he was quoted as saying that he didn't think England could win the World Cup. But club and country are totally different matters. While Roberto di Matteo would not be playing for Italy, having earned himself a suspension in the previous match, the little, darting, pocket-battleship of Zola would be out there. It didn't matter for any England fan which club the Italians played for, as for the 90 minutes in Rome they were fair game to be hoofed ten feet in the air.

The build-up to the match was certainly tense. All Glenn Hoddle talked about was self-belief: 'Any English player who goes out to this match with belief in himself can win.' It would be a night for those players who believed, even more so than in Poland. Gazza believed in himself; he had played for Lazio and had been in the Stadio Olympico in many electrifying matches. He feared nothing. As ever, the old clichés about Christians and lions came to the fore.

The words of the Italian Pressman before the February match against England came back to me: ' . . . the English seem to like celebrating before, to get their joy and happiness in early in case the match does not go as well as they thought – at least then they have got something before they have lost.'

I look at the way some England fans drink before the matches and wonder if perhaps it is an inbuilt thing in the English psyche which prevents us from winning anything.

The Italians had put the game on in Rome. Nobody in the history of World Cups had gone into the steaming cauldron of the Stadio Olympico and come away victorious. In Fortress Rome, foreign football teams were Christian fodder for Lions; Italy played 15 and won 15, but to forget that England were lions themselves would be Italian folly. England now started to believe they would win there, even if history was against us. Before the shock victory in Le Tournoi, England had been the slapstick partner to Italy's winner. Now, especially after Manchester United had comprehensively beaten Juventus only ten days previously, England held the upper hand psychologically.

On a warm October afternoon (in Rome the temperature was a balmy 75°F), Carl and I sat in the departure lounge at London Gatwick with no other travelling England fans. Carl and I had decided to travel via Florence. Harry, Barry and the Worthing Mafia were going via Pisa.

'Bollocks to that country . . . I'm gonna give that tower the push it deserves to tip it over,' said Harry in his inimitable style.

We were all booked in the Hotel Elite, as travelling businessmen. It reminded me of a story I once read about the mercenary Mad Mike Hoare who, deciding to stage a military coup in Africa, had booked his mercenaries on the plane as a rugby team called the Foam Blowers.

There had been so many scare stories going around in the Press about deportations and refusal of entry at ports and airports, that the biggest worry was going to be getting a drink on match day and the previous evening. After all, we are talking about a country that designated alcohol-free areas 48 hours before England matches during Italia '90. It was only relevant to those with English accents, mind you.

Carl looked like a football fan with his trendy dress sense defying his expanding waistline and advancing years. Deep down, every fan from 30 to 70 was about to be 18 years old once again. It happens to every football fan. I've never met one yet who doesn't dance a jig or chant the odd 'England' under his breath once the wife or girlfriend has dropped them off with a 'be careful' warning at the airport.

'Be careful? I was born careful, darling.' Then as she drives away he says, 'Careful. Order me up a lager, we're on tour.'

Perhaps Mad Mike and his merry men thought they were going to watch England play football after all. Watching England is like a military operation what with all the undercover police at this end and the rows of armed soldiers at the other. I think Mad Mike and his merry mercenaries got only a slightly worse reception when they were rumbled in Africa than England fans often do. With the Italians fired up, we'd need a few Mad Mikes.

The pretty lady at the check-in desk looked up at Carl and his beaming smile.

'Where would you like to sit?'

'Nearest seat to the bar, because I'm being careful,' replied Carl. The gentle Florentine tourists of advancing age looked at us as though we were from another planet while we smiled at them because we were the chosen ones – with the best seats in the house for the biggest match in a decade, we had the chance of being a part of history while they would only look at history from the freshly delivered pages of their *Daily Mail*.

Perched at the back of the plane, the Italian steward latched on to us straight away. Never a nation to understate a game of football, the steward described it as the match of the century, saying it was something the whole country had been talking about non-stop for weeks. Vialli, the other Italian playing for Chelsea, had predicted that England would win in Rome. It made Carl feel good, but despite the excitement I could not get the same feeling of superiority which seemed to be affecting England. The Italians felt a new mood amongst the England players, but the Italian coach, Cesare Maldini, betrayed a smug sense of superiority with his words that the English players would revert to type when the going got tough. While the Italians would refuse to retreat ten yards at free kicks, hold and obstruct at every opportunity and roll around as though they'd been hit by a sniper when tackled, the English would play honestly, kick the ball hard and long and expend energy chasing every lost cause. But they hadn't reckoned on Hoddle, now as much a psychologist as a coach, who hammered the point about self-belief.

Revenge, say the Italians, is a dish best served cold. I had the feeling we'd be serving cold fare in Rome. Last time we played in Rome in

1975 the crowd had intimidated England and the referee, but now there would be 12,000 present whose belief in England and its Englishness was supreme. Added to this was the fact that Hoddle had at last admitted that he was wrong to have played Le Tissier in the first match.

The steward's final act of kindness as we disembarked was to recommend a family restaurant run by two fat brothers.

'The food is so good that you go in slim but come out fat.' The next day, the Worthing Mafia tried it out; they went in slim and came out sharpish – they did a runner without paying.

We emerged from the plane into warm Italian sunshine. Florence railway station is like many on the Continent with its high ceilings, open concourses of people seemingly going nowhere with numerous food and drink trolleys, and salespeople selling everything from chocolate to warm lager. It gave a gentle ambivalence to the milling people, but this being Italy, the ticket office was on strike. (It certainly makes the Eurostar journey to Rome cheap if you can't buy a ticket.)

The early evening temperature in Rome was 75°F. The weather was forecast to be warm the following evening. It would be hot, of that there was no doubt. The morose Italian taxi driver dropped us outside our hotel.

'Tomorrow, you'll get a chance to be *really* miserable,' said Carl, as he paid him.

As we got out we heard the distinctive buzz of small engined bikes and spotted our first gaggle of moped riders. As we walked into the marble-floored hallway there was a commotion going on and a small Italian man was at the centre of it, waving his arms and shouting at some English guys from Sheffield who were showing him their reservation card.

'I have told you that we're fully booked. Get out of my hotel.' The bags were piled up where the lads had dropped them, thinking they had at last found their hotel. Once more they showed him the reservation card.

'Look! We've booked a room for the night,' remonstrated one fan.

The little Italian was incensed. He stormed out from behind his desk, kicking the bags.

'Get your bags out of my entrance and get out of my hotel! What is the matter with you stupid English? How many times must I tell you to go somewhere else?'

I handed the female receptionist my fax. The man was just about to explode at me when the pretty young lady (she was too nice to be his daughter) took my reservation card and explained to our miniature Mussolini that I was a registered guest. This seemed to calm him down a little. Carl and I apologised to the other six English lads over our fortune, but we were happy to have somewhere to stay. The Worthing Mafia were already in the hotel. The fact is that this was supposed to be a businessman's hotel, and if that was the case, it is no wonder the Roman Empire collapsed – ours was the grottiest room I had ever seen. Just big enough to fit two beds in it, it had the sort of wallpaper that would do justice to the front cover of a Stephen King novel, it was so frightening.

'You couldn't vomit that colour,' remarked Carl. It looked as though someone had vomited raspberry, apricot and lime into a striped pattern. The bathroom door did not open properly either, as it hit the bed. Anybody with a 40 inch waist or more would not have got through. Inside the bathroom, the paint was suitably stained, a beautiful shade of city grime. The pièce de résistance was the bath – three feet deep and just wider than a shower base so it wasn't big enough to sit down in. Carl started singing the words,

'I'm living in a box, I'm living in a cardboard box . . .' Then he laughed and said, 'I'll tell you what, Colin, you really are a top man at choosing hotels. Don't take up a travel agency franchise.'

It's Rome and TGI Friday English fans drank while they enjoyed the moment. I had been in cities the night before matches when fans got so drunk they could hardly stand, but the atmosphere here was one of tension. The bars were always in play. Outside was his; inside, and the piece of concrete directly outside, was ours. The mopeds sped past.

'That's it, keep moving,' shouted Carl.

Moped mobility. If ever a phrase summed up a city, then that was it. Sometimes a few exceptionally pretty girls would go past and wave, but mostly there were scowls and shouts from young Italians. The English were in town. Drink with us if you dare!

Ten minutes later we bumped into Harry in a little bar which was precariously situated in the middle of two one-way systems. The pavement was barely wide enough for one person to sit safely yet now four chairs were arranged outside. For the privilege of smelling the garlic breaths of the Italian car drivers brushing past us – they really were that close – the resourceful owner charged us an extra premium (on top of that for being English). However, after two lagers the hotel was a paradise lost, a veritable oasis. After all, thousands said they would be here but we were among the fortunate ones. Even at nearly £5 a pint, there was only one place to be. It was a scene being created at hundreds of bars all across the city. The early evening sunshine was being enjoyed by the thousands of England fans who arrived full of hope and good humour. Not that everybody was happy. Barry summed up the mood of a number of fans:

'I hate these people. They treated us like shit in Italia '90. If England lose tomorrow I'm gonna have it.' Quite what Barry was going to have was difficult to say because Barry was not the fighting type, but Matt and Steve, who would soon be arriving, were known nutters. The locals were wary and perplexed as a steady stream of 30-somethings rolled into town and sat down outside a bar, taking off their shirts to reveal varying degrees of beer belly and fading tattoos.

As the evening wore on, we moved into a wonderfully decorated bar with a colourful painted ceiling and classic decor. It was here that Motty took over. Motty was Barry's partner and owned his own theme bar in Worthing – the Czar Bar. Barry liked to be centre stage but that was impossible while Motty was around.

Motty had a story for every occasion and told them with such plausibility that you didn't care whether it was the truth or not. I am sure that other countries have characters like this, but it seems as if England churns them out on a production line and I always meet them when I travel abroad to watch England.

Motty was a rep for Club 18-30 and had slept his way around half the female population of Europe. His party piece was the story of how he forged coaching papers and worked as the Saudi Arabian Under-21 coach for a year. He was currently sleeping with the wife of a famous Premiership player. Watching Motty and Barry try to outdo each other made for great entertainment as we sat at the bar.

Later in the evening we walked up towards the central railway station. All along the main street the bars were full of England fans who had spilled out into the street because of the heat. As darkness descended, the first blue flashing lights appeared – up and down the road they sped, skidding to a halt outside the bars and screeching away with sirens blasting. Huge armoured wagons raced along and stopped abruptly; the back doors were flung open for fully equipped and armed riot police to jump out and stare aggressively at the benign England fans having a drink. One bar near the station was shut for no other reason than prejudice, the crime of the England fans being that they were enjoying themselves too much.

Opposite the railway station is a wide open concourse which forms the main red light district. The previous evening it had been teeming with girls. Now, as we walked across at around 11.30 p.m., it was empty save for the 40–50 England fans who had just seen their bar shut. (You know that a city is afraid when even the pimps and whores take a night off.) One England fan refused to accept the situation and stood with his shirt off, singing defiantly:

> *God save our gracious Queen*
> *Long live our noble Queen*
> *God save the Queen*

His voice screamed defiance. He dared the riot police to hit him but they looked on aghast as did all the Italian taxi drivers and a whole busload of people who had disembarked to gawp along with the driver.

'Tomorrow we take your football team but tonight we drink vodka,' shouted one young fan at the open-mouthed bus queue.

We all sat down outside a kiosk which was selling cold beers when a car with three Italians pulled up. One of them leaned out of the window.

'Hey, you English pig,' they shouted, looking at Harry who returned their look disdainfully.

'You motherfucker,' one of them shouted.

Harry lifted his arm and slowly waved at them as the queen waves at her minions.

They shot off but two minutes later they were back.

'Hey English, I fuck your mother and sister.'

'Good,' replied Harry in a weary go-away-you-tiresome-fool sort of voice, 'that makes you and me relatives of a kind.'

The Italians left again with a perplexed look on their faces: surely this could not be the mad English they had read about.

Back they came for a third attempt. The Italian driver leant out with a scowl on his face and put all his expression into his words as he put his fingers to his lips.

'Oy, English, I hate you.'

'Why?' said Harry laconically, then added, 'Do you have interpersonal problems?'

With that, everybody fell about laughing and the Italians drove off, never to return.

By now, anybody arriving in the city would have thought it was a war zone. Sirens were echoing around every street and no police vehicle could go anywhere without its blue light flashing. Camera bulbs were going off everywhere and the ubiquitous camera crews were charging around looking for stories of mayhem. Meanwhile, England fans who tried to get a quiet drink saw bar after bar closing in a domino effect. Tensions started to rise and one young female reporter felt the rush of wind as a bottle missed her head by inches. As it smashed, she froze against a backdrop of jeers and calls for her to leave.

Barry suddenly wanted to check out a nightclub, especially when a group of Italians ran down the road and threw a bottle at us. When the pursuing police car realised they were Italian, the siren was switched off and the chase abandoned.

The Italian techno club was a new experience for me. It consists of repetitious, thumping music with flashing lights going on and off to the rhythm of the music which has no sequence save for a thump, thump, thump which scrambles the brain into a jelly, leaving you a disorientated mess. You can't dance to that; all you can do is twitch with the vibration.

'Great music, eh?' shouted Barry at me.

'Haven't they got any Tamla Motown?' I asked.

It was easy to spot the English – they all wore their shirts outside their trousers. The Italians looked on scornfully as they drank cola or orange juice while the England fans stood at the bar trying to make small talk to girls who didn't understand a word we were saying, and even if they did they weren't fancying us – they were more concerned with flirting with the Italians who were watching. Present were a large number of young England fans from Manchester who spent most of their evening gyrating wildly. Had the roles been reversed and a large number of Italians invaded their club in Manchester there could have been a fight, but the Italians were safe in the fact that we were too enthusiastic in our drinking and dancing to impress the chic Italian girls. I knew it was time to leave when the transvestite on stilts (making him nine feet tall) bounced on to the dancefloor and purple, blue and white strobe lights flickered, giving me nausea.

Ciampeno airport is like any other international airport around the world, designed to be functional, rather than attractive. But on 10 October it changed and became something else. These were not tourists arriving, they were football fans. To those who had not experienced it, the brutality of being clubbed, strip-searched and then beaten was not a pleasant experience. Having duty-frees confiscated and accusations hurled at them shook some people's perception of what they were expecting, but surely there had to be a reason. It reminded me of the first time John Barnes played in Italy. Claudio Gentile knocked him to the ground with the epithet: 'Take that, you pig.'

I staggered downstairs on the Saturday to be met by my barking hotelier.

'Room number.'

'I am not a number; I am a free man.'

'Room number.'

'129 Ward reporting in for a jug of water, Sah!' I shouted, as though I were a private answering the regimental Sergeant Major. Then I saluted and clicked my heels. He grunted and pointed towards the kitchen without a flicker of humour.

Around midday, Carl and I caught a taxi up to the four-star Metropole where the Press were staying. In the spacious foyer, the FA people sat next to boards instructing everyone as to where they had to be and at what time. It was like a jolly school outing for the Press boys (the Travel Club members had no such instructions, not even a tube map). As we left, Paddy Barclay spotted us and bounced over with a cheery hello.

'What's the Press view, Paddy?'

'The English have decided that England will win, but they may well have passed the limit of over-confidence. Me, I'm not so sure. Italy don't lose in Rome, that's why the match is being played here. Glenn has described his players as relaxed and focused, and Adams as serene. This I look forward to seeing.' Then he added his own rider: 'But the prize for the losers is so good. A place in the play-off. It's like getting to a cup final for losing a semi-final.'

It was warped, Paddy, Scottish logic, but he said one thing which gave me hope: it was his description of Glenn Hoddle as being totally confident, almost to the point of being eerie in his self-belief. Glenn had convinced the sceptical English Press about England, which was no mean feat. If he had done that then it must have rubbed off on his players. Certainly it seemed as if the Italians would be the underdogs in their own citadel.

All day the English fans arrived with great expectations only to find their duty-frees taken away and themselves stripped to enable Italian police to laugh at their colourful boxer shorts.

Two fans in the local café had been arrested at midnight then released at 3 a.m. after the riot police walked into their bar and smashed their glasses with their riot sticks then arrested them for smashing glasses. At the same café, the waiter informed us that the momentum was with England but Italian players are better. He didn't sound to me as though he was altogether sure, especially as he considered the win at Wembley a historic conquest. Climbing Everest for the first time, the exploits of Julius Caesar or Napoleon, these are historic conquests, but not a bloody football match. This whole nation was shitting itself despite Zola stating categorically that there was nothing to fear.

Jonathan Pearce came blinking into the sunlight, looking as though he'd had a tough previous night. He was in Rome working for London Capital Radio, so it was his voice that needed to be on form. Jonathan was a man who had put a new slant on the word *GOAL* with his extravagant verbose pronunciation. He chatted to us for a minute or two, warned us to be careful after the match and then left.

The afternoon settled down to a drinking marathon and the looks of bewilderment on the faces of the Italian police and passers-by told the whole story. How can they drink so much yet remain upright? Why do so many of them have tattoos and beer bellies? The aggressive way in which fans talked to each other shocked many as insults between friends were barked across tables to be followed by raucous laughter.

One of the most famous landmarks in Rome is the Trevi fountain. Young couples go to the monument before their wedding. On this day one young couple got out of their limousine and walked towards the fountain through the England fans who started to applaud. One wag shouted out: 'It's a life sentence mate. If you murder someone you get out after 15 years but with marriage you don't get any time off for good behaviour.' The other England fans laughed. In one of the English newspapers it was stated that England fans were insulting and abusing people around the Trevi fountain.

People drink for different reasons. Today the England fans drank time away because staring us in the face was the irrefutable fact that the Christians would have to go into a hostile atmosphere and survive: something that had never previously been achieved in the Colosseum. As kick-off approached, the Glenn mentality got through to us. The English are invincible. After tonight Rome would be conquered. The words of Ian Wright came into my head. 'Italy are easy to break down if you've got the right midfield player and a forward willing to run. No defender likes running towards his own goal. At some time he'll lapse in concentration and then it's up to you.' Now it was our time to confront this logic at the stadium.

With kick-off approaching, it seemed that everybody in Rome wanted a taxi and every taxi in the city was reserved. Carl and I stood in the middle of the main road and vainly tried to hail one. A Danish woman hurried past us looking harassed. We did a deal with her. It seemed as if the taxis were not stopping for England fans so if she got a taxi we would pay her fare to the Hilton then take the taxi up to the ground. Being chivalrous Englishmen, we helped her push her way to the front of a queue of Italian men. The Danish lady told us that there was to be a party in the Hilton later (it was Bobby Charlton's 65th birthday party) and invited us for a drink back at the hotel. We accepted, but it was a date we had no intention of keeping.

Our taxi driver was not best pleased to have to drive to the ground with all the traffic, but we had spent the last two days listening to scowling taxi drivers so one more disgruntled Italian would not matter as we were about to put a whole nation into mourning.

As Carl and I walked towards the ground we felt good. The dark foreboding of what would happen later started to unfold as English fans tried to enter the ground. The clubbing started at least an hour before kick-off.

An elderly English gent sporting his best blue blazer walked along with his England rosette – here was a throwback to the glory days of chivalry when men wore suits and ties to the match. Suddenly three young Italian teenagers burst out of the dark treeline shadows. One of them clubbed the elderly man to the ground with a large stone. In a flash they were gone, leaving the man dazed and bloody. The watching riot police stood and shrugged their shoulders, almost smiling. Elsewhere, their colleagues were shamefully hitting men with children and women saw their handbags emptied of perfume and mobile phones while uniformed thugs stamped on the contents and laughed. A pervading darkness surrounded the stadium which had become a black hole where human rights and dignity for English people had become taboo. Italians spat in the faces of Englishmen and when they retaliated, they got clubbed and arrested. In the face of such brutality which could not be tempered by reason, Carl and I became Australian if anybody asked.

Alighting from a coach was the 'hooray Henry' tour: people who had never attended a match before but were trendy types who have to be where the action is. These are the flash city brokers who ski in St Moritz, scuba dive in the Maldives, drink beer at the Munich beer fest or bungee jump off some far-away bridge because it's the in thing to do and they have the money.

'We're here for the futhbool, we're the bloody champhoo tour and boy will we drink some of that tonight,' one of them laughingly remarked to me.

'This a fookin "A" event, a must see,' shouted another. Each person getting off the coach had to make some remark which outdid the previous one.

They worked on the money markets and had wads of cash – the previous evening they had done the hostess bars and 'sploshed a few slappers'.

When they walked down the road into the biggest shitstorm they'd ever encountered and got their heads cracked and mobile phones smashed to pieces by morons in uniform, it turned into the non-vintage claret tour. Carl and I had a good belly laugh. We were just humble England fans watching our team, honorary Aussies for the evening. Thanks to a six-hour drink with the Worthing Mafia, we even had our accents.

Whilst others had problems getting in, Carl and I sailed through. Now we stood on the forecourt of the Stadio Olympico. Twenty-seven years previously, my hero Herb Elliott, the Australian miler, had come into this stadium and buoyed by his invincibility and self-belief, had gone out and destroyed the rest of the field in the Olympic 1500 metres final. Now 12,000 Englishmen felt the same as he did all those years ago. As long as the 11 who counted matched us then we would be okay. Even now, with 30 minutes to kick-off, the atmosphere was heightening. Every seat had a blue bib so that the crowd would look a solid blue Azzurri mass to the players. By chance, I was wearing a dark blue shirt. Everybody had joked to Carl before he left that he had a chance of passing off as an Italian, but I had no chance.

Our seats – right in the middle of the Italians – were at the back, so we had to climb hundreds of steps into the gods. Every Italian looked at us bemused, some with stern faces and some with cold stares of anger. One said something to Carl, who retorted: 'English numero uno geezers.'

A black singer belted out songs to rouse the crowd into an even greater frenzy. With just ten minutes to kick-off, the first chords and words of a song came out which caused the crowd to go crazy. I think it was 'Kumbaya'. *La la la, oooh la* . . . It had a catchy melody which got inside your head even in Italian. When he sang the chorus, 70,000 Italians sang with all their might. Sung with the passion of 'Auld Lang Syne' but with the sober jauntiness of 'Lord of the Dance', it was deafening. The sheer power of the delivery sent a shiver up my spine. Then the jumping started. *Italia! Italia! Italia!* It felt like an earthquake as our seats shook along with our cast-iron resolve.

Carl and I looked at each other and wondered if the two sets of England fans in each corner opposite us were beginning to have doubts. In amongst these two groups were the Sheffield Wednesday band, now being sponsored by *The Sun* newspaper.

When some semblance of quiet settled down upon the Italian crowd, the first muffled lines of 'Rule Britannia' could be heard. It was soon to be drowned out once again, however, by the forceful roar of *Italia! Italia!*

Matty and the Worthing Mafia were scheduled to be in the opposite corner. For some reason the Italian authorities had separated the England fans and placed them in two pens at either end of the stadium. For Matty and the rest, getting into the ground had been difficult as the Italian riot police had attacked anything and anybody. Women, children – everybody was fair game. Once inside, the police only allowed people up the steps two at a time and clubbed people for daring to do anything else.

Consequently, when the teams came out there was a huge, empty space in the stadium. The noise which had previously been loud, was now ear-splitting with crimson candles exploding everywhere. The match kicked off. The first 20 minutes would be crucial. We had to survive since chasing the game against this sort of passion would be practically impossible.

But the fears engendered by the frenzy proved unfounded since England played to Glenn's vision of confidence and belief from the start. Fancy triangles of passing and movement unfolded with blind side runs coming from everywhere. It was poetry in motion. Our 'futhbool' friends must have realised under their bruises what the phrase 'beautiful game' actually meant. Normally it takes 20 minutes to quieten down a crowd, but that day a continued frenzy could be heard from the English with the band starting a rhythm going. Then Gazza got the ball and did a party piece, turning one way, then another, each time sending the chasing Italian the wrong way.

'*Olé!*' we shouted. When Beckham, Ince and Gazza combined to send Batty on a run, it was left to the majestic Zola to chase Batty. When it came to football, Batty was like a carthorse with Zola a thoroughbred. Now Nijinsky was chasing Trigger and Trigger was moving away with panache. Zola fouled Batty and looked at the Italian bench with a look of bewilderment bordering on terror. Batty was the man the Italians had dubbed *Il Cattivo* – the bad boy – whose main attribute was biting the calves of opponents. Carl and I sat there laughing, unable to believe our eyes.

'It's in the bag now, mate.'

Then the sound came up like a hot, bubbling geyser and exploded.

> *Rule Britannia, Britannia rules the waves*
> *Britons never never never shall be slaves.*

Young Italian ultras put on their masks and started throwing missiles. That was all the riot police needed to launch a vicious attack on the England fans in the far corner, but a few lads fought back and pushed the Italian riot police back. It was hardly a fair fight when the Italians had full protective clothing and batons while the English lads had shirt sleeves and bare arms.

Matty took one blow to the front of his arm and reeled back in pain. Back he went as the blows rained down. On the floor next to him, a fan had gone down and the stick blows went in, one after the other, aimed at his head. One officer thought he had time to stand and take aim but he was hit by a flying kung fu kick which put an end to his plans.

Matty took stock: he was in the front line now. He spotted an Italian policeman with his visor up. He sprang across the rows of empty seats and felt his fist land plum on the nose of the Italian policeman. Bullseye. Cop that you plimsoll-wearing, backfiring-rifle Italian coward!

As he retreated, police came after him. One policeman ran but slipped and fell heavily. In went the boots until his Italian colleagues rescued him. They called for a stretcher and the twitching policeman was rushed through the front gates one England fan shouted, 'I hope you die, you bastard.' There were plenty there who felt the same. That was the cue for more riot police to come in and attack with even more gusto. One England fan even found himself being hit while he was on a stretcher. Still the young Italian ultras ran up to the police lines and launched missiles at England fans while the police, far from stopping them, took it as a cue to attack the English fans once again.

People squashed up against the fence, facing the terror of feeling their breath slowly being squeezed out of their bodies while their cheeks were pushed through the mesh as they were pressed even harder from behind. Women and children were among the crowd, yet *still* the Italian thugs attacked and hit. The looks on their faces were the same, fearful; looks I had seen on the faces in the pictures at Auschwitz. Fear, like football, is an international language.

For a few minutes the crowd lost sight of the match as the events behind one goal shifted the focus. Ince went off to get stitches for a head wound and returned bandaged, looking as though he'd been in the crowd for a few seconds, but England supremacy was once again evident when he strove forward and only a brilliant save by their keeper spared Italy. More close passing. Ten passes and one final movement to Beckham whose shot just eluded the upright.

It really was poetry in motion.

On the terraces the police beatings abated but the missile throwing of the Italians did not, and the police were happy to let it continue. After all, weren't these English hooligans? – that's what the British authorities told them.

Half-time came and we were smug. For 45 minutes the Italians had done nothing while England had completely dominated the field.

The thoughts of those who'd been battered black and blue were perhaps elsewhere.

The Italians around us were shaken and silent. A small gaggle of Englishmen gathered on the pathway at the top of the stadium. The view of the silent eerie streets outside belied the tension inside this huge bowl of emotions, but the noise had now been replaced by a hum of hushed voices speaking.

By the time the second half started, the temperature had risen to the 80s.

The second half started as the first had finished – with England in command. Then the band started playing the tune of *The Great Escape*. Now the England fans were out of their seats, doing the dance, their arms flailing upwards, slowly punching the air and chanting. Five, ten, fifteen minutes passed. In between a trumpet blast. *England Rule Britannia . . .*

Every time England lost possession or simply had tinges of self-doubt they only needed to look into the corner to renew their strength of purpose.

The temperature was now so hot you could have sat there with no shirt on. Nevertheless, we could see a middle-aged Italian stand up repeatedly to implore his countrymen to be more passionate and create more noise. He was wearing a smart suit with an overcoat draped over his shoulder as though he were attending the opera in midwinter. He threw his arms upwards in desperation while the rhythmic beat echoed from the England fans. He turned to us with an anguished look on his face.

'Sit down, Mafioso,' shouted Carl.

The Italian's wild gesticulations and exhortations brought a few weary chants of *Italia, Italia* from the natives but they were sapped of energy as the rhythmic jungle beat and slow tempo dancing from the England section matched the rhythm and passing on the pitch. England players, meantime, were using the ball with speed and skill. This wasn't the brainless, lung-busting stereotype the Italians had anticipated but a thoughtful, measured performance. When the ball did come through there was the Rock of Gibraltar Tony Adams – a man who'd fought the demons of alcoholism and come out even, so a few frantic Italians held no fears now.

In the midst of this frenzy, Gazza was laying his own ghost to rest. Despite being a favourite when he played for AS Roma, he had left Italy in tears. The Roma president insultingly informed him that next time he returned to Italy it would be for a holiday. Now he was having a ball. When, during a break in play, the Romans threw bottles on to the pitch, Gazza picked one up, took a swig and threw it back laughing. Well, Gazza was definitely on his holidays now as the dish of revenge was mighty cold. It was so cold the Roman president would freeze his hand if he picked up the plate.

Time was running out for Italy and, with the pressure on, their football took on a frenzied appearance. They had long since tired of shouting at the Dutch referee who made every decision correctly and with a strength of purpose, so the Italians resorted to cheating. Del Pierro ran into the box and dived over a tackling leg. Eighty-thousand people sucked any remaining oxygen from the air then held their breath as the referee ran into the box and produced a card. It was yellow and Del Pierro held his head in mock shame.

'You cheating Italian bastard,' I shouted, but my heart had just missed two beats in fear. Around me Italians held their heads and threw up their hands as if they'd been robbed or cheated, as if it was their divine right to win by cheating. They had after all spent the last two days cheating money out of England fans.

I looked at my watch and saw that time was up. Suddenly Wright burst through and by sheer force of will, got himself in front of his man and past the Italian keeper but the ball was eluding him. Back he went towards the goal making it bigger to aim at. He measured his shot as an engineer puts a micrometer to metal. As he did, 80,000 leg muscles twitched and rose slowly upwards. 'GOAL', screamed the England fans. Now with the whole stadium standing open-mouthed, the ball bounced off the inside of the post. At that point, steaming in like an express train, Sheringham appeared with the ball right in front of him.

Hit the bloody thing. If it goes over the stand it doesn't matter because it will all be over. But Sheringham dillied and dallied and gave us one trick too many. The Italians sprinted forward for one last chance. Seconds later, a perfect cross into the English box and time stood still as Christian Vierri rose and headed downwards.

At that moment, Harry, Carl, myself and 12,000 other English people inside the Stadia Olympico foresaw a dream die. But the ball slithered past the post to groans.

Then it was all over. The England players ran towards the band section where the sound of 'Rule Britannia' echoed victoriously. For a few moments we hugged and shook hands with fellow Englishmen or friendly Italians but the final moment seemed almost anticlimactic after the tension.

Carl and I now had the onerous task of walking the lonely walk to the metro on our own. Outside, the streets were filling up as Italians poured out. Off we went with the old maxim close at hand: a moving target is harder to hit.

Later in the week, a female journalist for the *Guardian*, Lynn Truss, wrote that she tried to look glum. Why? Because she was frightened? Why bother attending if victory means you have to look glum? Carl and I grinned like Cheshire cats while we walked along the middle of the grassy central reservation, with a shirts-out, English pride.

Within minutes, the streets were beyond berserk with bikes and cars alike weaving in and out of pedestrians. The night air was full of hustle and the thousands of mopeds gave it a buzz-like sound, but no cheers or excited chat abounded. The Italians were muted. The mopeds streamed past like fleeing lemmings. Buses were packed so tightly that perspiration ran down the windows like floods of tears. But no flags waved or horns tooted – all that could be heard was the monotone sound of thousands of buzzing engines. Even the flags which trailed behind the mopeds hung limply.

Down in the metro we were too cocky for our own good.

'Inglese'. It was a shout from a watching Italian to a waiting group. The streets looked safer. Back on to the streets, we walked with some fear, at speed with demons inside us and the edge of fear coming back into our walking, always watching to make sure we knew what was going on around us, but there was still a smile etched on our lips. We let the part-time fans pretend they were Italian; we'd just be alert Englishmen. In any case everybody who saw us knew who we were. Further down the road a bar beckoned where we joined two Canadians sitting outside who were full of praise for the English.

Two young Englishmen came along looking nervous. They were pleased to see us and looked surprised that we were laughing and joking. One of the two was Italian-looking with his slick, black hair gelled back, but when he went for some beers his mate told us that he had spent the last two weeks on a sunbed to look the part in Rome.

When Mike returned, he told us a story which saddened me.

Mike had played in the same Arsenal youth team as Tony Adams. He had been a star striker in that team, but had thrown his talent away on birds and booze. Now he was sitting outside this Roman bar looking to us for protection, when if he had worked harder to change his fortunes he could have been out there tonight representing the hopes of millions. At the end of the match Ian Wright had cried with joy along with us all. Mike had been born with talent yet sat there drinking beer, thinking of what might have been. Looking at him with his sleek athleticism made me feel sad. I've never had much football talent, so living my aspirations as a spectator is as good as it gets for me.

A group of young Italians was also in the bar. While we laughed and joked and danced *The Great Escape* one more time, they looked glum. A carload of six Italians pulled up, giving us daggers.

'Cheers, boys,' we shouted, and lifted our glasses to them. They replied with abuse before driving off.

We suddenly remembered that we had agreed to meet Harry and the chaps in a bar after the match. As midnight approached, we needed a taxi. At the rank opposite the bar, the arrogance of the Italians shone through. Two of the five waiting Italians had lived in England for a while and spoke perfect English.

'You did not beat us. We are not unhappy.'

'England outplayed you. You were second best in all departments and I don't see too many of you dancing in the streets tonight.'

Their arrogance, which had permeated every Italian utterance before the match, oozed out of their pores. They had grown up to believe in the superiority of their own land, and it showed more than ever that night. All the rubbish the Italians had come out with before the game – that England are easy to read; they play with their hearts but they deserve a pat on the head anyway for trying to be like Italy; that in the end, Italian superiority will win the day – all of this was now nothing more than a sham. Whilst we may have a 'British is best' arrogance, these Italians, like everybody else, are undeniably attached to their own sense of self-importance which is perhaps why the police dished the beatings out after the match – we had humiliated them on their own territory. A taxi pulled up and we jumped in before them. Mike wound down the window.

'Second best again, garlic breath.'

Back at the intersection pavement café we sat outside and waited. Within ten minutes we had attracted the attention of the moped riders. The back pillion rider spat as they zoomed past so that a full mouthful of spittle hit Carl and Mike in the face. Mike rushed into the toilet to frantically splash water on his face and hair, while seconds later a bottle was viciously pitched at us so we retired to the bar inside. As night turned to early morning, fans drifted in. We had been drinking for over two hours but still the arriving fans told us endless horror stories of their attempts to leave the football stadium.

Stuart had grown up on the rough side of the track but he'd got out of his violent council estate, which was now a drug-infested slum, to rise to be a director of a public company. Stuart was there as a corporate hospitality guest of Terry's. He had been the victim of a pickpocket on the metro where he'd lost his wallet containing his match ticket. At the ground he'd bought a ticket off a tout, gone to the Italian end, been struck by the riot police when he ran away and then got into the England section just in time to get another whacking. Leaving the ground he was treated to another battering. Now, at 2 a.m., he was still shaking with fear. He spoke in bursts, uncontrollably, and at the speed of his racing pulse.

' . . . it was brutal, horrible, police were just hitting, I was up against a fence, I couldn't breathe, I felt my legs buckle and I thought I was going down, then they started whacking us again . . .' Stuart lifted his beer and gulped it back as though it were his last beer on earth. Stuart had reached the age of 50 and had come to Rome to watch England play football only to be confronted by his own demons of terror and hearts of darkness of a far worse variety than anything Conrad had ever written about.

Al from Stoke-on-Trent gave his opinion of the Italians: 'Pasta-munching gigolos who are so full of bolognese that they couldn't run away from a war fast enough to save their handbags,' then he lifted his shirt to reveal weals and bruises from over 40 truncheon blows. They had been inflicted the previous evening. Looking at those bruises made me flinch and I could see why he was a little upset with the Italians. By the end of the evening, I had heard so many stories of beatings that I doubted there were any more English people left to beat.

Harry and the boys never showed up. They had been kept behind for nearly three hours and when they emerged to a five-mile walk back to the centre of Rome, it made them so tired they went straight to bed. We moved on to another bar where the England fans had spilled on to the pavement. Within minutes, five vanloads of riot police arrived with police staring through the grilled windows at the fans who glared back. England fans inside the bar looked on the marble tables as weapons and stools as clubs. This time we've got weapons to fight back with and a wall to stand with our backs to.

The police officer in charge spoke to the owner who apolo-getically announced that he was being forced to shut within five minutes.

Another taxi, another bar. But our taxi driver this time was friendly and took us to a 24-hour pavement café. As we alighted we were immediately accosted by a spivvy-looking man.

'You like girls?'

'Sure we do; we're English,' replied Carl.

He produced a card. 'I have lots of pretty girls waiting to meet you.'

'Jig-a-jig,' said Mike.

Our spiv friend smiled. 'Yes. Plenty fucky fucky,' he said moving his hips back and forward.

Carl looked at him and smiled: 'No need mate. Tonight we fucked the whole of Italy, so we can afford to give your scrubbers a miss.'

We sat outside the bar laughing while our friend walked away shaking his head mumbling something incomprehensible.

Then we set about celebrating as the sun slowly came up over the horizon. Groups of weary England fans traipsed past; some joined us in animated conversation while others waved a tired arm and gave a triumphant smile. As celebrations go this was not the dancing, singing type but a more studious, reflective type. All our physical energy had been left in a pool of sweat on the stadium floor but we still had our nervous overflow to keep us going.

Back at the Hotel Horrible we were greeted by our aggressive host.

'Keep the noise down, English.' I pulled him up by his lapels so he could smell my beer breath.

'You miserable old Steptoe. All you've done is bitch since you rented us your room cupboard. Now shut up and go and tell your grandchildren that you were privileged to have England fans in your hotel.'

We shouted and danced up the stairs to wake up any other England fans who were stupid enough to sleep. Bursting through the door of the room occupied by the Worthing Mafia, we opened up their beers spraying them with foam, and wondered why they had all thought to retire to bed, especially as they had obtained VIP passes to a party hosted by the BBC Radio 1 DJ, Pete Tong.

Barry was not amused and, had he mustered the strength, would have thrown a punch.

'This country's shit. Twice I've been here and twice I've been treated like dirt. It's the last time they get my money and the next Italian customer in my bar gets charged double,' muttered Barry before falling back to sleep.

We left the room whooping and shouting, collected our bags and checked out. Our little Steptoe Mussolini was not present so we bade farewell to the pretty girl on the desk with big, slobbering, beer-breath kisses.

We spilled out on to the streets to banner headlines. Cesare Maldini told the Press that England were not dangerous but the Italian Press knew the score.

La Stampa – 'An English lesson . . . from the masters.'
Corriere Dello Sport – 'Poor Italy.'
Gezzetta Dello Sport – 'England dominant in midfield.'
The city of Rome was left with nothing but its heritage.

At Florence airport, the small group of noisy England fans congregated at the bar and regaled each other with stories about the match. One of the fans opened a sports paper and looked at the list of teams who would be going into the hat for the sudden-death play-off matches with Italy. The returning tourists looked at us in bewilderment as we all chanted RUSSIA RUSSIA RUSSIA . . .

Four days later we got our wish: Italy drew Russia.

7

Ticket to Ride

The aftermath of the violent attacks on England fans took a different course from that of previous events. The Italian authorities blamed the English fans and the Press chipped in, but when horror stories started to emerge from middle-class people who normally spent their Saturday evenings cheering their lottery balls, the FA were forced to wake from their habitual soporific torpor and listen. For once they actually acted.

A specially set up hotline received so many calls that the FA could not ignore the weight of evidence and the subsequent report came out against the Italians. Later FIFA chastised the Italians, but the Italians didn't apologise, and Tony Blair stated that he didn't want it to harm diplomatic relations. The Press, led by Jeff Powell of the *Daily Mail*, led the chorus of ' . . . this report will unleash the barbarians in France.' I thought of the terrified female faces of nouveau England fans having their perfume bottles stamped on, only to be called dregs by the paper they revered and all I could do was file it with the rest of my unfair memories of injustices and chuckle.

So a few English football fans got a beating. So what? – Did anybody die? Did it harm our balance of trade? How will it affect Tony Blair's popularity? Shout loudly and brush it under the carpet if you want, but if it had been the other way round, with fans attacking police, then everyone including the politicians' dog would have been munching on a media sound bite.

The picture of Matty being surrounded by Italian riot police was reproduced in most of the English dailies. Other pictures showed older English faces from past hooligan battles in the front line looking angry and perplexed. They were there to watch football so why were they being attacked. Why? Whilst it would be churlish to describe all the England fans as innocents abroad, it was a proven case of the shits hitting the fans on this occasion.

The real justice which would have seen Italy knocked out by Russia never happened. Italy, unlike Napoleon, survived their winter retreat from Moscow and triumphed to advance to France for the draw proper. Not only that: they made Italy one of the seeded teams for the tournament above England who were not. Even before the draw, every England fan who had been to any England match abroad knew where their first match would be: the furthest geographical point from Calais. Anybody who doubts that politics plays a huge part in football is more simple than Forrest Gump. Examples abound: at the previous World Cup draw, Pele, the greatest player ever, was banned by the president, José Havelenge, over a political argument in Brazil.

At the finals draw on Thursday, 4 December, Michel Platini, one of the most graceful players ever to don a France shirt, and now the President of the organising committee proclaimed that the '98 Coupe du Monde would be the fans' bonanza. Then in the draw, England pulled out Tunisia, Romania and Colombia for their group while Scotland landed the dubious honour of playing Brazil in the opening match.

The next evening, every male in England in every pub in the land between the ages of 21 and 40 declared his intention of travelling out to France. The reality, of course, would be much different as tickets were rarer than hens' teeth. The French authorities had already asked the French to go to a ballot and this accounted for 60 per cent of the tickets. The sponsors had 20 per cent, while the fans were well down the pecking order. England, with 27,000 members in their Travel Club, would never satisfy demand.

Oh, the madness of it! The Coupe du Monde had become a corporate beanfeast. Those who wanted to gatecrash would have to swim through the sea of circling sharks from the black market to get to their promised land. Later, fans would be left high and dry as unscrupulous individuals profiteered on people's dreams while Argentine superthugs, sponsored by the Argentine FA, would sell their official tickets for £1,000 to desperate Japanese fans. You couldn't invent a story like that. In any other area fans would have given up, but this was nationalism, tribalism and the chance to be part of the greatest human drama on earth, so the sea of sharks with the odd piranha and cocodile thrown in was not as daunting after all.

The marketing people spoke: 'The way companies like to talk to their consumers is through their enthusiasms and football is a ubiquitous enthusiasm.' As Harry said: 'Call me "ubiquitous" again and I'll smack you in the teeth.'

Now the World Cup fever could start in earnest and Harry would get to live his dream. Every night for the next few months the talk would be about how good the Africans would be, how much flair the Romanians could bring to the pitch and whether or not England would face the brilliant or useless Colombians. But in the back of everybody's mind was the harsh reality that there would be no tickets. Frantic phone calls were made to friends, relatives and anybody who lived or travelled in France. With more 'Nons' than a Charles de Gaulle speech about the UK entering the Common Market, it soon became obvious that this World Cup would not be known as the fans' bonanza. Unless, of course, you were prepared to sell the family silver and take your chances on the streets. Harry recounted the words of an Amsterdam prostitute: 'The more money you have, the more you get to party.'

In a move designed to infuriate, England fans were allocated only a few thousand tickets for each venue. The FA wrung their hands and insisted that they wanted more, but this was FIFA – an undemocratic body which on a bad day makes corrupt African dictators look good and on a good day makes the English FA look good, which is an almost impossible task. Not that other nations fared any better. The Dutch, Germans and Danes were all complaining loudly, but it cut no ice. Every day, fans opened a newspaper or switched on their TV to be told that some corporate giant had tickets to win.

Tony Blair had a conversation with French President Chirac and sought more tickets for the England fans.

'But who is paying for the World Cup – the English taxpayer or the French taxpayer?' asked Chirac.

'Well, the French I suppose,' Blair is reported to have said.

'So whom should the tickets go to?'

And thousands of French people rubbed their hands at the thought of all that tax-free money they would make from all those English people looking for entry into stadiums that were too small for their collective requirements. All of it extracted with the conniving acquiescence of the French President. Seldom has a president said no and seen his stock rise so much.

So with England matches set for Marseilles, Toulouse and then Lens, the scene was set for the political posturing. The English police were off to an early start and soon briefed the media that Lens was only 70 miles from Calais and that the fans would be drunk and full of duty-free lager. There were not enough tickets so there would be thousands of hooligans storming through the towns en route. Soon their political needs were put into context when it was discovered that they were lobbying for over 100 undercovers to follow England around France. The police felt so confident that they were telling the press as early as December '97 how many undercovers they wanted – yet not once did they produce one shred of evidence that the violence was planned. I thought back to Poland and Auschwitz and how the German propaganda machine had painted the Jews and saw similarities. Weren't the same people who only a few weeks previously were battered innocents in Rome now being painted as thuggish lowlife? The words of C.P. Cavafy summed up the police attitude: 'What are we waiting for assembled in the forum? The barbarians are due here later today.'

Phil worked as an undercover in drugs work in south London. Having a young child, he had no interest in being in France for a whole month, but there were plenty of others who wanted this trip. He'd sat in cars on eight-hour surveillance jobs listening to young PCs eulogising about France '98.

'Following England as an undercover is the best number many of the young fellows can get. They have to use the young single guys so they can actually drink in the bars with the hooligans to get the information. Can you imagine it, just standing around drinking lager all day, joining in the songs about England, insulting foreigners, getting involved in whatever argy-bargy breaks out, and then a guaranteed entry into the matches. Then you file a stupid report the next day '. . . identified a suspect by his NF tattoo, drinks lager . . . observed another suspect drinking lager and chanting papal obscenities . . .' – and it's all paid for by HM Government! Sometimes if they're charged with following one person in particular they get pulled in by the local plod and get a bender for free. Who says the police force doesn't prosper under a Labour government? They're practically fighting to be invited to France '98 as an undercover, especially for the trip to Marseilles. Lager on tap and whores paid for by HM government! One of the guys who's looking for an invite is the biggest plank you have ever met. He actually asked if he could travel first class.

'The super said to him,

"PC Plank. How many of our illustrious hoolyfans travel first class to the matches?"'

Phil once asked one young PC what the objectives against the hooligans actually were, but he was met with a quizzical look. The words of the American general in Vietnam sprang to mind when he was questioned by a baffled Pressman who said he couldn't grasp the objective of a particular exercise against the Vietcong: ' . . . you're brighter than you realise – there weren't any objectives. The purpose of hooligan-watching is to observe.' But to observe what?

So the PCs planned their French holidays while their senior officers lobbied for political favour, which was easy to arrange as all they had to do was mention Lens and the potential for trouble. As Harry remarked: 'I'd like a pound for every time the Press mention the close proximity of Lens to Calais.'

The Press printed verbatim whatever the police said. Police methods of information release continued to astound football fans yet the Press gobbled it up without questioning. In April 1997, a Fulham fan was killed as a result of a head wound sustained by his falling during a brawl at Gillingham and the Press release put out by the police stated that his cause of death was stab wounds after a mass brawl involving 50 fans. It was then that I began to doubt the credibility of the police and their system of gathering information. My doubts would surface in a few weeks in Marseilles when the police information was so far removed from reality that while the world was watching a few hundred people charge up and down a street in Marseilles on their TVs, PC Nero sat in his bunker fiddling and informed the French that none of the main hooligans had yet departed England.

English people were terrifying long before cheap air travel and increased lager consumption. Now, the mass marketing of consumption has given us international drunks. For Southend and Margate, read Marseilles, Toulouse and Lens. When the whole premise of a World Cup revolves around increasing consumption, and when one of your sponsors is Budweiser, then the conclusion of drunken cities should have been anticipated.

Harry and the boys hunted high and low for tickets, but to no avail, and decided to go whether they had tickets or not. As soon as the UK Government caught on that this was the prevalent attitude among fans, they spent £1 million on a TV advert which stated that fans buying black market tickets would not gain entry because the ticket would have the owner's name on it. On the other hand, the French said that fewer than 40 per cent of tickets would have names on them and that they had no plans to check everybody's. In fact, they wouldn't bother as a matter of course. It seemed as if the UK Government and police were living in some sort of fantasy land which bore no relation to the reality of the actions of football fans. Knowing they had only a slightly better than evens chance of escaping a truncheon between the eyes, 15,000 went to Turin for the semi-final with Italy in 1990. Did they seriously think that some crass advert would stop fans embarking on the French adventure of a lifetime? This was the World Cup not the bloody Chelsea Flower Show. You can arrange your intelligence gathering, undercover plods and oppressive policing methods against England football fans; you can batter fans then state that you had to batter us to save us from ourselves and that you had to oppress the majority lest the minority spoil it (the English way of doing things), but you won't stop fans travelling, no more than the Berlin Wall and 50 divisions of Russian troops could stop East Europeans escaping to the West.

Besides, they were talking to fans who whiled away many a boring hour being shut in grounds every Saturday by jobsworth policemen, so they would be more than prepared to take their risks on the streets and let the French have the headache of policing their ingenuity for gaining entry to places they shouldn't. Getting battered black and blue is a lesson in risk assessment a regular English football fan learns to adapt to. Like it or not, it's just the way it is. Only the new football fans struggle to come to terms with restaurants closed to English accents, dry cities, and rows of unsmiling riot police conditioned to batter the flag of St George.

But it wasn't all bad news as the Football Supporters' Association obtained sponsorship from Mastercard. They would have an advice bus on hand every time England played. On the very day Jack Straw warned us not to go without a ticket, the French Tourism Minister told us to come and be welcomed in France without one. So the Government spent £1 million telling fans lies they didn't believe anyway, while corporate money gave the fans some information via their own people. It's no wonder some fans feel unashamed when they lash out at provocation: the suppressed anger, built up over a period of months, is partly due to the increasingly alienated state in which fans find themselves.

The French were phlegmatic about the World Cup and doubled hotel prices while the labour unions planned strikes in essential travel industries. Within hours of the draw being made, flights in Marseilles were sold out, so the lads booked low-cost airlines into Nice.

'Sounds nice to me!' shouted Harry, as he walked into the pub clutching his low cost Easy Jet ticket to Nice.

Gradually, as the opening match drew closer, the 20 million strong army of fans who stated on 12 December that they would be in France dwindled to a division and finally a battalion. Yet this battalion would still be around 20,000 strong. The Press, once again, started looking for their hooligan stories. The News Rotters sharpened their pencils while the French doubted the wisdom of putting England and Tunisia in Marseilles for the group opening match considering the tensions that surround such matches along with the racial tensions which already exist in Marseilles.

Paul Dodd was a tabloid hooligan monster who'd made a name for himself as some sort of superthug. Rather like his late predecessor, Paul Scarrott, he existed to fill the pages of the *Daily Mail* and other newspapers to frighten heartland England. People like Paul were the reason why 100 undercovers could get money from the Treasury to go drinking. I first saw him in Stockholm in 1990 when he was just a lad. With his mop of black hair and incessant use of the F-word, I found it impossible to take his ramblings seriously.

'Come back and see me when you learn to read and write,' Hickey once said to him when Paul told him that Chelsea ran from Carlisle. There were plenty of people who did take Dodd seriously, though. The Home Office had, and has, categories of hooligans: a Category C hooligan is one who is likely to perpetrate violence against other Category Cs or Category Bs – those who are often involved in general high spirits or boisterousness but who rarely cause trouble. Category B could actually describe anybody who argues loudly with his wife and jumps up and down when a goal hits the net, but they are probably worth another 50 undercovers. Category A constitutes the two other fans not covered by B and C.

The tabloids gave word space to Dodd and other cronies who were so far removed from the reality of football fans travelling to France that they might as well have been marooned in the Sahara.

' . . . everyone's going, even lads who haven't gone for years. Imagine if England are in the final over there: there'll be 60,000 locked outside. It's closer for the cockneys than coming up here to Carlisle. It'll be mad. There'll be a lot of people saying, "This is the last one."'

Then they dragged out other hooligan faces, like half-caste Mickey

Francis, for example, who'd had his exploits ghost-written into a hooligan book, like the Skinhead series of books in the 1970s.

'Do I think it's going off in France? I know it's going to go off in France. If it doesn't go off in France, I'll wake up white in the morning.'

Then they would add the inevitable little piece of Freudian psychology about why they do it in the first place. And the interview is always carried out in a windowless pub on a grim, drug-ridden housing estate where young girls outside are either selling their bodies or putting broken bottles under their car tyres. Fact it wasn't, but it served to frighten the pants off the England of the *Daily Telegraph*, *Express* and *Mail*, England now basking in the cool of Britannia. I hadn't seen any of these alleged hooligans in 25 years of following England. They existed only in the fertile imagination of shock journalists and encouraged the criminalisation of every England fan. Many journalists went on like that, and all in the name of having to earn a living like everyone else. Nobody ever got rich by underestimating the people's desire to read half-truth and innuendo. Fans saw only too clearly that this kind of journalism was only adding to the tension surrounding them. Respected TV commentators like Mark Lawrensen stated with conviction, as if he knew, that one per cent of England fans are hooligans. If you add the statistic that one in ten are homosexuals, I would like to know which Liverpool player in his team, when he played at Liverpool, was a poof, then?

The heady days of qualification in Rome seemed more distant than ever as England played some putrid football in their warm-up games. Ian Wright and Gazza, along with the others, were struggling to regain fitness. England lost to Chile at Wembley in February in a manner which chilled the bones; only the debut of young Michael Owen gave any warmth. 0–0 draws against Saudi Arabia and Belgium and a narrow win against Morocco followed an unconvincing win against Portugal, whose clever moves had cut huge swathes through the England defence like a combine harvester cutting through a virgin wheat field. All of this made me fretful and nervous about our chances. England's team had no shape and Shearer had returned a shadow of the player he was before his injury. It augured badly. Only young Michael Owen looked as if he had that something we needed to make an impact on the biggest stage. In the final Wembley warm-up, fans left the stadium shaking their heads. The walk back down Olympic Way had no spring in its step and after match analysis, things did not look good for France.

Glenn Hoddle took his squad away for training and friendlies against Belgium and Morocco. The squad would be based in La Manga, flying in to Africa for the friendlies being held in Casablanca. Glenn had the Press holed up in a timeshare complex well away from the players. One of the players complained that being away with England was like being on a 'flipping moonies' convention' with the accent on togetherness and spiritual healers. Not that the players knew what Glenn was thinking any more than the Press did. As Matt le Tissier said, 'I don't know what goes on inside his [Hoddle's] head.' He had allegedly had meetings with Uri Geller then denied it, and it was he who was in charge of the fans' holy grail. We'd only lent him the right to represent us: now he acted like some tinpot dictator making rules which benefited Glenn only. When Owen scored with a natural flair which had Pele singing his praises, Glenn replied that Michael was not in fact a natural goalscorer and had other things going on around him which he needed to cut out.

Paul was synonymous with Chardonnay and prawn cocktail dinner parties. He had his job as a policeman, a wife on the school PTA committee and a Surrey house which was once a vicarage. Protecting middle England had enabled him to buy his house for £30K and then sell it for £250K. Having sons and a boss who was head of the France '98 football liaison committee, meant that he was also a fan of football whatever his views on the travelling football fan. He happened to be in La Manga with his family at the same time as England. He spent a pleasant afternoon watching England train, admiring the skills of Gascoigne who stood out amongst all the talent on display. At the end of the session, no one was left apart from about 60 people with 20 autograph-hungry lads. All the players walked away and got on the coach except one. Steve McManaman stood and signed autographs for every lad who wanted one. After about ten minutes Glenn got off the coach.

'Come on, Steve, we're ready to leave. We're all waiting for you,' he said.

McManaman spoke just loudly enough for Paul to hear him:

'Go away, Glenn, I'm signing these lads' autographs.'

Steve McManaman, number one Scouse scally, stood up to the overbearing teacher as only Scousers do. He stayed until he had signed every last book before jogging over to the coach and jumping on with a spring in his step. Football fans are animated by meeting their heroes even if they never have anything to say to them. Only older people or other fellow athletes can talk to them without the glazed eyes of hero worship. Did England's ultimate destiny in France '98 depend upon them ignoring young children? No it didn't, but the sad truth was that Glenn had lost sight of that fact because he was so wrapped up in himself.

As opening day approached it became obvious that many fans had purchased tickets from unscrupulous suppliers who had no intention of delivering them. Hundreds of Japanese fans sat crying at Tokyo airport when their dreams were cruelly shattered at the last minute and their plight was shared among many throughout the world. In England, a company was closed down after fraudulently taking millions of pounds for non-existent tickets from fans all over the world. In Argentina it emerged that the Argentine FA had sponsored the 'Barra Brava' hooligans in return for not being threatened. Hooligan groups such as those had been responsible for 37 deaths during the Argentine season which had resulted in the suspension of the league. It seemed a mad world had gone completely off its trolley. In Cameroon one senior official was arrested for selling his entire country's allocation back into the black market. The lunatics were running the ticket distribution asylum now. Nowhere did it state that corporate tickets would not be supplied. Getting a ticket for an ordinary fan resembled the chaotic scenes in the Klondike when speculators descended on the claims office for a stake.

The announcement of the final England 22 produced the biggest talking point since a Labour Government ousted the Tories – Paul 'Gazza' Gascoigne was left out of the final squad. Gazza had played in his first and last World Cup in Italia '90. True, he'd been struggling with his fitness due to a number of injuries and yo-yo weight problems, but his omission split the nation into two camps, pro and anti. It made the main news and leader comments of every newspaper. The sports Press, who loved to fill their pages with his antics, came out on Glenn's side. Later I was to find out why. I remember watching Rob Shepherd in Poland spend two days writing stories about Gazza. If he was out now, who or what would they write about? The comments from Glenn summed up the man, epitomised by what he said to McManaman at La Manga.

' . . . some of his [Gazza's] lack of fitness is self-inflicted . . . there are a lot of things he could have done to get himself into better shape.' ' . . . his fitness levels are probably lower than they've been for a long time.' 'Modern top-class football is as much about athleticism as it is about technical skills.'

Athleticism *doesn't* win important matches in World Cups – flashes of sublime skill and inspiration do, but Glenn wasn't listening to anybody because his self-belief had become a dangerous arrogance. Glenn wanted to talk about players who had responded to his arm around the shoulder like Rio Ferdinand who had been thrown out of a previous England squad after a drink-drive charge.

' . . . his game has got better over the last four months since I've asked him to improve his defending,' said Hoddle. The message was there for everybody. Listen to me and I'll judge your mettle by your reaction to adversity.

Two days later Teddy Sheringham was spotted in a disco at 6.45 a.m. with a drink and a blonde. Fans understood the need to relax. We weren't a nation of monks. All this deprivation was for foreigners who were used to it. After all, we've seen what a dysfunctional Royal family we have produced from a reclusive existence in single-sex schools. Fans needed Gazza, who needed a drink or two to relax. If we could play, we'd all be Gazza.

Gazza was devastated. One drink or one kebab doesn't make me a worse player, argued Gascoigne: 'There's plenty of time to get fit for the World Cup.' Gazza had played, and lost, the biggest ever poker hand he would play in the last-chance World Cup saloon. Whether other countries would have left him behind is open to debate. Didn't the Saudis include Saeed Owairan, even though he had once been jailed for being caught in the company of drink and women? England might fail, but that's okay so long as we are fit failures.

One thing was sure: Gazza and Sheringham would fill the topic of conversation in every airport lounge, ferry terminal and bar between here and Marseilles.

'Should Gazza stay or should he go, Glenn?' belted out Harry to The Clash tune during the Frog Pond karaoke evening. To every travelling fan there was no doubt. Gazza should have gone because he was one of the lads and England had always relied on the lads in previous French campaigns.

When Terry Venables and Bobby Robson stated that they would have had no hesitation in taking the risk on Gazza, everybody waited for the result.

8

Madness in Marseilles

When the draw was made, the proprietor of the local Bookham Bistro, Eric, the Toulouse Chef, implored the lads to steer clear of Marseilles.

'Do not go to that city. It's so violent. Even when it is calm in France, Marseilles is full of violence. French people do not dare venture into parts of the city at night.' Eric had expressed his thoughts on this so vociferously that it made me think.

By the time I arrived at the departure gate in Luton Airport for my flight to Nice on a Sunday afternoon flight along with at least 200 other football fans, there had already been sporadic outbreaks of violence in and around the old port area.

At the departure gate, the officer looked me up and down.

'Going for the football?'

'No, I'm working,' I replied.

He looked at me questioningly then checked my name against a list of undesirables. When he'd satisfied himself that I wasn't on the most-wanted list he turned to me.

'You are going to watch the football, aren't you?'

'Why bother asking the question if you already know the answer?'

By the time the England fans left for Marseilles, the World Cup had already been on for four days. Scotland had opened the festivities and narrowly lost to Brazil. Matches were being played in a competitive spirit yet no team really stood out. Anyway, the group matches were the phoney war. The World Cup proper didn't start until the knockout stages in 12 days' time.

'Then all the dross teams deemed worthy of inclusion by FIFA will be gone,' said one learned fan at Luton in the departure lounge bar. He also had a view on the World Cup which I tended to agree with: 'Travelling to the World Cup is about the anticipation of arrival. Once you're there and the first match is gone, it's about filling in the boredom before the next match.'

My flight had been switched three times by Debonair and now it was an hour late. French air traffic controllers had slipped up: they had gone back to work after a strike, thus preventing the best way of keeping the English hooligans out of the country.

The travelling England fans going via Nice, like myself, were a motley crew, mostly in their 30s and 40s, some with their wives and children. None could be described as hooligans although I had no doubt that we were all classed as one category or another. The flight itself was pleasant with the England fans responding to the captain's best wishes for England with a hearty cheer. Nobody got drunk, although some of the younger lads were so full of excitement that they could be described as boisterous – and yet this was the travelling division which had mobilised a whole army of police. Only a few days previously I read that Gottfried Dienst, the Swiss referee in the 1966 final between Germany and England, had died aged 78. His death had prompted an obituary in the *Daily Telegraph*, something only the rich and famous usually achieve. For those old enough to remember, his goal award changed the lives of those watching and playing. Whether he understood one word that the Russian linesman spoke to him was never asked, at least not by an English journalist, but it didn't matter because this man understood that it was necessary for England, the host nation, to win that cup. Now, 32 years later, England had awarded Dienst with the establishment status of obituary celebrity. I sat on the plane wondering if his death wasn't some sort of good omen for France.

Movability, that's what France was all about for the England fans on the trains, planes, automobiles and bus tour. Keep 'em moving, never have them standing in one place too long. Marseilles one week, next Toulouse then Lens. Just like the Clint Eastwood line from *Rawhide*, make them use their energy in arriving rather than getting there and relaxing with a cold beer. This had never happened before. England fans had always been given a static base, allowing them to mix with the local people. Rome might have been a motion match where everything in the city moved but the long, straggling lines of shaven-headed Englishmen arriving at the station and moving slowly off to the nearest bars looked like columns of prisoners of war from old newsreels. Only the beer bellies stopped them being extras in an adaptation of *One Day in the Life of Ivan Denisovich*. For those intending to stay inside France the need to be mobile was more important than anything else except the search for available tickets.

From experience I have learned the trick of booking an aisle seat, so that should I ever find myself beside a 15-stone-plus beer monster, at least I haven't got to clamber over his belly to get to the toilet. Across the aisle on the flight sat salesman Rob, Essex man right down to his designer socks. He was going down to the south of France for a week and was looking to do a bit of serious posing. Staying in a posh hotel near Antibes, which his travel agent mate had got the lads for £40 per night, he was ready to rock and roll.

'I mean, we're talking serious discounts here, me old mucker.'

Catching the England game was a serious side show for the main event. It was only when he arrived at the luggage carousel that I realised that he meant business. He had more luggage than a travelling Hollywood film star. Two bulky cases and a suit bag: ' . . . especially for my Armani shirts. It's all about looking the part.'

Watching him struggle along to the luggage trolleys, his every stagger watched in awe by the younger northern lads on the flight who were getting ready for a two-week stay with less luggage among four of them, was the highlight of the journey.

The weather in the south of France had been unusually wet and cool for the time of year. We had to hope that it stayed cool for the next 24 hours, as England could ill afford to play an African team at 2.30 p.m. and have the weather as an opponent as well.

There was a recruiting poster for the French Foreign Legion at the train station in Nice ('We are neither mercenaries nor outlaws, but men of action and élite soldiers,' said the poster). Reading those words and looking at the pictures of the French Legionnaires with the same haircuts as many of the England fans who were at the station, they could have been the same people. Four of us had shared a taxi to the station. The latest fashion accessory for any travelling football fan is the mobile phone. Eddie, from Somerset, almost had his glued to his ear. As the train pulled out of Nice station, the shrill ringing tones made everybody look at Eddie who loudly proclaimed to the carriage that trouble had just kicked off in the Marseilles port area. Everybody huddled round the phone as his friends relayed dispatches from the front line in graphic detail, like a conference call.

' . . . bloody hell they're firing tear-gas. Shit, that bottle just missed me!' It sounded absolutely chaotic.

Suddenly the line went dead. Everybody speculated as to what they were going to do when they got to Marseilles and whether it would affect everybody's ability to obtain tickets for the match. The rumour was that tickets were available on the black market. Rumour and football fans travel together like Steptoe and Son, strange bedfellows locked together in an uneasy alliance, both needing and relying on each other to co-exist.

Two of the young lads had decided to skip the train fare and spent the whole journey walking up and down the train dodging the friendly ticket collector. As we sped along, the wealth that emanates from this region of France became obvious. Huge, plush, freshly-emulsioned, gleaming apartment blocks and a vast array of sparkling white yachts adorned the elegant waterfront while refined women strolled along the platforms every time the train stopped at stations. The usual array of clichés regarding French women were trotted out, and while we'd all heard them before and knew that none of us would solicit a second glance from these women, we all laughed anyway. The laughter was more on account of the nervousness we felt at being less than 24 hours from the start of the '98 World Cup. England's last kick in anger at a World Cup had been Chris Waddle's fateful penalty miss against Germany in Turin in 1990. We'd all aged a little since that night. Gazza had aged and bellied up so much that Hoddle had left him behind, while we'd all left someone behind who'd said they were coming to France. Now, cruising along the rich playground of Europe, their loss wasn't worth thinking about. While everybody had certainly aged, the little boy in us was starting to get excited by the thought of seeing England on the big stage once again.

Terry had met us in Rome and now he had arranged to meet me on Monday morning as I had his match ticket. Terry took off from Gatwick travelling on the British Airways 7.30 p.m. direct to Marseilles. The flight had extended the business-class section nearly three-quarters of the way down the plane to accommodate the demand created by hospitality England. Most of the people travelling business were on a corporate freebie. I am sure that these people have a great feeling for England but they were not around the last time England kicked a ball in the World Cup. Football was all about the fans, while these new-money types had upped the ante for most of them. They might not have taken the seat of the average Joe Bloggs though they sure had increased the price of flights, hotels and black market match tickets. For the true cynic, this World Cup had ceased to become a fans' bonanza and had just become a junket which generated larger television revenue, watched by fans consuming ever-increasing quantities of alcohol and snack foods. The quiet Sunday calm of the travelling business class was about to be shattered by a reminder that however much the new fan encroached upon the game, there would always be lads on a beano as long as England played. Ian and Steve had just passed their 20th birthday and their mum had won two tickets for Marseilles in the many thousands of free trips that were being offered by every sponsor of the World Cup. Their excitement meant that everybody in the plane was about to share their experience, as well as their Canning Town vocabulary, which necessitated prefixing and suffixing everything with 'fuck' or 'fucking'.

'I've never been abroad before. Well, I've been to Torremolinos, but that's not abroad is it, that's fuckin' Blackpool with sunshine,' shouted Ian to a smiling Terry.

'Nah, it fuckin' is abroad 'cos you have to get a plane,' shouted Steve. And so it went on. Sitting across the aisle from the two lads was an old man.

'All right, Grandad? Still getting it?'

'Yes, thank you.'

'You dirty old bugger – I thought you had a glint in your eye.'

By the time Terry got off the flight he knew the names of their numerous sexual conquests, how much they could drink 'wivout chundering and how posh birds liked it up the arse.' Not quite what the good citizens of Hospitality Habitation had in mind when they said yes to their tax deductible bribe. No doubt the lads' incredulity at being offered free wine with their meals was noted for future marketing promotions.

'Free wine darlin'? I might just have a couple of extras for later, eh?' said Ian, winking. The hostess did not bat an eyelid. No doubt she'd heard far worse from some drunken oik in business class before.

Just before take-off, they too had received a call. Once airborne, they announced to the whole plane that it was revving up in Margate Frogland and they determined to tell all the passengers their plan of action.

'Oy, Grandad! Those Froggies are tear-gassing our boys. We've got to get down there and reinforce our boys. Bloody 'ell! We're fighting them on the beaches. It'll be like Dunkirk all over again.'

'Dunkirk was a defeat,' replied Grandad, wearily.

'Read your history, Grandad, it was a great victory. We showed them Krauts how to organise a day trip to England on a cross channel ferry,' replied Steve excitedly.

Once the plane touched down the lads were off and sprinting across the concourse. The last time Terry saw them was when they shouted to a confused taxi driver to get them to the front line 'pronto pronto'.

As the train got closer to Marseilles, the architecture got progressively harsher. No wonder it is not recognised as a tourist area. By the time the Canning Town lads arrived, the main skirmish involving some stupid posturing by some well-meaning but drunken English lads had got completely out of hand. I arrived in the early evening and caught a taxi down to the front. Huge mobs of French Africans were roaming the streets. For added organisation, scouts were patrolling the streets on mopeds and any England fan they spotted was chased, which called for some nifty moving. Other bikes were patrolling the street with a pillion passenger at the back with clubs. Any unfortunate to be spotted wearing an England shirt was the recipient of a club to the back, sometimes even to the back of the head.

At one time, the English visitors to Marseilles were a curious spillover from the shaded terrace verandas of Nice and Cannes; a curious relic of white blazers, Panama hats and Empire snobbishness. What they had in common with the fan visitors was their belief in English being the best. Now, smart blazers were replaced by baggy shorts and three-lions T-shirts while lager was preferred to Pimms.

At every England match there is a congregation bar, a place where the fans have an impromptu meeting and get together. Any outsider looking in would assume that the meeting place is pre-arranged since everybody seems together, but this just isn't the case. For the match in Marseilles, the Vieux Port area became the meeting point. It also, unfortunately, became the focal point of the local underclass of French Africans who started harassing the English fans as soon as they entered the town on the Friday. The following day, one of the lads, much the worse for drink, jumped up on a car and fell down, breaking his leg. When the ambulance arrived, the English lads hurled abuse because they didn't feel it had arrived quickly enough. Hearing this story reminded me of the stories my wife tells about her past work in the casualty department of south London's St Helier hospital when Saturday nights became fight nights and stab and glass wounds were attended to while drunken mates would start the fight all over again in the waiting room. Drink isn't the cause of these problems, but rather arouses some peculiar basic anger which seems endemic in the English.

Since these boys are not into sightseeing or other refined activities unless there is a bar opposite, the drinking began early on Sunday. The beer culture is a natural consequence of the attempt to achieve an identity. It is a culture as much a part of England as London Bridge – a monster who has broken free of the Frankenstein laboratory controlling ethos and is running wild. Beer culture is derided by the rest of England, probably because it reveals too much about a society which craves conformity yet enjoys the humour surrounding the cult which has created mini economies in Spain, Cyprus and Greece.

Above the Marseilles harbour is a church with a gold angel on top. Quite what the angel made of the shirtless tattooed England fans is hard to imagine. You see these lads at Goodwood, Torremolinos or even on day trips to Blackpool. When the English beer monster talks about culture he seldom means historical ruins – he's more likely to mean a new designer brand of lager to be drunk from the bottle.

The first car, full of flag-waving Tunisians, went past at around 11 a.m. It stopped and the horns tooted, not just once, but incessantly. It fairly grated on the nerves.

The lads sat chatting about football, for the most part. One of the lads brought an interesting story with him which emphasised the thoughts of the travelling England fans.

'You know that Tunisians are bum bandits.'

'You can't say that.'

The younger lad telling the story got quite animated.

'I'm telling you. This lot are dodgy. Did you know that they beat up a Scotland fan in Paris then pulled his trousers down and gave him a seeing to afterwards. Remember that Tunis was the place the bum bandits used to go to when it was illegal to be a bum bandit in England.'

People sat up and took notice.

'Fuckin' hell, imagine getting a right kicking then one of them gives you a rogering with the old pork sword.'

Nervous laughter followed and everybody gave unspoken agreement that it was a frightening scenario. Once upon a time, the phrase 'Tunis boys' to the Panama hat class would have had totally different connotations to that which was being bandied about the Bar Olympique. The English lads always want to know how the local boys shape up against their machismo.

As a succession of cars pulled up, the shouts from the English became more offensive. The Tunisians replied in kind, but they did not shout at the England fans so much as bark at them. The constant tooting of the cars outside the bar area was becoming tiresome. A combination of heat and strong beer changed the mood from one of benign verbal abuse to one of English xenophobic nationalism. The light sea breeze belied the strong heat of the sun which was beating down on the lads. At around 2 p.m., the sensible people felt it was time to move on as the mood outside O'Malley's Irish pub started to get a little aggressive. Somebody tore down the Irish tricolour and the chant went up.

No surrender. No surrender
No surrender to the IRA

We are talking Premier League drinkers here: 'Who cares about Monday afternoon's game – this is all about showing people that we are English.'

The fact is that if you wanted to go crazy you'd sit there with a shaven head and no shirt on and drink a dozen six per cent strength lagers in a fierce Mediterranean sun for six hours – I'd defy Tony Blair to think rationally if he did that. And yet this was the organised scenario the police National Criminal Intelligence Unit came up with and briefed the media on. Meanwhile, on the other side of the harbour opposite these well-meaning Anglais buffoons, sat the English police masterminds telling their French counterparts that they knew all the main faces who might cause trouble and had categorised them for easy recognition. Don't worry, Mr French Policeman, the English have the hooligan strategy all worked out . . . It would have been comical if O' Malley's bar in which they congregated hadn't been listed by the Lonely Planet guide as one of the in bars. Some intelligence operation that one! And people wonder how 60,000 British and Commonwealth troops got killed and wounded on the first morning of the battle of the Somme.

A camera crew came up and started filming. James Shayler, a 34-year-old father of three, responded by singing to the camera at the top of his voice while slapping his St George stomach tattoo to show how proud he was of his country.

'*Ingerland Ingerland Ingerland.*'

Then he upped the decibel level until he was screaming at full blast.

'*INGERLAND INGERRRLAND.*'

At that point, a timely intervention of two or three English bobbies and a few French policeman could have averted the riot by shutting off the road to through traffic, but these things seem to have a life of their own. The Tunisian cars constantly drove past. A comment was made. 'If they do that one more time then I'm gonna stick one on them.' It had probably been said a hundred times before without anything happening. But this time something did happen because drinking six hours in that sun was the tolerance limit. Quite what happened around 4 p.m. on the Quai des Belges, and who threw the first bottle will be discussed forever (even those who were there are undecided), but a march past of some Tunisian flag-waving fans sparked off a short flurry of punches followed by an ungainly charge of English beer bellies pursuing the fleeing Tunisian fans along the Quai de Rive Neuve. Marseilles is the repository of France. Beneath the beautiful veneer of yachts, luxury restaurants and wealth is the toxic waste of a forgotten underclass of French Africans. The French Africans and Tunisians soon responded by throwing bottles and the England fans were quick to reciprocate. The massed ranks of cameramen and TV crews were on the scene within seconds. This was the moment they had been waiting for. Within seconds the first images flashed up on the screens and the wires screamed out that disturbances had broken out in the port area. More cameras and reporters followed. Reporters left their beers and sprinted to the area. Mobile phones went wild as every reporter in Europe grabbed the story.

Some of the pressmen later remarked that the riot was organised and orchestrated. If that was organised then I'd hate to see disorganised. Fans stood around while others scurried around shouting at others to get themselves together and do it for England.

'We're English and proud of it,' they chanted. If they were planning a riot, then to dress in shorts and trainers and sit there drinking until they were almost too drunk to stand up would seem a trifle poor in terms of planning. Everybody loves a conspiracy theory, though, and it's good form to say that it was pre-planned because there is no right of reply to a conspiracy theory that doesn't exist.

By now, the police were standing in a line and the French Africans stood behind them holding bottles. Local lads were soon pulling empty crates into position for a stream of ammunition. English fans tried to get the lads going. It was one thing to make a charge along the road but they had their backs to the sea and nobody wanted to get nicked before tomorrow's match.

'Come on, you wankers – let's go at them,' shouted one tall lad wearing a white shirt and shorts.

'Let's fuckin' show them we're English,' shouted others.

'Come on, let's go! The fish and chips, the whores, the beers, all the good stuff will be hot tonight. Who really gives a toss about tomorrow afternoon anyway? This is the time. Do it. Fuckin' do it. Do it now!' shouted another.

And the collective drunken tabloid mentality of England and Empire charged down the road in the most disorganised, chaotic, ridiculous way you could ever imagine. Passers-by, locals and tourists together stood back and watched in awe.

INGERLAND INGERLAND INGERLAND. A short charge led to most of the lads being out of breath. A second charge was met by a withering barrage of bottle fire. The heavily weighted English lads retreated. It was like Agincourt, with the heavier English knights being cut down by the skilful French archers, in this case veteran bottle throwers, their skills honed by countless skirmishes with the CRS. The English lads had no idea that the others were as skilled at rioting as they were at drinking – and it wasn't their town and they had nowhere to go. Normally the French Africans were on the receiving end of a beating from the riot police but now the riot police were lining up alongside them blaming the English bad guys. Some lads used lulls in the skirmishing to phone their friends or even their mums. One lad was heard shouting to his mum.

'Hey mum, watch the news, I'm in the middle of a riot. Oy! cameraman, point this over here. Which station are you from? Swedish TV. Christ, that's no good to me. Oy, mum – I'll phone you back if Sky or the BBC cameraman get me into shot.'

One of the lads who was upset by the camera flashes ran forward with a chair and pitched it at a cameraman, a move that earned the camera crew a bonus of £5,000, due to the image being sold all over the world.

Then the tear-gas was fired. One or two of the fans started dancing around in the gas.

'I'm singing in the gas,' to the tune of 'Singing in the Rain'.

Through the haze of tear-gas, the faces that stared back from the English side were not ones of hatred but of gentle bemusement. Little did they know that they would become the biggest anti-establishment figures since the Birmingham Six were falsely arrested.

To make matters funnier, the wind was behind the England fans so the gas blew in the face of the Tunisians and the riot police as well as all the diners sitting outside the restaurants further down the road.

Dean Whiting was there on holiday with his girlfriend, sitting outside a plush fish restaurant when he tasted the bitterness in his throat. He immediately jumped up along with everybody else and started to retreat, as did the restaurant owner who was desperately trying to get the bills out first. As Dean walked up the road still holding his serviette, he was snapped by a photographer from *Paris Match* magazine. His picture was reproduced under the headline, *CARTON ROUGE AUX HOOLIGANS* (Red Card for the Hooligans).

'There's something really beautiful about an exploding tear-gas canister, what with all its amazing pyrotechnics,' somebody later remarked to me in a bar in the station.

One of the fans who was spotted dancing around in the gas and generally shouting his defiance to the police and TV cameras was James Shayler. With his shaven head and flag of St George tattooed on his stomach, he portrayed the image of a thug leader. Really he was just another travelling England fan who got carried away on too much beer, sun and English attitude. When a snatch squad moved in and grabbed him his persona of shaven head, bare torso, sullen look and sunglasses became synonymous with riot. To the London fans, he was just what we call a Goodwood racer – a sensible guy who gets on a coach to go racing in July, yet who after only five hours of drink and sun, turns into a raving lunatic, usually getting involved in some sort of fight or rollaround brawl. He then goes home to the wife and kids, and arrives at work the next day with a hangover and an ear-bashing from his wife. For James Shayler, the reality of being branded by the British media as a superthug, organiser and starter pistol of the Marseilles riot would be an instant three-month prison sentence. The harsher punishment would be reserved for his wife and family, being subjected to the Diana paparazzi doorstep treatment.

The English lads were just having a punch up and being English. England on tour, piss-up and punch-up: one doesn't necessarily follow the other, but now it's happening, let's have a laugh. They just wanted to dish out a few smacks in the teeth to those who dared to insult England, not hurt anybody. The French Africans, however, had other ideas. They intended to up the ante. Now, in greater numbers, the African front-line lads were looking to swap punches. Behind them were harder, nastier cases with knives and more. Cue more stupid scuffles. One England fan ran forward, kung fu kicked the air and then fell on his backside. The Tunisian punched him. His mate tried a kick and also fell over. Fighting after a five-hour lager session always seems like a good idea but the reality is totally different. Some of these lads were probably seeing five faces to punch on the same person as they ran up the road. What did the media expect? Choreographed fist fights. Nobody gave journalism a good name on Drunken Marseilles Sunday. Like the westerns of popular memory, the English fans were the baddies.

I looked down that road and saw lads running back and forward, not punching, just shouting, gaining territory and then relinquishing it. My mind flew back to primary school where we played British Bulldogs and ran up and down the playground. The English weren't being nasty – just playful – because they'd swapped the playground for a street in Marseilles.

You're up, you're tough, drink fired, English. Bollocks. CHARGE. The English have charged to their failure many times before. Hastings, Balaclava and the Somme spring readily to mind, yet history records these lads charging to failure as being glorious. In their own minds, they were charging for England once again. These lads thought they'd get a medal, not mass condemnation. The media rehashed the script for England back home using the tired old clichés that have been written so many times before, they could have come from a journalistic hooligan manual: 'You don't want to let your mates down ... the buzz ... control the lads around you ... lead them into battle ... you can't resist the thrill of the charge.' It could have been written at any time over the past few hundred years. It's the same old song.

A young fan stood on the corner looking on in bemusement. A camera was thrust in his face. He pushed it away then gave an eloquent speech through clenched teeth:

'The media call us a disgrace, the locals attack us, the touts rip us off, then people wonder why we do it and don't care about our actions or apologise for our behaviour. All we've got is a few quid in our pockets and our respect as English.'

Some of the cameramen and journalists were also getting a big-time buzz from the aggro. That's what they came for. It was keeping them young. Seeing the English fight made their week and kept them enthusiastic, and, more importantly, kept them in work for the remaining weeks of France '98, maybe even beyond. If the army of anthropologists and sociologists who have earned a fortune writing about England fans had stopped and asked one of the front-line puncher lads why they were doing it, they would have been met with a giggle and the words: 'It's a bit of a larf, innit? – rough lads enjoying themselves.' Because, despite the reams of analysis that have been written, that's all it was. Other fans were not quite so eloquent. 'SCUM, SCUM,' shouted one lad, looking at the camera with obvious venom. The next day, Rob Hughes wrote in the *Herald Tribune* that these words had been directed at him, although I was perplexed that a *Times* football correspondent should be working as a rotter news reporter. When I questioned a journalist about this later, he told me matter-of-factly that events were often reported *in situ* when the writer wasn't actually present at the scene. The papers reported it as they saw it – perhaps . . .

'Vindaloonies' – *The Daily Star*

'A disgrace to England' – *The Sun*

'So ashamed of our yob fans' – *The Express*

'Louts, thugs and mindless' – *The Mail*

One fan who was there but never got nicked nor got his name in the papers told me his view the next morning: 'I love the feeling of power we invoked in Marseilles. Just for a few minutes, they all backed off us. Two hundred hand-picked geezers went forward – what a mob. Rag-heads and riot police together were absolutely powerless in the face of our togetherness. We were kings for 15 minutes and famous forever. I'm bleeding notorious! To think they'll be talking about that in our boozer for the next decade and I was in the front line.' He clenched his fist and moved his arm back and forward in mock celebration, then punched the air.

'Superb. But later when I ran for me life it was a different matter altogether. I used muscles I didn't think I had, gulping air into me lungs while my stomach ached with that retching feeling. Once you're clear, though, you're ready to go back in again with another dose of adrenaline. I didn't even think about the risks – being nicked or done was something that happened to somebody else. Mind you, I can still taste that horrible taste of tear-gas in the back of me throat.'

He'd created his own bit of history. In beer-monster England, everybody wants to be a somebody. Now he was a somebody who could bask in his reflected glory and fellow beer monsters would give him the respect he'd earned in Marseilles. Other nobodies would want to know him now. Was he a thug? No: he was just a little – how shall we say it? – *misinformed* as to how English people were expected to behave in Marseilles. Was he ashamed? No, not a bit of it. I could see his point of view, even if I disagreed with what he said and did, because, as he put it:

'Where I come from, you only take so much grief before you stand up to be counted.' I asked where he came from. 'England, of course', he replied then gave me a look which made it clear that he thought my question ridiculous.

'It makes no difference who caused it 'cos we caused it whether or not we caused it. It's always grief for us,' added his mate with a sense of urgency, as though he had to get it out quickly or else it wouldn't be told.

As night fell, the riot took on a different turn as the French Africans turned it into a gang warfare situation. Sitting outside the Marseilles bars on Sunday evening was like being an insect going too near a Venus fly trap. You think you're okay then suddenly you're sucked in and ambushed by a nasty little mob of knife-wielding French. Fear kept me moving, kept me alert. I didn't consider myself a coward for getting the hell out of the Vieux Port area when darkness fell. What had been safe by day suddenly became dangerous by night. I retreated up to the station where you could have been in a different city it was so calm, almost as though it was sealed off from the port area by an invisible force field. This end of the street was safe but that end wasn't. Not everybody managed to get out as easily as I did: two of the Worthing lads had come early and were sitting in the front window of a restaurant near the port area when bottles started hitting the front glass. The owner pulled the shutters down across the main windows and locked them from the outside. The shutter over the door could only be shut from the outside. The owner pulled it down and stood on the lip while outside the mob bayed for their blood when they eventually ventured outside.

Every time the owner pulled the shutter up across the door, dark faces surged forward, up against the glass, salivating with excitement, almost sexual, knives being drawn across throats to show them what they should expect. The owner then tried to pull the shutter down, while outside, and the mob tried to lift it up. The mob started throwing bottles underneath while two enormous bouncers inside whacked shins the other side with baseball bats. The lads had been looking for kicks but this was ridiculous. Eventually the owner got the shutter down and stood holding it down while all hell seemed to break loose on the other side of the metal. When the owner sounded the all-clear three hours later, they emerged shaken. Tentatively, they walked up the road towards their hotel. Within seconds, a moped rider shot past screaming 'English pigs' at them. From a sidestreet, dark faces emerged and all that could be seen was their white eyes and teeth as they smiled a long, forbidding smile.

Run English! Run English! Run, Run, Run!
Don't give the locals their fun, fun, fun!

Two girls screeched up in an open-top sports car and rescued them – it was fear beyond panic – and then out the other side.

Everything was spooky on the streets of Marseilles that Sunday evening – it would have been spooky whether there had been a riot or not. Just when you thought you'd got clear of the darkies another group would appear from a sidestreet. Fear and loathing walked those narrow dark alleys hand in hand. One English lad came past the bar at around 11 p.m. completely smashed and started to walk towards the port area. He could hardly stand up.

'Don't go down there, mate, you'll come a cropper in that state,' I implored him. Three times I tried to stop him walking down the dark road through the African quarter leading to the port area, but he was so determined to go down there and so convinced that being English was some sort of shield against physical attack and injury, that I gave up dissuading him. He told me he 'liked danger' in any case.

For Harry and St George.

A short while later, just after midnight, an England fan was found in the road near St Charles railway station with his throat cut. Only the skill of the French surgeons saved his life. Other fans suffered stab wounds. There it was for many England fans: the worst nightmare. Getting on a plane in England and being found in a dark alleyway with your throat cut; the English Press label you 'low-life' and say that you were a deserving victim; some darkie doing the unspeakable to you while you lie there dying. Much of the venom of the riotous England fans was aimed at the media who seemed to be revelling in the fans' predicament.

Two fans charged up the road, holding beer in one hand and a metal crowd-control barrier in the other between them, and threw it at the camera. It bounced harmlessly two feet in front of them. It was a gesture of contempt. For their trouble, they were photographed by 20 different cameras giving them a notoriety with the English police which they would never live down and would probably live to regret.

Sitting outside the bar near the St Charles railway station I really was in a different city. All the England fans inside were watching the Jamaican Reggae boys play Croatia. When Jamaica scored, the bar erupted. Every England fan had an affinity with Jamaica because Jamaicans plied a lot of their trade in England. People talk about racism in football, yet in all my time I have only ever met a few morons who cannot see that skin colour is irrelevant once the football shirt goes on. Two cars pulled up outside the bar at the lights with the occupants hanging outside waving flags. The horns of the cars blasted away in tandem. The lights changed but the cars sat there. A door flew open and two skimpily-clad, attractive, French African girls jumped out. Their hips gyrated back and forwards like simulated sex and belly dancing combined.

The provocative dance led to a few shouts and wolf whistles from the bar, but this dance wasn't for us – it was for the men inside the cars. You could see from the looks on their faces and their body language that they were in a highly excited state. The English looked on in awe. Some even put their beer down. After two minutes, the girls jumped back in and sped off with the car horns blasting.

'Jesus Christ,' exclaimed a fan. 'She was so worked up she was practically having an orgasm.'

'I bet they've got hairy armpits. All French girls have got hairy armpits.'

'And a smelly snatch, all African girls have a smelly snatch.' The guys who said it then turned to the TV and went back to their beer. Their comments said more about some English attitudes than anything else I had heard during my two days in Marseilles.

I was staying in a French suburb so I walked up to the station to get the metro out that way. As I went through with my ticket, security guards with large guard dogs checked the entrance barriers. Once on the platform, I was met by five armed Foreign Legionnaires. The platform was deserted. They looked me up and down. The captain asked me in French where I was going.

'Je vais au St Marguerite Drommel.'

He spoke in English. 'We will accompany you. Things are very bad out there.'

That had not occurred to me as I, too, had the imaginary shield of St George protecting me. At the end of the line they bade me farewell and boarded another train back. As I went down the stairs I was confronted by five young Africans. Perhaps I could pretend to be French. There was another security guard on my side of the barrier holding back a very agitated dog as he attempted to hold them at bay and stop the Africans getting over. I decided to walk through with a sense of purpose. They were onto me immediately. My heart skipped two beats and I was struggling for breath.

'Can we have your ticket?' asked a young African in good English.

I passed it to him. They could have had my money or any other tangible thing they so desired. Perhaps they were going back into the city centre where the riot was really getting fierce.

The hotel which looks out on to the harbour had a number of Englishmen staying in it and as usual they had their flags hanging out on the balcony. The French African mob were trying to storm the front of the hotel which even for the guys three storeys up was still pretty frightening.

I left the station still shaking from my African experience. My hosts for the evening were the elderly parents of my French work colleague. His mother is half Italian. When I arrived, they had enough food to feed every England fan in town and enough drink to sink a battleship. They told me about the news bulletins they had seen which were all about the trouble in Marseilles. It was generally agreed that the hard-drinking English combined with the Africans living in Marseilles was a riot waiting to happen. I retired to bed around 2 a.m. and lay awake for two hours as the heavy meal I had eaten rested on my stomach.

The next day I was up around 8 a.m. and down to the stadium. I spoke to Paul Hayward of the *Daily Telegraph* who was with his colleagues watching the CNN news.

'It looks pretty bad. They are blaming the English for starting the trouble,' he stated to me on the phone.

All through the day the image of James Shayler flashed up on the screen. The barbarians, epitomised by this image, were indeed in town. The next day James Shayler got three months in prison while others got two months after a fair trial of ten minutes. *Liberté, égalité, fraternité* indeed – for that's what it said on the front of the coins in those lad's pockets. The proud French sentiments of liberty and justice are obviously irrelevant if you are a drunken England football fan. The French police were not looking for anybody involved with the throat slitting of the England fan. One fan even pleaded not guilty but his defence was denied him when he was asked this one question.

'Are you an English football fan?'

And when he answered that he was, the response was no different from the rest:

'Send him down, three months, guilty as hell.' In the words of W.B. Yeats, 'The blood-dimmed tide is loosed and everywhere the ceremony of innocence is drowned.'

The English police and Government applauded this approach. After all, it worked when IRA bombs had gone off in England.

With the Mediterranean sun spreading a warming glow on the city, I headed back into the port area. I expected to see total destruction from the previous evening's exploits, but the port area was remarkably quiet and undamaged. I sat down opposite the area where the trouble had been and the waiter served me a coffee.

'Pretty bad last night.'

He looked at me and shrugged his shoulders.

'This is Marseilles. It was Saturday night again.' His demeanour indicated it was nothing out of the ordinary for this city.

Normally after a day of violence there would be an uneasy calm over the whole area with fractious police watching every move and acting in an oppressive manner, yet exactly the opposite was true of Marseilles. The riot police were nowhere to be seen and the fish sellers with their plastic trays did business as usual from the spot where, only four hours before, a screaming mob of over 2,000 French Africans had bayed for English blood. I laughed at the irony of this. Back in England, my friends were under the impression that every shop and bar had been smashed to smithereens. I pottered along the 250 yards around the port to the Rue Forta corner café restaurant/bar which had three windows smashed and three with impact cracks where bottles or bricks had been pitched at them with extreme force. The English had done this, of course, although I wondered if this had been the restaurant where the English lads had been trapped and the mob had tried to break in, and if that was the cause of the damage.

Nothing else mattered because the media had decided who was to blame. Journalists filed report after report on their mobile phones. I saw a photographer, on edge and looking tired, but snapping at the windows from every angle. Other people stood looking. A *Times* journalist finished his report and approached me.

'Who did this bar?' I asked.

'English fans.'

'Are you sure?'

'Yes, they have it on camera. I've seen it.'

'Well if that's true, then it's a black day for all the good English fans who are on their way here,' I stated.

In the next morning's edition of *The Times* that journalist managed to twist what I said : ' . . . at least Colin Ward has the decency to show remorse for his previous actions.'

I purchased a Marseilles newspaper which had a colour picture of the overturned burnt-out car which had contained journalists. This was a front page leader for the *Daily Mail* back in England. No wonder fans are angry at journalists when all they read are twisted words and half-truths. If *The Times* twists words to gain an angle, then where does that leave tabloid truth?

The blonde female bar owner was photographed and asked to pose from various angles for the cameras. How many different angles can you photograph a broken window from? Was it really necessary for the photographer to lie on the floor to get one? Next, the lady was asked to recreate the moment when the crazed England fan ran along breaking her windows with a piece of metal table support. It was like a film set with directors barking orders. Lights – camera – action!

'Okay, lets take it from that angle. You walk up the road slowly towards the smashed window looking glum. Stop. Hold it there for five seconds. Spread some of that glass around in front of the camera lens. Point at the broken window. Good angle. Camera, do you need another take or have you got enough? Right, thanks very much,' and then a call on the mobile and off they shot to the next flashpoint area. These guys are making movies. No cameramen were on the streets when it was really going wild out there around 2 a.m., and anyway, it was already decided that England fans had caused the trouble. Category Cs had organised it. The fact that the BBC had obtained a report that Argentine hooligans and French neo-Nazi MVA members were in Marseilles looking for a violent confrontation with England fans was never looked into. All the English media needs is a one-word answer and a drunken, shirtless England fan to get the ratings up.

Unfortunately for them they could find no more repeats of that violence and were stuck for a story. All they could find were hordes of Tunisians making a huge din as they rode around in cars, waving flags. The bemused England fans sat around drinking coffee, eating croissants and looked shocked when a camera was stuck in their face.

'What effect do you think the violence will have on you?'

By 11 a.m., the English were sitting around in different bars in the usual half-naked pose, drinking and topping up their tans and alcohol levels. Those arriving by train were searched, put on buses and dropped some distance from the port to prevent it becoming a mass-congregation area. The violence had frightened the Mayor. But if the violence hadn't, then I bet the 50-strong journalists machine gun firing him questions about further violent confrontations did. It would have taken a brave man to keep his calm among that braying mob. I have actually witnessed a press conference where the levels of violence increased during the period in which the questions were asked. Scary. The knife-wielding Tunisians from the previous evening looked like pussy cats in comparison. Mr Mayor did what he felt he had to do which was declare Marseilles a drink-and-enjoyment-free zone from 11 p.m. that evening. The original idea of letting the bars stay open till 4 a.m. after the match was now shelved. I sat down outside La Samaritaine café along with a few other England fans to enjoy the morning sunshine. I ordered my first beer of the day and got talking to three lads from Huddersfield. Two of them had tickets and had paid £150 each for them. The third had a theory which said that once the stadium held 60,000, then demand would drop just before kick-off and he would get a ticket for around £50. His theory was to prove right on the day. One thing was for sure: there were plenty of tickets available on the black market and plenty of English folk heading into town. Estimates had been upgraded from 10,000 to 20,000. Later, I believe, the total was closer to 25,000.

I had arranged to meet Terry and the Worthing Mafia, but sitting there enjoying the bonhomie with the England fans I was in no rush. By now the corner of this bar had become a focal point for a very noisy crowd of Tunisians. Suddenly two motorcycle outriders sped past with their sirens wailing and their blue lights flashing. Immediately behind was a motorcycle speeding in their slipstream. Standing precariously on the back and swaying from side to side, there was a young Tunisian waving a giant flag who was followed by a red van full of riot police. It was an incredible sight. As the red van tried to overtake, the Tunisian weaved from side to side. They sped up the hill into the distance. How the man with the Tunisian flag managed to hold on is beyond me. I flinched, waiting for him to come to grief, but as far as I know he didn't. Two lads sat complaining about the differing treatment being dished out.

'They stood there last night while England fans were getting beaten up, yet when we retaliated they nicked us.'

'What do you expect? They have to co-exist with this lot 52 weeks a year,' I replied.

The fact that the stab count in the French Press was 2–0 to Tunisia was not open to discussion. I ordered another beer but the owner was getting nervous about the amount of interest his bar was attracting and stopped serving alcohol. With that, all the England fans moved on.

Terry turned up around 1 p.m. and we settled down outside a bar near the port with a large group of fans from Reading. We talked about football with a knowledge which would have astounded the Press. Glenn Hoddle might not understand the fans but we sure as hell knew which team we wanted even if everyone thought differently. Would he play Beckham or Anderton at right-wing back.

'Definitely Beckham since I reckon he fancies Posh Spice and he's good at nicking other blokes' wives,' remarked one guy laconically, referring to Hoddle's marriage break-up. Coaches full of England fans swept past, giving us enthusiastic waves. Eddie telephoned me from the seafront, where a Radio 1 roadshow was in full swing.

The atmosphere at the seafront where the giant screen was situated was one of friendly bonhomie between the Tunisians and English.

'Come on down – the water's lovely,' he shouted down his mobile at me.

I meant to go to the seafront but ended up whiling away the final hour before we left making small talk in the sun. By the time we got on the underground we had only 40 minutes to kick-off. As we boarded the train, Terry was accosted by a strange-looking England fan who was drunk enough to talk us to death yet not enough that he didn't know what he was saying. He wasn't the strangest fan I have ever met, but his self-created facial tattoos told me that he'd done a lot of time in prison. He had LANCASHIRE tattooed across his neck in huge black letters as well dots on his cheekbones. There was a large number on his arms too, including the words 'Manchester City'. All were done in Indian ink and were smeared enough to look as if they'd been done by someone who'd taken to drink and gone blind. The ACAB (All Coppers Are Bastards) on his four fingers spoke volumes. He soon told Terry his life story.

'I've just done an eight-stretch in Strangeways and I've used all me discharge money to get meself down here. You can't be called an England fan and not be here. I was banged up for Italia '90 so I was determined to be here for this one. I've only been out three weeks and I've kept out of trouble to get meself down 'ere.'

You could see that he was right proud of it. France '98 had kept him going, given him a zest for life in a grim institution, then given him a purpose to propel himself forward. As a kid, he'd been battered by his dad. He then went to a borstal, fathered a child, saw Manchester City a few times and went straight to prison. His future looked bleak but the next two hours would give him unbridled happiness, proving that no matter how far corporate greed encroached, it wouldn't stop people's dreams. We called him Lancs (after his neck tattoo) and remarked on his huge fat lip.

'I got that last night. Some young Turk swung a lump of wood at me from the back of a moped as I was staggering home, but I was so pissed that I didn't realise he'd hit me until this morning. Have you got a ticket, then?' he asked.

Terry nodded, thinking our friend might be upset but he was genuinely pleased that we would be getting in. His *modus operandi* was to hang around outside the ground and hope that someone would give him a ticket. His method of being understood by the French was also quite novel.

'I aim to get so pissed that when I talk they won't know whether I'm speaking French or English.' He took an instant liking to us and was especially pleased when he found out that I was an Arsenal fan. His support of Manchester City, which was tattooed on his right arm, extended to thanking Arsenal of the league and depriving Manchester United of it. He liked Terry so much that he kept kissing Terry's cheeks in French style. This alarmed Terry so much that he couldn't get away from our friendly fan quickly enough. He was a harmless friendly drunk with an appearance that could frighten anyone, whether English or French.

At the ground, we were confronted by a huge wall of England fans in England shirts, singing, dancing and making noise, but again the police seemed to be completely relaxed. Many fans were wearing those silly plastic English bowler hats sponsored by *The Sun* newspaper. Each hat had a red cross of St George on the top. We had come to the wrong entrance so we made our way round to the other side. I had purchased my tickets in France so they had a French name on it and I was worried that there might be a check against the name but my worries were unfounded as we sailed straight in. Our entrance was through glass doors where stunningly pretty French women in red suits ushered me in with a huge smile. Men dressed in immaculate green blazers and beige slacks directed groups up to the hospitality suite. I had lost Terry on the way, but I soon realised that one of the hostesses, seeing the lost look on his face, had personally escorted Terry to his seat. It was friendliness of the highest order, and it was happening all around the ground. The English fans reciprocated by turning the ground inside the stadium into a giant carnival. I got to my seat to be met by the sight of the magnificent arched stand of the Marseilles Velodrome, running the length of the pitch, and 25,000 English people having a celebration.

Dean was sitting there with his girlfriend, both now recovered from their tear-gas ordeal. Before kick-off, a minute's silence was given to remember the death from cancer of one of the organising committee. Everybody, except one or two England and Tunisian fans who felt it necessary to puncture the stillness with stupid calls, observed the silence.

Then it was time for the national anthems. I will not sing 'God Save the Queen' but the rendition by the England fans was so powerful and passionate that pride swelled up in me. Call us terrible names, and drag us through the muck, but we'll still be there with a love of our country and football which defies reason.

The only downer was that the lack of any cover meant that most of the atmosphere was being lost into the air. The England band played the music and everybody sang along to their renditions of 'Rule Britannia' and the theme from *The Great Escape* film, which was becoming the national anthem of England fans of France '98. If you were disposed to being angry, then the folly of the ticket allocation which forced all these good people to resort to the black market was there for all to see, yet the spirit of fun and football shone through. Sure you're pissed off at paying over the odds but once you get the ticket, the cost is overtaken by the feeling of joy and relief knowing that you will be in the stadium witnessing one of the greatest events in the world. In amongst this carnival, the small matter of England winning their opening game needed to be approached. Bobby Robson had stated previously that Tunisia were no special hurdle to England and as the match kicked off, it soon became obvious that England were far superior. After 30 minutes, Paul Scholes was bundled over. Penalty. Our stand rose, shouting and swearing with one voice, yet the referee waved play on. Then there was a free shot for Scholes. The goalie saved it. England looked assured and confident. A free kick was played in front of us and the ball went in to the crowded penalty area. Shearer rose. The goalie had made his decision to fling himself to cover the header but he dived too far.

The England players flung their arms skywards and the whole stadium seemed to rise in a sea of pure white lava coming out of a volcano.

SHEARER SHEARER SHEARER!

As he ran towards the fans, thousands of arms moved back and forward pointing one finger at him in synchronised movement. Let the party begin. At half-time, the England fans felt very satisfied. This was what is was all about. England were playing within themselves and it was the same in the second half. For myself it was like I was there but I wasn't. The tension which everybody had felt had been replaced by a sort of melliferous haze. This was the World Cup opener for England yet it didn't have the vibrancy which it should have had. It was more like a Wimbledon tennis crowd being entertained by Cliff Richard. Some of the England fans started to create Mexican waves to keep the fun going and the band played *The Great Escape* while others just sang their hearts out solo. A bonus was the performance of Paul Scholes, who filled the gap left by Paul Gascoigne. With minutes to go, the fans let out a poignant roar as young Michael Owen warmed up. Only ten years old the last time England kicked a World Cup ball, he was now entering the world arena himself. Already the youngest-ever England goalscorer, he ran on to the pitch with cheers from England fans, most of whom were old enough to be his dad – and all of them remembered the recent praise from Pele stating he could be the star of France '98. But in the last minute, the star of the day, Paul Scholes, instinctively curled a superb shot past the flailing Tunisian keeper and England fans cheered loud and hearty. Before that, one pass too many meant that Sol Campbell's perfect match was spoiled by a yellow card.

On the beach, where a giant screen surrounded by two temporary stands had been erected, England's second goal was greeted by a barrage of missiles from the Tunisians. England fans backed off, those with children ran. The riot police fired tear-gas into the fray which promptly blew into the faces of the fleeing England fans. That was it: the beach was shut for any subsequent parties.

At the end of the game, the England fans filed out feeling as if it had been a job well done. Yeah, we had played well, but it was more like a controlled performance than anything else. Tunisia hadn't tested England, that would come later. As Terry and I walked towards the beach we were unaware of what had happened. To our right were

English coaches by the dozen, stretching as far as the eye could see. The first smashed English car window was about 50 yards into the rue Prado. As we continued to walk along that street, it became obvious that during the match every car with an English number plate had been targeted and systematically had their windows broken. In the papers, Jack Straw had talked about paying blanket compensation to bar owners who'd had their windows broken during the fighting without any evidence as to who had done it. I wondered whether he would do the same for these hapless people on their holiday of a lifetime. Ten yards further on I heard the first echo of a bottle smashing . . . *pop, pop, crash!* like a dull roman candle on fireworks night. Over the top of the coaches they rained. The woman next to me in her England shirt looked at me, terrified. Suddenly people behind started running and the woman grabbed her husband's arm, shouting 'Oh my God, help!' Both she and her husband broke into a panic-driven canter. Terry was off, too. All around, English people ran. These weren't the thugs of popular myth but the honest burghers of middle England who'd looked at the French World Cup as an extended holiday. Now they were being subjected to an unforeseen attack by an invisible enemy lurking on the other side of the road (later, when I walked back up the road, I saw massed crates which the French Africans had stockpiled). More people gripped by terror ran past me saying that the Tunisian mob were behind me. I turned and ran backwards looking for the Tunisian mob, my eyes roaming left and right thinking on the move. I too was running, something I hadn't done for years and for no real reason other than the fact that everybody else was running. What was the matter with me?

'Stop running, you idiots, there's nothing there!' I shouted, but nobody heard me due to the mass hysteria which had set in for a few short seconds. The woman ran round a corner and into a metal post, doing more damage to herself than any stray bottle could do. I wondered how she would tell that story at her next sophisticated dinner party. I ran up to Terry. 'Slow down, Terry, there's nothing there,' I said. Famous last words: for at that moment, another barrage of bottles rained on us, sending everybody running again. Sirens wailed and bottles smashed and a few English lads ran at a small group of Tunisians who had pitched their bottles and run. Glass was everywhere underfoot and we scrunched as we walked. By the time we got to the beach, though, everything had calmed down.

'La plage est fermée,' said the man on the gate. About 20 riot police stood around while the England fans started to congregate. Whilst the

French Africans might be at home in their port, this was now England territory. Groups of lads turned up. There was nothing to do except find the nearest bar.

Robinson's bar on the front was getting very crowded so they put a large Frenchman on the door to let one in as another came out. Now that he had shut the doors and windows, the heat inside the bar became oppressive. The resting England fans stretched along the street like a rag-tag army. Terry and I sat in the sunshine drinking chilled Heineken. Local vendors came down selling cold beers. As we sat there, Graham Kelly, Chief Executive of the Football Association, walked past. He had lost a lot of weight since I last saw him on the TV criticising England fans. He too had walked down that road with his wife, so he must have experienced the fear that other people on holiday with their wives had experienced. He didn't look at ease amongst the shirtless beer-drinking fans.

'Hello, Graham. Enjoy the game?' I said and stood up. I was only making mischief by making him feel uncomfortable yet I saw something of the fear in his wife's eyes that I had seen in others' only minutes previously. Perhaps I would attack Graham? Perhaps I would tell everybody that Graham was a traitor who'd sold us down the river? All I did, in fact, was make banal small talk.

'Not a bad performance, Graham, but now – about my World Cup Final tickets . . . ' I smiled and Graham started laughing if for no other reason than to keep moving and make sure he was not a static target. There were plenty of fans there who had bones to pick with the Football Association's Chief Executive. Graham's wife gave a sigh of laughter that people give in relief when they have just survived a scary ordeal. Having walked down that road, Graham had seen the injustice which innocent England fans had suffered yet he chose to keep his own counsel to the Press, preferring the party line of English hooliganism rather than the truth.

On the seafront was a Sky news team. They asked me for an interview and I gladly accepted but just before they were due to run it, they got word of more violence breaking out in the port area so the news team was back on the move. The news that there were now 2,000 England fans on the front quietly enjoying themselves with a cool beer and that England fans had actually been attacked by French Africans but had not retaliated, was not newsworthy enough. As it transpired, the reports of violent fan clashes in the port area were false and were actually the result of Tunisian anger at their team being beaten.

After an hour or two, Terry and I decided we needed to look for a restaurant and as we walked towards the centre of town we bumped into two young lads. They were looking for Chris Waddle's (ex-England player who used to play in Marseilles) football pub on the Prado front while we were looking for a fish restaurant near the port area.

'I wouldn't go down there – there's a frightening atmosphere,' one of the lads said abruptly.

'Aye, it's as tense as hell. There's going to be one hell of a bundle later,' added the other.

They were right, although the whereabouts of the battle was slightly inaccurate. The French Africans had amassed a huge stockpile of bottles and rocks near the station. Added to this were now petrol bombs. When the England fans didn't go back to the front, the French Africans advanced to the station, tooled up to their white eyeballs, and the fans waiting at the station to get out of town came under attack. Once again the English charged, but this time they were met with petrol bombs. Sensing that this could ignite a problem beyond their control, the French CRS riot police did the only sensible thing: they attacked and clubbed the English fans back onto the station concourse. A small crew of Tunisians got too cocky and were caught in a mass charge. One of them went down and in went the boots, stamping like a rugby front row rucking the ball.

'Do his head.' 'Make him have it.' Within seconds the CRS were at his rescue and one poor England fan, who was still kicking the prostrate African, was lashed around 20 times on the back and legs until everybody backed off. For a few seconds there was chaos as petrol bombs exploded and bricks and bottles filled the air along with aggressive shouts from the French Africans. The CRS riot squad held back the England fans while the petrol bombs exploded with huge whooshes of energy then burnt out with a fading beauty.

Barry and Motty, who were trying to get hold of me, were driving around town looking for the restaurant Terry and I were in. At one point they were surrounded by French Africans with bricks, bottles and clubs. Having been caught in such a situation once before, I know how nerve-racking it can be. They left town as fast as they could without trying to find me. The trains finally came and some of the English left, while those who stayed were greeted with a town which was fast shutting down. The normally vibrant streets took on a deathly quiet.

Terry and I settled down in Les Echevins restaurant with its gentle ambience and subdued lighting. We were the first customers but it was still only 9.30 p.m. Shortly after we had settled down, two casual but well-dressed men in their late 30s came into the restaurant and sat at the next table. Terry was an Essex man, a self-made wealthy man but not quite a millionaire – described by a fellow Essex man as being worth a bob or two. With his short beard and quickfire patter, he was thought by some to be Terry Venables' half-brother. He sold sausage skins all over the world, generating enough money to have a huge manor house near Cambridge, and was so Essex that he'd once played football for Leyton Orient as a professional. You don't come more Essex than that. Terry was past his prime now that he was over 50, yet once upon a time he would have been down on the Cannes promenade posing with his best shirts like the salesman, Rob, I'd met on the previous day's flight. In fact, Terry used to sell or talk about selling even when he was talking about football. He soon struck up a conversation with our fellow English eaters who were hard-core hospitality. When their two friends joined them, they regaled us with stories about their day. I have nothing against people having a great day out but this was a free lunch with *attitude*. The young bright-eyed guy who had brought over 30 people to Marseilles was also planning to take 20 to Toulouse then another 20 to the World Cup final, and didn't he want to tell us that.

'That's big bucks,' I said. He smiled at me. His company could afford it because, after all, they were into computers and that is where the serious money is now being earned.

'I live in Berkshire and work in Silicon Valley,' he stated matter-of-factly, as though he were telling me something profound.

'Its a long way to commute to California,' I replied, dryly.

'No, Silicon Valley, Reading, Bracknell,' he replied.

Terry laughed. 'Take no notice of Colin, he's one of your lot – he lives in poncy, commuter-land Surrey.' That was all they needed to know. I was now accepted because I was one of the boys living in a four bedroom, detached house in stockbroker belt with two children and a responsible job. Yet in terms of our attitude to the World Cup, we were galaxies apart. The World Cup for me was a religious experience; not some jolly to take customers as a thank you. Hospitality Hotel is where guys take customers out to the Far East and lay on Filipino prostitutes to clinch a deal. All he was doing now was prostituting my beautiful game and I was sitting in the same restaurant as him, finding it difficult to get annoyed with him.

He produced a match ticket which had been signed by Ray Wilkins and Emlyn Hughes. Ray Wilkins was his hero as he was a Chelsea fan. At least he used to go to Chelsea when there were terraces which is more than could be said for the other three. The white-haired guy had been to every corporate hospitality bash going, proudly ranking this trip among the best of them, if not the best. Only one thing had pissed him off.

'We were all having a celebratory glass of the old bubbly after the match when the team coach pulled out. Sitting there all haughty was Alan Shearer. We all cheered and chanted at the man but he completely ignored us as did all the other players. The only players who acknowledged us were Steve McManaman and Les Ferdinand. McManaman gave us a huge grin with a thumbs-up.'

'If that's the worst you've encountered, then you're doing okay. We've spent years being told we're slightly less welcome than Hitler on a lightning trip to Poland,' I stated. This caused the hospitality lads to fall about in raucous laughter, unable to discern the seriousness in my voice.

'We,' he asked quizzically, 'Who are 'we'?' I then explained who and what 'We' were, using 'Lancs' as an example. They enjoyed the stories but looked at me as if I were talking about people from another planet.

'What about the real fan?' I asked.

'Bollocks to the real fan; or do you mean the organised thugs who caused all the bother yesterday? If my money eliminates them once and for all then I am sure that everybody will thank me for it.'

I meant to put him right about the level of organisation amongst the England fans but didn't bother. He'd read in the *Daily Telegraph* that these people were organised so it *must* be true. One English guy was lying in hospital fighting for his life and all this guy was concerned about was being ignored by the England players. At least the English Football Association liked their money. Should they completely oust the real fan then the game will be finished but for now, their profile was higher than that of the real fan whose destiny was inexorably entwined with that of the 200 idiots who'd charged yesterday afternoon. Hospitality profile was high. Our own government was spending a million pounds telling ordinary fans not to come to the World Cup while these guys were being pandered to by Mastercard, Cannon, Budweiser and a host of other corporate giants. Cool Britannia was epitomised by the all-encompassing, consuming, corporate guest. It must have made Tony Blair feel good to think that these people were being feted, but if 18,000 England fans hadn't purchased their tickets on the black market, who would have filled those seats? Perhaps the British Government saw the stab victim as a necessary casualty. I am sure that the parents of this poor man wouldn't thank people for calling him an organised thug and disowning him.

I tried to get angry with the Hospitality mob, but they were great company and the white-haired guy kept ordering quality wine which he topped up my glass with repeatedly. I suppose that in the end I prostituted my anger for a bottle of quality claret. We left them on the brandies: I knew it was time to leave when Terry started trying to sell them natural sausage casings. We were staying about 20 km away in Aix-en-Provence. We asked our taxi driver to give us one last tour of the port area but it was all shut down, just like the rest of the city. It was only midnight yet every bar was shut, giving Marseilles a ghostly look. It looked more like Margate on a windy December evening than Marseilles in June. Our taxi driver claimed that Marseilles had never, ever shut before like this.

'Not even the Vichy French Government dared to shut down Marseilles.' I took no pride in the fact and saw it as a taste of things to come. While the rest of the World Cup was getting down and boogying, England were shutting down and brooding. We pulled into the square at Aix-en-Provence and the main bar was humming to the joyful chat of England fans having a good time. It immediately restored my faith in true England fans. The next morning at the Holiday Inn, a group of England fans stood and watched as their Renault Espace had its windows replaced. Despite it having French number plates, one of the lads had left an English Sunday paper on the back seat which meant that its windows had been smashed. Now that really *was* organised football thuggery and it didn't even rate one line in the tabloids.

For England fans to complain that they are treated like dumb animals and herded like sheep from one insensitive police force to another is the cliché of clichés, in the same way that every England fan who arrives back with DEPORTED stamped on his passport and shouts, 'I never done nothing,' at the camera, doesn't tell the full story. When 'nothing' describes shirtless drinking from dawn to dusk and acting in a manner which offends by the coarseness of its delivery, then it should come as no surprise that the recipients of this 'nothing' react unfavourably. The resulting English media outcry and eyebrow-raising (which states that the culprits are not very English after all) would signify that most of the people writing such balderdash are unaware of how most people are educated and live their lives in England today. After the horror comes the brow-smoothing by our ambassadorial coterie. On every level it would make you sick. The drinking fans are England today: you and me, upper, middle and lower classes, united by centuries, divided only by their varying ability to influence their macro environment. England fans influence their micro environment by their actions. They'll take what they get when they arrive and ask for no more than bars to serve them till they fall over, but to try and distinguish them from the other inhabitants of middle and upper England who drink alcohol until they can't stand in locations as different as White's Gentleman's Club and Sandals, Jamaica, is facile – too ridiculous for words.

Despite the supposed mass destruction, I left Marseilles as I found it – rough, tough, dirty yet strangely seductive and attractive. The young locals would have stories to tell about the day they met the England fans. One gleeful journalist even wrote that the English football hooligans had traded blows with the French Africans and got more than they bargained for. I could almost picture his smile as he wrote it. I wonder if the Press cheered when they found out that some poor fan had his throat cut. It was the sort of gutter journalism which saw *The Sun* print that Liverpool fans were robbing bodies at Hillsborough.

It certainly looked as if the media attention focusing on the drunken antics of a few England fans was beginning to have an effect. The Mayor of Toulouse was talking about a complete shutdown of the city when England fans arrived. The media didn't help by cruising the streets and comparing the other countries' fans' behaviour with that of England's. The Scots seemed hell-bent on drinking France dry yet they were feted and applauded wherever they went. While in the past England fans were given the benefit of the doubt, there would now be rigid adherence to the fear factor.

The train pulled out of Marseilles slowly then quickly gathered speed as though it, too, realised it was leaving a bad place and speed was necessary to put distance between them. The gentle countryside rolled by. Four young lads in their early 20s walked through. One sat opposite me. He was from Preston and had the bulk of a drinker and Big Mac fanatic, rather than the bulk of a body builder. He looked up and noticed I had a copy of *La Provence*, Marseilles' newspaper.

'What are they saying about us?'

'They're saying that the England fans are equally to blame for the clashes with the locals due to the amount of beer they had drunk. The French are calling the English xenophobic.'

'Anybody throws a bottle at me then I throw one back. English people don't back down. That's why the French aren't Krauts.'

I could see myself getting involved in a very tiresome conversation with a Brits-is-best-bore, but he changed tack immediately.

'Two England fans are dead you know.'

I pointed to the paragraph in the paper. 'It says in here that a lad is critically ill but stable, and I heard one of the taxi drivers remark that one lad is dead, but it's just a rumour.'

'No. It's a fact. One had his throat cut and the other died on the beach immediately after the match. Lad who had his throat cut were on our coach. He's with one of our lot. He's a mate of a lad on coach.'

I looked at him.

'Did you know him?' I asked.

'No; but he was on our coach coming out.'

I meant to ask him who identified the body and also inform him that I was on the beach until 7 p.m. after the Tunisian match and never saw any trouble but I found it easier to shrug my shoulders and go back to my paper. Fans like him wouldn't take kindly to being informed that his imagination had run away faster than that of a *Sun* journalist. He moved away, pleased that he'd spread this rumour. What sort of an idiot walks up and down a train carriage telling people that an England fan is dead? Perhaps it was a badge of honour that he travelled and pretended he *nearly* knew a fellow England fan who'd died supporting his country – the ultimate fan, akin to the unknown soldier.

As I sat on the train back to Nice, I was joined by two far more sensible England fans from Bedfordshire. Their incredible journey showed just how much this match had meant to the average Joe Bloggs, and why the antics of a few hundred seemed even sadder because the fun factor would be missing from now on. These two guys were not huge earners and had been unable to get any of the cheap flights into Nice or any other point close to Marseilles, so they had booked a cheap flight to Geneva then saved on hotel bills by snatching sleep on the overnight train. It didn't matter that they had been reduced to physical wrecks, because they had fulfilled their wish to see

England play in its opening World Cup match. The indomitable spirit of the average England fan can never be broken. I had a short flight back to Luton in front of me but they had a return trek that frightened me far more than the baying mob of Tunisians had on Sunday evening.

At the airport, the England fans huddled around a TV watching the Scotland *v* Norway match. Some cheered the Scots, some cheered Norway. Most, like myself, were indifferent to all other teams in the World Cup unless they were a perceived threat to England. If Argentina or Germany had been playing, for instance, then the match would have taken on a completely different complexion because we saw those as teams we would have to beat to win the Cup. Scotland scored and few England fans cheered. Most were at the bar getting yet another drink down their necks or phoning home on their mobiles. One really flashy guy was phoning his girlfriend in the US. Looking at him in his ridiculous garb of striped England T-shirt (complete with beer stains) and baggy shorts, it was hard to imagine him as a senior executive in a computer company. One of the small party travelling back to Luton struck up a conversation with me. He was incredulous at my knowledge of France, especially when I told him that he could eat a good three-course meal with a beer for £12.
    'You don't mean to tell me you wasted good drinking time by sitting down and eating a proper meal?'
    'You're not being serious,' I replied.
    'Bloody right. At £4 a pint you can't afford to dilute the alcohol with food. I've spent the last day living on beer alone. It enables me to top myself up and get into drunk mode much quicker. Mind you, it does give you a terrible sore throat, this French lager.'
    I walked away shaking my head but his ghost followed everybody around the airport as his chants of 'England' filled the air during our three-hour delay. Thankfully his friends, though not any less sober, were at least witty and perceptive. They were led by a large Chelsea fan and his smaller blonde friend. As the delay lengthened and people got more drunk, the chanting started:
    'One man went to mow, went to mow a meadow.'
    Immediately six armed riot policemen appeared and spoke to the barman.
    'You must keep the noise down or I'll shut the bar,' implored the barman who was enjoying the banter. So they played a stupid game. They sang the song quietly while the riot police watched. As soon as

the police turned their backs, they raised the volume then turned it down immediately when they turned round. Everybody laughed, especially the French people who were in the airport waiting. This was how it was supposed to be: bawdy, eccentric, slightly risqué fun, but as soon as our young food-free zone drunk lurched across the shiny floor shouting, 'Ingerland', 'No Surrender', then the French expressions changed to trepidation. When we finally got on the plane and took off, the mood amongst the fans was one of great hilarity. Some of the guys needed to go to the toilet because they had drunk too much. The stewardess in charge looked muscular so the large Chelsea fan immediately nicknamed her Martina the Essex Arm Wrestler.

'Is she butch or what? Would you want to get a right hander off her?'

Out from the seat sprang a 30-something and waddled at full speed down the middle aisle like a pregnant duck, trying to get into the toilet before Butch Martina got a grip on him. Martina, on spotting this man who dared to defy the 'fasten seat belts' sign, charged down after him grabbing the back of his shirt.

'Oh no you don't – not until the fasten seat belt signs are unlit.'

She frog-marched him back to his seat with the rest of the plane cheering and laughing. It was one of my funnier travelling moments. Another guy was waiting for her to turn her back. As he half stood up she turned round.

'Don't even think about it,' she shouted with a steely voice. He slunk back into his seat. Martina marched down and informed us that we would not be served any alcohol. Nobody argued.

Next to me sat a father and son. They were on a hospitality trip. He was an advertising creative director who had been responsible for the recent Renault ad where Claudia Schiffer has seemingly stripped naked to get into the car. He had a view on hospitality.

'In my line of work I get offered it all the time. I am a big Manchester United fan and I always feel that those people who aren't football fans should offer it to the ones, like myself, who are – but we all know it doesn't happen like that. Look at this trip. I felt guilty about taking it because my true allegiance is to Ireland but then again, I am a football fan and my son wanted to go so I thought, why not? and I took the trip.'

I asked him about making small talk with the people with whom he had to watch the matches.

'Yes, that is a problem. Once, we were all invited to the boxes at

Arsenal. Now they really are great because you can go outside and catch the atmosphere of the match as opposed to those at Manchester where the boxes are enclosed by glass and the sounds are piped in. On this day at Arsenal, the wife of one of the guests asked who the man in black was. Her husband told her it was the referee. When she asked why he was being called a wanker I looked at the floor. Her husband told her to go back inside and eat some more food. In my business there is unbridled hospitality, almost a religious zeal to partake in it, but I never feel guilty about taking a freebie to watch sport because I love being around sportsmen. I have even directed some of them in adverts.'

I meant to ask which ones and what they were really like but that would have been another cliché. I did ask him if Claudia Schiffer had cellulite. He laughed and said that she was even more attractive in the flesh than she was on TV. At Luton, everybody disembarked quietly and said goodbye to Martina, while the large Chelsea fan demanded, and got, a kiss. We then drifted into the car park to find our cars in the pitch black.

Next stop, Toulouse.

9

Fansville

For those fans able to get tickets, France became the trip of a lifetime. As the tournament unfolded, the flags of St George and St Andrew appeared at grounds where neither England nor Scotland were playing as football became a drug to be ingested every day. English fans who went to the World Cup returned home with their own views on the tournament and the behaviour of England fans. Any claims that they hadn't seen any rioting were met with utter astonishment.

'The Reggae Boyz make the most noise and the Jocks might like a drink and dress stupidly with their tartan kilts, but nobody parties like the Danes,' said Harry the day after he attended the Denmark v France match in Lyons. Despite the Danes losing the match 2–1, the party started as soon as the lads arrived in Lyons, never letting up until they finally left exhausted the morning after the match. Not that the people they were drinking with needed an excuse to party, as they were the very chaps who would be having a dancing party on the slopes of the Alps during the Tour de France a few weeks later. The fact that they had produced a winner of this gruelling race in one of the flattest countries in the world was an even bigger reason to celebrate. I don't know if it's because they live in a country where they have to trade the natural resources of their richer Scandinavian neighbours, Sweden and Norway, or perhaps because they live next to Germany, but whatever the reason, they live to have a good time. One Friday I phoned a Danish company I was doing business with only to be told that they could not speak because they were receiving their Friday afternoon beer from the company. With a weekly ritual like that, it is not hard to see why they enjoy life. I had watched Scotland's opening match in a

bar in northern Denmark. One minute I was in the furthermost point
of Denmark where the North Sea meets the Baltic and the next I was
sitting in a bar with happy Danes drinking pints of Carlsberg. Work
had stopped in this town for the more important business of the World
Cup opening match, not the opening ceremony that was summed up
in the following way by my Danish host:

'Opening ceremonies at football are similar to unfair ticket
distribution practices: they are there to massage a corrupt ego and
justify the existence of someone who should be spending their time
doing something creative for mankind instead of holding up the start
of a football match.'

I'll drink to that – and being in the company of Danes, that is
exactly what I did.

Two days later I was sitting in the Nyhaun in Copenhagen, which is
the Danish canal version of London's Covent Garden. Many Danes
were sitting outside the bar with red-and-white wigs and painted faces.
It was certainly the fashion these days but the match wasn't until
tomorrow.

Beyond the brave, new mirage of good fans, the old image is still
there, only more tired, more pathetic and living amongst the outdated
fantasies of violent confrontation. After Marseilles, journalists queued
up to interview hard-core hooligans. In a pub in south London you
could find the whereabouts of Lord Lucan if you paid someone £50,
so it was no surprise that someone got a spokesman with plenty to say
for the front pages.

'Lots of the boys are still at home. There's plenty of time yet. Don't
forget, we might get Germany or Argentina.'

He was tall and articulate, of course, had a good city job and for
good measure, had plenty of category C hard-core chaps' numbers
stored on his mobile phone. 'Every one a "kick-off geezer"' was how
it was reported. All around England that evening, dinner parties would
make hushed statements about thug organisation, new recruits to the
terrible mysterious twilight world of football violence and a new
phrase they'd learnt – 'kick-off', which signified violence was starting.
And all the while, Jeff Powell, spokesman for the fan condemnation
classes in the *Mail* was reinforcing the prejudices of obese England by
calling England fans SCUM, using the word more than a detergent
research chemist.

Clive and Monty were not regular football fans. Neither of them had ever attended an England match, yet they wanted to see at least one World Cup match. When they failed to get through on the notorious English hotline, they decided to go to Paris anyway and watch a match on the big screen. They cycled to Paris via Dieppe and camped in the huge Bois de Boulogne campsite alongside every other nationality who was competing in the World Cup. They watched the Norway *v* Brazil match on the screen situated underneath the Eiffel Tower. The relevance of this match was that if Brazil won and Morocco beat Scotland, Morocco would go through to the knock-out stages. Consequently, Clive and Monty sat in a crowd that was nearly 100 per cent African, all of them going absolutely berserk. It was a crowd made up of the Paris beyond the Boulevard Périphérique – the Africans from St Denis, Sarcealles and La Cité des Tartarets.

'It was like being in Africa,' said Monty. Brazil scored first and the Moroccans celebrated. Then Norway equalised through Flo. Being a Chelsea fan, Clive cheered as his Chelsea hero slotted in a brilliant goal. Then, with two minutes to go, Norway won the match through the most dubious of penalties. It meant that Morocco were out, a realisation that made their fans mad and had them smashing up everything in sight.

'I never thought I'd be in trouble with Africans in Paris,' shouted Monty to Clive, as they scrambled to get away for fear that their white faces would be mistaken for Norwegian.

Soon England would be playing Colombia. England fans with their painted white faces would be playing a country where white powder meant something other than face paint. The fact that cocaine could corrupt even the power of football showed clearly just how far reality had departed from everyday life. Who knew what future fate would befall a Colombian player after they played England. Andres Escobar scored an own goal in USA '94. One week later he was shot dead in his home town. The trigger-happy assassin mimicked the South American commentator shouting 'gol' after each one of the 12 shots he pumped into his body. All Harry and the rest of us had to worry about was perhaps a feeling of emptiness; our lives didn't depend on it.

In the crowded Toulouse bar, he wasn't unusual but his lean, gymnastic, muscly build and confident cockney manner said that he knew what he was about and that made him stand out. There was a tight clique of around a dozen drinking, not drinking for the sake of it like the Marseilles Sunday mob, but drinking to socialise. Nobody would catch them off their guard, drunk: they knew me; they'd read my other stuff. His mate had long brown hair in a ponytail. One of his other mates didn't like me very much or the 'garbage' I wrote. Undercover police and numerous newspapers had his card marked yet here was a category C top man on display. No journalist would ever get a quote from this guy because what he had to say was too expensive for them, and he didn't have anything to say anyway. All the while we were talking, he knew who was coming and going around him. At one point someone came in who didn't fit any category they felt safe with, so one of the group was dispatched to check him out. That is how I got involved in conversation with him. After a few beers, he dropped his guard to a 'poncy writer' and told me that he was indeed a category C and that his route into France was via Belgium.

'Do you think the French border police were looking for a cat C smartly dressed driving a 7 series Beamer?' he asked me mockingly, not expecting a reply because that was the answer to his own question.

'No', I replied, nevertheless, 'because they're sitting in Calais waiting for goons like Paul Dodd and other media-friendly hooligans. When did you ever see a top hooligan interviewed on the TV? That Dodd is a sandwich short of a picnic in the brains department.'

'I've done some real serious stuff in the past,' he said. 'Attacks on the main faces of rival gangs as they sat in their local pubs, Saturday night ambushes, the full Monty . . . '

There is a legendary story etched in hooligan folklore about the time the main Spurs faces were met on the Seven Sisters Road by a transit van, the door of which was flung open to reveal crazies with blowtorches coming towards them. Months later, the Spurs fan who told me about it was still in shock: 'Jesus, they had blowtorches.' After that, all other stories about football violence seem to pale into insignificance. (Cat C liked the military planning of that episode. They laughed a lot about that one – and it never even made the papers.)

'Makes paintball look like a Teletubbies' tea party! Now look at me: a successful businessman living in a five-bedroom detached house in sleepy Surrey, commuter land, with my two kids at private nursery school. Last Christmas, at the school black-tie dinner, I sat at a table with the chief accountant of the biggest brewery in England and he told me how terrible football hooligans were for his industry. Then he leaned over and informed me that prior to Euro '96, Carlsberg lager was at number 13 in the marketplace, but during the competition it was the number one standard lager. He was right proud of that. Who the bloody hell does he think drinks the stuff in such large quantities to take it to number one – little old ladies? And what does he think the lads do shortly after they've been coerced into consuming all that wobbly juice? Play ruddy scrabble or talk about the price of paint at B & Q? When lager sales are three times higher than for the same period the previous year it might well be that a few of the boys get on the turn. Later in the evening, accountant-face asked me if I knew anything about football hooliganism. I laughed, winked at the wife and started talking business.'

My friend loved to play the crowd just the same as Motty and Barry but, unlike the fun the Worthing mob perpetrated, behind Cat C's veneer of humour was a nasty side that I'd seen too often in the past and didn't care to be around. After a few too many wobbly juices of their own, his mates now started to comment on arsehole writers. I knew category C from of old, like the ageing disco stars of the '70s and '80s. Now as disco fever swept the dancefloors once again, the media talk was all about hooliganism also making a comeback. The proof that this was wrong came right at me in the words of this former nutter who stated that we'd all grown too old for that kind of funfair ride (I never got on the scary rides, so the 'we' was for someone else). As I left, he called after me: 'Remember to tell everybody that MB is thug-retired. I've hung up my knuckleduster. You write that down and you also tell them that my wife is on the PTA along with a few very, very posh ladies.'

That got a lot of laughs. He liked people laughing at his jokes. They probably laughed the same sinister laugh when they chased those terrified Spurs lads with blowtorches or kicked prostrate bodies during their famous ambush days. I suddenly realised that I had nothing in common with these people. I doubted whether I ever had, and that went for nearly every real fan here. Nostalgia for everybody else meant Bee Gees and flared trousers, not the flare from oxyacetylene. I meant to ask him what business he was in but it seemed irrelevant, and I left them as they basked in the sewage of a violent hooligan past.

Eric and Valerie Vanderville ran the small French bistro in Bookham. On Friday evening, two days before the final, Eric heard one comment too many from an English commentator about the French World Cup.

'Do you think I want to stay in England and listen to a stupid

English commentator talking about my country?' he exclaimed to the bar. 'I will return to the greatest country on earth to watch our destiny.' So the Sunday dinnertime bookings were cancelled with the trademark Gallic shrug: 'The English will understand.' Eric didn't realise that Great Bookham isn't the pulse of middle England, but rather the heartbeat, and they would not look very kindly on their well-defined existence being disrupted by a patriotic Frenchman. Eric didn't care, however, because in France there's always another customer, while there may never be another World Cup Final.

Eric set off late (of course he set off late, he's French) and didn't arrive in Calais until 5.30 p.m. on Sunday. The original intention of going to Paris was abandoned, but as he headed towards Boulogne, the magnitude of the transformation in France really hit home. There were flags everywhere. Cars drove along tooting their horns and everybody was dressed in something blue, red and white to represent their country.

'I had never seen so many flags in my country. Normally France has no interest in football, but now there were young and old, standing on their balconies waving and shouting as we drove past.'

Eric checked into a hotel in Boulogne and headed for the Caesar café with the giant screen.

'The noise was incredible, even the fire engines were driving around, sounding their sirens to add more noise and colour. Inside the café, everybody was packed like sardines. Some food was eaten but the tension was tangible – a new experience for many French people [they'd arrived in fansville and found it to their liking]. They drank, not like the English before a match, but with the French enjoyment of savouring every mouthful. I myself never had a drop all day because you cannot enjoy football with a dimmed brain. Inside the café, it was not like the English pub with lads, lads, lads, but women, children, old and not so old. I am 38 years old and I have never seen anything like that in France. When France scored the first goal, everybody jumped up, screaming, kissing and shouting, 'We win! We win!' Then we drank. When the second goal went in there was even more emotion, yet despite everybody going mad, not one glass got broken – that's just the French way. Even in the second half when Desailly got sent off, nobody was scared.'

I asked him about the French President.

'Yes, that was very big with everybody. Seeing the French President waving the number 23 shirt and cheering along was great. When Petit scored at the end the French President was not Mr Politician; he was a Frenchman going berserk like everybody else. If he called an election tomorrow, everybody would vote for him because he threw his arms up and sensed emotion like all of us. Now we know he understands, unlike Prince Charles who politely clapped when Beckham scored. At the end of the match the bar went silent so we could all observe the joy of the players. We waited till the Cup was lifted, then the whole bar sang 'La Marseillaise' followed by 'We Are The Champions'. France was one big happy family. Everybody spilled outside, kissed each other and shook hands. 'On a gagné! On a gagné!' (We won! We won!) the crowds chanted. France was a country reunited and the reunification party went on until 5 a.m. with the champagne and wine flowing.' The last thing Eric remembers was falling down the stairs at his hotel.

The next day, offices closed all over France as only a quarter of the workforce turned up for work – most of the country was still celebrating. Eric and Valerie returned to England in a state of excitement. They may have made their living in middle England but their hearts were still in France – the wonderful togetherness they had experienced with their French compatriots would stay with them forever, even if Eric was so hoarse he couldn't tell anybody about it.

Paul and Ben caught the Eurostar train down to Marseilles for the quarter-final tie between Norway and Italy. They were nervous about being English in a city where England had been involved in so much trouble. Arriving on the Thursday, they booked into the same hotel that the English had seen besieged in the early hours of Monday's riot. On Thursday evening, the Norwegians started drinking and continued to drink until they were beaten 1–0 by Italy three days later. The Norwegians celebrated and drank even more after they had lost, yet throughout the singing on the same pavement cafés where England had fought the French Africans, there was none of the animosity. Not that the tension was not in the air, it was just that the Norwegians got to a certain level and held it at the top. Paul, being a plumber, put it like this: 'The bath got to the top but the overflow stopped the water spilling over.' One night they sat outside and spotted a dangerous-looking character lurking behind, just waiting and watching. As Paul turned, he gave them that all-knowing, evil smile just to tell them that this was their town and they were there keeping an eye.

10

To Lose in Toulouse

Due to the huge media coverage of drunken Marseilles Sunday and my previous writing about football fans, I was asked to do a number of interviews. I missed out on *London Tonight* as my plane was delayed by three hours. Central TV had been on my mobile all day previously, begging me to do a live appearance on *Thursday Night Live* with Nicky Campbell, offering me £100 plus travelling expenses and a night in a hotel to boot (complete with mini bar). It was only when the producer phoned me and started going through the sort of questions I would be asked that I realised I was being set up as a Lee Harvey Oswald hooligan patsy.

'We want you to say why the England fans charged back down the road at the Tunisians and why you [me personally] started all the fighting because we will have people there who will be saying that you shouldn't have done it under any circumstances' . . . 'What do you mean you are not a hooligan? I was told that you were on the front line leading the charge.'

I'd been an England fan in Marseilles, so, of course, I was involved in the trouble. Wasn't everybody? I corrected my learned idiot quite forcibly. Later they phoned to inform me that they were sorry to have to drop me from the line-up because I wasn't the type of fan they wanted. As far as they were concerned, everybody in Marseilles that day was a hooligan. All they wanted obviously was someone (although any fool would have done) to say we did it because we are English and we're proud of the trouble we cause. It was a pointless call as I'd already made that decision anyway. The BBC also phoned to say that they wanted me on TV.

'Could you do the interview on Wednesday afternoon?'

'Sorry, but I'm going back to work.'

'You have the chance to be on the BBC.'

You could hear the indignation in her voice. As if I really care whether or not I appear on the BBC to be asked some moronic questions by some ignorant journalist with a pre-determined agenda. Then BBC Radio 4 asked me to appear on a phone-in the morning of the Toulouse match, adding ' . . . if there is no trouble then we may not use you.'

I was glad to tell them that I would be in Toulouse with every other England fan worth their salt.

'You get me a business-class return so I can do your phone-in and still get to the match, and then I'll do it.' That usually shuts up most TV companies because they think the average fan is stupid, and yet when you see the average fan being interviewed they speak with startling clarity and coherence. On the other hand, if you re-ask the same question in 20 different ways until the fan responds in the way the media wants them to and then only show the two seconds where the response is sensational or confrontational, you are naturally going to give the public back home a distorted view. 'It doesn't happen like that,' shouts shocked England. 'Oh yes it does,' reply the fans on the front line. If only the authorities would listen to fans and embrace them instead of ostracising them all, then perhaps the final furlong to eliminating completely English football violence could be achieved.

My World Cup trip was based on many fans, many of whom were limited by fiscal restrictions. Only corporate England could live now, worry later: the average England fan was watching his centimes. Terry had arranged a sausage skin meeting in Lyons for Sunday so I booked onto a cheap Ryan Air flight into St Etienne. It was my intention to watch England in Toulouse on the Monday, then travel up to St Etienne to watch Scotland. The following day I'd travel to Lyons to watch Denmark v France, then up to Calais to write about the England fans, then on to Lens on the Friday – in short, a week of rural France, catching the football. Things started to go wrong when it became obvious that the people of Toulouse were getting very frightened about the impending arrival of the England fans. Early arrivals from Marseilles were greeted by massed ranks of media. Just as the bell ringer used to announce the arrival of the removers of the dead during the Black Death epidemics, so the arrival of such a huge media entourage meant that the barbarians were indeed coming, bringing destruction and aggression in their wake. Even if the barbarians had a day off the very presence of so many cameras meant that the tension hung in the air like a dense smog. I had no worries as Terry was driving his car around France but the world of sausage skins moves in mysterious ways and, at the last minute, Terry decided to fly business into Toulouse on the Sunday, leaving me stranded at Stanstead airport with numerous travelling Scots. At the departure lounge bar their drinking habits could only be described as cirrhosis in transit. Quite why people would want to drink half a bottle of gin during a 30-minute wait is beyond me; nor was that an isolated incident.

On the way down to the plane I struck up a conversation with two young Scots.

'Win or bust for you boys tomorrow,' I remarked.

'Aye, but we're full of hope.'

They had worked out all the permutations of what everybody needed to do in order for them to qualify. However, you couldn't help but get the feeling that their destiny was pre-ordained to end in glorious failure, which seems to be the way with the Scots in World Cups. If they hadn't been such glorious failures then I felt that much of the cheerfulness of that travelling crowd would have diminished. The fact that they knew they would fail meant that every last second of the trip had to be wrung dry for enjoyment. Even saving the money for the trip was part of the fun. The Scots fans remind me of the Barmy Army England cricket fans who know England are going to lose yet still they go and make a carnival. Some days – sorry, most days – they are more entertaining than the England cricket team itself. England football fans were going to see their team win, so every second in between matches was about waiting for the next match. Consequently, England fans were killing time while Scots were enjoying their time because they knew they'd be going home early. Even their World Cup song was entitled: 'Don't Come Home Too Soon'. Ex Scotland manager, Tommy Docherty, said the Scots would be home before the postcards. When Sports Minister, Tony Banks stated that he doubted England could win the World Cup, there was an uproar but all Scots agreed with Tommy Docherty and laughed heartily at this self-deprecating humour.

As I boarded the plane it was obvious that the Scots on board were drunk beyond description, but they were being applauded nevertheless as funny Scots. I found their in-flight, pathetic renditions of 'Scotland the Brave' and comments about English people abusive. The tunelessness and boisterousness of 'Flower of Scotland' merged into a sad lament as though they knew their own fate. Any group of people purporting to represent a nation which sings 'Jimmy Hill's a wanker' non-stop on a flight from London to St Etienne must have pretty shallow lives.

So thought one French woman who asked if she could have the spare seat next to me at the front of the plane.

'I have seen drunk people before but these people are paralytic. How they manage to stay upright is a miracle of science,' she exclaimed, with a worried expression on her face. I smiled, wishing that the same news media who were telling the world about the well-behaved Scots versus the thuggish Englishmen could have heard her comments. Would it have mattered? I doubt it. When a mould is cast it takes something exceptional to break it. Weren't we continually being told that English hooliganism had not been broken by the fans themselves but by clever establishment policing practices – so that when the English police and establishment cocked it up in Marseilles, they would have to find some instant factor to blame rather than the obvious shortcomings of their category C identification? The fact that they didn't understand the basic *modus operandi* of the English drinking psyche or the Goodwood racer factor was overlooked in the stampede to railroad a few easy convictions of James Shayler and his ilk. Bolting horses and stable doors sprang to mind. As the flight taxied to a halt at St Etienne, the sight that greeted us was one of huge rows of CRS and armed police. As the well-behaved English walked off, we all thought we were going to see the Scots get a belting from the riot police, yet I have never seen a flight shut up so quickly. It was a miracle that those Scots managed to walk across the tarmac. Once inside the terminal, however, when it became known that the police were waiting for the arrival of the German and Yugoslavian teams who had just played and were staying close by, the Scots came back to life. The bagpipes started up and some Scots began doing something similar to morris dancing around imaginary swords. Perhaps it's because I'm English, but the sight of grown men in tartan skirts dancing around rather too close to each other reminds me of San Francisco poofs.

My French host was waiting to meet me at the airport with his daughter. As I drove away in my hired car, the Scots were outside dancing to the tune of their bagpipes. My French hosts cooked me a magnificent barbecue with the most incredible technique of getting the coals hot with the use of a hairdryer. We drank fine wines while watching Iran versus the US. Watching Iran beat the United States was a pleasure because it brought spontaneous joy to the Iranian people without anybody needing to die, reinforcing the fact that the most powerful nation on earth could only field eleven against eleven on the greatest field of combat and was found wanting. Had Ronald Reagan still been in power, I've no doubt an aircraft carrier fleet would have been dispatched immediately to provoke an incident and redress the balance. The Americans were an irrelevance to this sporting contest because football is bigger than they are. The US had boycotted the 1980 Moscow Olympics yet no country touched by football dared to boycott the World Cup, since most countries understand that football is about passion, fervour and emotion and boycotting would run the risk of inciting insurrection.

On Saturday the Mayor of Toulouse announced that there would be a complete shutdown of all restaurants and bars at 11 p.m. until the England fans left town. The following evening, Terry booked into the Maeva Lattission which was surrounded by two beautiful golf courses. It was also the Hospitality Hotel exquisite. Sir Bobby Charlton and his wife were staying there, and sitting around the pool that afternoon, Bobby was subjected to attention which would have driven lesser men to anger. First there were nudges as people recognised probably the greatest player ever to wear an England shirt and one of the top five who has ever worn a football shirt globally. After a while people drifted over for pose photos and autographs and finally there came the inevitable conversation. One elderly couple who knew his brother Jack's wife and went to school with her ended up pulling some chairs over. Bobby's wife chattered away while Bobby was the perfect host. Even Germans spoke to him as though he were a friend and Bobby reciprocated. They wanted to talk about that goal and the Russian linesman so he spoke about it.

'Yes; that ball was over the line, but it didn't matter – we were the better team and we would have gone on to win anyway,' he said.

The Germans roared with laughter as only Germans do and talked about the famous English sense of humour. But Bobby was quite serious. Bobby was a proud man from a tough, north-east of England upbringing. He might be a gentleman and England's greatest ambassador, but England won the World Cup in '66 because they were the best team in the world at that time. The fact that people always mention that Hurst goal and the Russian linesman rankles with him and all the other players who won the Cup. People talk about celebrity-status and the pressure of fame, yet nobody could have achieved more attention than Bobby Charlton that day and nobody could have been more obliging to the fans. Bobby Charlton made people happy that day. They left him animated and enthusiastic because they had spoken to a legend. On other, trickier questions, he reverted to media speak and answered with diplomacy.

'Can we win the World Cup?'

'There are a number of teams who are well equipped to win it.'

'Can we beat Romania?'

'We should do, they are not that good a side.'

Later when Bobby went off to a restaurant, Terry sat in the hotel bar with three cheeky Scouse fans who took the rise out of everything that moved.

Then six Millwall fans entered the bar just after midnight, led by their 32-stone spokesman.

'Bleedin' 'ell, someone told me it was only three hours' drive from Calais. Ten poxy hours! It doesn't look that far on the map.' They had crates of warm lager with them which they proceeded to pass around the fans, and there was a brooding menace which seemed to hang in the air as soon as they entered. The Scousers would have been well advised to retire to bed along with the others, but they chose to swap banter and drink with the Millwall lads who started punching them at around 3 a.m. because they were 'piss-taking Scouse wankers'. In the morning the hotel manager explained that there was blood everywhere and due to this disturbance, the Maeva bar would shut at 5 p.m. instead of 11 p.m. The Millwall fans were asked to move out so I never saw them again.

I arrived at the hotel, checked in and then Terry and I drove the car back to the airport. There the day trippers were now arriving in full force. They were probably paying through the nose for the privilege of flying in and out in one day, yet penny for penny they were probably spending less than the fans who had spent two days in Toulouse and had to get tickets on the black market. Nobody begrudges these fans their few hours at the event but there is something wrong when tickets are made available for people to get a flight in and out while the travelling fan who adds colour to the proceedings and money to the local economy is left to negotiate his or her match entry on the black market.

Terry and I caught a bus into town around 2 p.m. We had arranged to meet the Worthing Mafia as I had two spare tickets for Toulouse and one for Lens. Very quickly it became obvious that England fans would find it more difficult to get tickets for Toulouse as the ground only held 38,000. Prices were being bandied around at £150–£300, and fans were paying them. As kick-off got nearer, the price wouldn't drop.

With its historic centre and vibrant night life, Toulouse was always going to be the best trip of the three qualifying matches. Eric, the French chef, had told us that Toulouse, *la ville rose*, (the pink city) would be ready to party as long as we were able. The Place du Capitol was always going to be the focal point for all football fans in Toulouse. For the England fans it would be no different. The magnificent brick-and-window fascia of the Capitolium with its huge, black, wooden door, like an elegant Buckingham Palace, dominated a huge square which was surrounded on two sides by numerous pavement cafés and restaurants. After the tension of Marseilles that comes with the opening match of a World Cup, Toulouse was a chance for people to renew acquaintances from previous football trips. When fans bump into each other they speak to each other as if the intervening period were days or weeks, not months or years. People who had last spoken on a beach in San Sebastian in 1982, met after 16 years yet recognised each other and talked immediately as if they'd always known that one day they would meet again. That's the togetherness and camaraderie of football fans. But Toulouse would not be without its problems. Whereas every other fan watching their team would be able to sit and eat a pleasant meal after any evening match, England fans would suffer the ignominy of everything being closed at 11 p.m. – to make them feel at home.

As Terry and I walked towards the square, every bar was full of England fans in various states of inebriation. One guy was giving everybody who walked past a high five, yet more often than not, he missed the hands he was aiming at. For most it was a pleasant drink to while away the hours and talk about football, while others were already in full stagger mode with three, nearly four, hours to kick-off. For the most part there was no hint of menace. On one corner of the square was a McDonalds, making many England fans feel at home. One fan told me quite proudly that he'd spent the last week in France on lager and Big Macs and his guts were still holding up. On the opposite side were two large hotels, the Grand Hôtel de l'Opéra and the Holiday Inn Crowne Plaza. Smartly dressed waiters scurried in between the pavement tables with trays full of beer and food. They might be forced to shut at 11 p.m. but they intended to take as much as they could between now and then. Some of the bar owners had protested to the Mayor, Dominique Baudis, that they didn't want to shut but he waved them away. The signs went up. 'Par arrête PREFECTORIAL le Bar fermera à 23H 00!' All over Toulouse, the iron curtain would descend on enjoyment for one evening only.

The specially constructed Toulouse village of culture, Prairie des Filtres, was shut down. These English boys weren't culture vultures, but even if they were, the French weren't prepared to risk it. Fans drinking around the square, which was overlooked by the Mayor's office, were arrested and deported without charge on the word of English police spotters that they were category Cs.

As Michael Caine said in *Zulu*: 'Two disasters in one day looks bad in the newspapers and puts people off their breakfasts.' Two outbreaks of violence in France would be very off-putting for the good citizens back in England so arrest and deport a few without trial for good measure. It never worked in Northern Ireland when we tried it for decades. Try it anyway.

Barry, Motty and the rest of the Worthing Mafia were waiting to meet Terry and me and had found a small bar run by a friendly French couple who thought England fans were the best-behaved, most polite fans she had served so far. The lads drank the beers as fast as she could pour them. Mad Matty, who had punched the policeman in Rome, came over and relayed an interesting story.

'I was in the square last night. It was full of Christmas trees [fans dressed up in England shirts waving flags] having a good time. Three of us were looking for tickets when we were approached by a nasty piece of work.

'"Oy! Long Hair – we reckon you're an undercover, old bill," said a voice.

'I turned around and standing there was a vile-looking man. On his left arm, I HATE MILLWALL was tattooed in large black letters. On his neck, down the left side, was WEST HAM. He confronted me: "Are you an Elephant Boy? 'Cos they suck cocks." [People who live on the north side of the river Thames refer to those on the south side who support Millwall or Charlton as Elephant Boys, after the landmark Elephant and Castle.]

'I shook my head to deny it. "Worthing," I said. I don't think he knew where Worthing is. He seemed to spend the rest of the conversation trying to remember if anything about Worthing had ever upset him. I looked at this bloke and thought that he was beyond category C – more like category N for nutter or LU for loose upstairs.

'"We've been watching you in this square and we reckon you're undercover, so why don't you clear off before we stripe you good and proper," said West Ham.

'"Don't be silly," I said, I'm just looking for tickets."

'With that West Ham said: "We'll be keeping an eye on you, so watch your step." He then added this little soliloquy to tell me what a great achiever in life he'd been: "Do you realise that we did what Hitler couldn't do? Years ago we shut down the London Underground through fear and now I've done it to Marseilles. That's two countries, three if you count the complete shutdown in Luxembourg."

'No doubt he went back to England and said that he turned Toulouse into East Ham High Street on a Sunday evening. The neons might be going out all over Toulouse at 11 p.m., but they went out upstairs a long time ago with his bloke – if they were ever on,' mused Matty.

'He was away with the fairies. He must have been one of these care-in-the-community types, although in his case it was *don't* care in the European Community at large.

'He looked at me with a sickly mad stare, and I looked him back in the eye, but there wasn't too much in there. The lights were on, but no one was in.

'"I'm waiting for the Argies, so you'll keep." With that West Ham gave a chilling Vincent Price-like laugh which was all menace and no humour.

'It was pure intimidation on his part,' said Matty, 'because we looked like we knew what we were about and he wanted us to know that his little firm were the "guvnors". In Rome, the Chelsea Headhunters ran the show, but these guys were a step above that. I mean, if you walk around with I HATE MILLWALL on your arm then you've got to expect to get into one or two fist fights and more.'

Then Matty went back to his beer, filing this character away in his memory reference library.

Touts and desperate fans abounded. Prices on the streets were rising. The price of tickets had now reached £300 as it became obvious that demand was exceeding supply. The touts felt no menace and flashed their tickets quite openly.

One walked past and pulled four from his briefcase. 'I hope you get rolled, you cocky bastard,' shouted Barry. No doubt touts were getting set upon but there was no fear among them. Enterprising English fans walked around with cardboard signs written in French explaining that they needed tickets for that evening's match. As the afternoon wore on, groups of touts descended on the road we were encamped in. I had two spare tickets and sold them to two of the lads I knew from Worthing but that still left two lads short. Matty had the answer. A tout approached.

'Combien?' asked Matty.

'3,000 francs each,' replied the tout.

'2,500.'

'Oui,' replied the tout, smiling.

'Look at this rip-off merchant; I'll make him smile in a second,' said Matty, like Robert de Niro in the Russian roulette sequence in *The Deer Hunter*.

'Let's have a look at them to make sure they are not forgeries.' Gripping them tightly, the tout held them up to the light. Matty pointed a finger at an imaginary blemish on the tickets.

'They're duds.'

'Non, monsieur.'

Matty took a closer look and took hold of them raising them up to the light for further examination. Then he was off up the road, shouting as he went.

'Hum diddle dee, a snatcher's life for me,
Hum diddle day, a snatcher's life is gay.'

The tout never gave chase as everybody clapped Matty.

One of the pre-match rituals for the Worthing Mafia is a hearty meal, usually Chinese. That day we settled for a western bar just over the bridge near the ground. As everybody sat around, the conversation got quite animated. Matty said something to his best mate, big Jamie, sitting opposite.

'Say that again and I'll throw a bottle in your chops.'

'Go on, then.'

With that Matty pitched a bottle full pelt right at his face. It bounced off his forehead, smashing a plate and landed in the lap of another in the group who got covered in beer. The two protagonists laughed at this fun. The French people in the restaurant looked horrified at the brutality exhibited between fellow England fans. When I asked him why he did it, he replied in such a way that implied they behaved like that all the time, and I don't doubt it.

'He dared me, so I couldn't lose face,' was his cogent reply. Small wonder that the English invasion had left France frightened and worried. After all, if even friends perpetrate such violence among each other then it must run in their blood. Small wonder that the Mayor of Toulouse had dismantled the big screen which had been showing all the previous matches.

Everybody streamed towards the stadium. A group of England fans marched alongside the road waving the flag of St George. Buoyed up by the effects of too much alcohol and a belief in their invincibility, they sang as they staggered. As Terry and I walked past, one of them growled at me in a friendly manner.

'These colours don't run.'

I smiled at him. I've heard that hundreds of times before but I didn't hear it when they were coming past me like Linford Christie in the back streets of Marseilles. As we turned the corner, two elderly Americans had a cardboard sign up. 'Tickets for Lens – 3,000 FF the pair.' It was expensive; in a few days' time it would be cheap. Quite what two Americans were doing in France with two tickets for Lens was beyond me. What it did sum up for me, however, was the complete unfairness of the ticket distribution system.

'Oy, Yankie! when in France, do as the French do,' shouted the colour non-runner.

'Tossers. Hope you get rolled,' added his mate for good measure. Then they were gone and forgotten, a blur amongst the other circling sharks and touts.

The Toulouse Municipal Stadium is situated on an island in the middle of the river Garonne in pleasant surroundings, a short walk from a tree-lined park. As Terry and I walked towards the stadium we were met by hundreds of ticketless English fans lining the bridge, still asking for tickets but with a weary air of resignation which signified that they were just going through the motions. As we approached the barrier, a young father came back past us with two tearful young boys wearing a full England kit.

'Tickets, spare tickets please,' he pleaded. He then picked up the youngest boy who was sobbing uncontrollably. I averted my gaze.

'That was sad,' remarked Terry.

We negotiated the first barrier. The French names we had on our tickets didn't bother the CRS; all they were bothered about was the fact that we had tickets. As we walked towards the ground a group of fans were walking behind a man on a mobile.

'You wanker, why are you slagging us off again?'

'Go on, shitbag, make some more garbage up.'

One of the lads spoke to me. 'That pillock is from Sky and he's probably doing a number on us.'

I walked up to the reporter who was chattering into his mobile and introduced myself.

'What have you got?' I asked.

He looked at me, nervously.

'Statistics, reports,' he said. 'This lot behind you are ready to give you a slap so why don't you tell them exactly what has been going on.'

'Nothing has been going on today,' I said. 'It's been really good natured with absolutely no arrests anywhere in the city. Everybody has behaved really well.' I could see the look of disappointment in his eyes as though he didn't want to believe it.

'Bet you don't bloody well report that though, you tosser. That's not news to you wankers, is it?' shouted one of the irate fans. The BBC reporter went hastily through the barrier into the press enclosure with the catcalls still ringing in his ear, never looking back.

We sailed into the ground past three lines of security and searches and arrived just before kick-off to hear the national anthems. Not that it had been plain sailing for all the fans. The man sitting next to me complained that there had been an almighty crush at his barrier and the police seemed intent on causing problems for the England fans going in. They had even snatched the white plastic hats from the heads of England fans which everybody had worn quite happily without any trouble in Marseilles. Terry and I looked out around the stadium which was awash with the white shirts of England. Once more, England would be playing a home match in a foreign country. Another tax-free bonanza for the honest citizens of Toulouse. Taking up the whole top tier of the main stand, running the length of the pitch, was the section reserved for the Press.

'Disgusting that; they could have put real football fans in there,' shouted a furious fan.

Looking around at the huge support from England, it was obvious that there were at least 20,000 England fans inside. With the covered roof extended all the way around, the party started early with rhythmic clapping to the monotonous tune of *The Great Escape*. Fans sang and clapped in unison. This was the English at their best.

'If only they could let the party spread to their hearts and be less aggressive with their drinking,' a Frenchman later said to me.

Unfortunately, the Romanians had not read the script. All through the day, the spectre of being defeated by this team had never reared its ugly head, but during the match their touch and movement made England look pedestrian. Every time they got the ball they released their players with crisp passes while England looked prosaic by comparison. After 20 minutes, one moment stood out: Shearer backed into the Romanian centre-half then waited for the foul. When he didn't get it, he ran across to the linesman just in front of us.

'Come on, line,' he shouted in a broad Geordie accent.

I always get worried when players start looking for a linesman to give them something they should be taking for themselves. Sheringham looked slow while Batty looked totally predictable. Shearer couldn't make any runs and the Romanian shooting, whilst not very accurate, showed that they were confident. The Romanian fans started to chant as they dictated the tempo of the match. Hagi was directing the pace of the match by picking up loose England passes from a line of six men strung across midfield. Suddenly Ince went down and was carried off. On came Beckham, the face of English football, the man with flair who could compete with Hagi on level terms when it came to hitting long passes. and shooting from distance. Half-time came and Terry looked worried. The singing continued unabated but with only two minutes into the second half, the ball was looped in and Adams failed to spot the Romanian stealing a yard behind him. As time stood still, Modlovan volleyed the ball ferociously past Seaman. The Romanian bench was off its feet while the full-back ran along our touch line in front of us, beating his chest.

A 1–0 lead had never been more deserved. England huffed and puffed while the England fans beat out an incessant rhythm: it was uncoordinated noise spurring on a disjointed team.

The tickets I had sold to the Worthing lads had positioned them right behind the England dugout. Close enough to touch the players sitting on the bench, the players and management could hear their comments. Joe Foley was a bouncer at Barry's Worthing club and a West Ham supporter so his joy was unconfined when he found himself sitting next to Harry Rednapp, West Ham's manager. Harry Rednapp was really one of the lads who just happened to manage a Premier League football team. Once, during a pre-season friendly, when his West Ham team was at the receiving end of a bout of incessant barracking from one West Ham fan, he snapped at the fan, 'If you think you can do better then get changed and get out there.'

So the fan got changed and actually went on to play alongside his heroes.

In the second half when England squandered a half-chance, Joe turned to Harry.

'Ian Wright would have got that.'

'I know,' replied Harry, and added with a smile, 'I've signed him from Arsenal for next season.' And sure enough, Ian Wright left Arsenal and signed for West Ham on 13 July.

Not only did Joe get to sit next to his hero, but he also got autographs from the England players sitting on the bench. Harry Rednapp organised one from Rio Ferdinand, who played for him at West Ham.

With 20 minutes to go the England fans started the chant:

ONE MICHAEL OWEN
THERE'S ONLY ONE MICHAEL OWEN.

The chant crescendoed. Hoddle was up off his seat doing his arm movements as in an irate-Rome-traffic-cop-meets-classical-conductor scene. Nobody knew what it meant, least of all the players.

In his exasperation, he went back to the bench and turned to his assistant, John Gorman. 'You have a word, they're not listening to me.'

As John jumped up, the mass chanting for Michael Owen continued.

Joe knew John Gorman could hear him.

'Oy, John! Get Owen on; get your act together. We'll bloody lose this if you don't get your finger out!' Gorman looked at him.

Finally Owen stripped off as the roar from the crowd nearly took the stadium roof off.

'About bloody time, Gorman,' shouted Joe. A dejected Sheringham trooped back to the bench: all the cheers were for young Michael Owen.

As soon as he came on, a new hope inspired the England fans who upped the decibel level. Suddenly the Romanians looked worried, even if England could not put them under the sustained passing pressure which other top nations seemed to be able to do. With the clock ticking away, Shearer pulled the ball back, which Scholes stopped. The first to react was Owen.

OWEN! GOAL!!!

Relief with a capital R. Twenty thousand England fans thanked the Almighty for sparing us.

As the ball hit the net, John Gorman jumped up out of the dugout and turned his snarling roar of defiance on Joe.

'Oy, Blondie! Yeah you, bigmouth. See? We know what we're doing, so get off our backs.'

Joe couldn't hear him above the roar of the crowd but he knew that John was telling him that he knew what he was doing and didn't need grief from guys like Joe. This was England's assistant manager behaving like a Sunday-morning pub manager, like a real fan.

Further down in the stand there was a fan with a giant red rose in one hand and a giant World Cup in the other. He ran along the front of the stand like a man possessed, urging the crowd into a greater frenzy.

A nation roared, as much in relief as anything else. We had not played well but at least we had scraped a draw when all had seemed lost. Not that the girl in the next row seemed to care. She had spent the whole of the second half asleep. Tired and emotional through the effects of too much drink, she was slumped forward wrapped in her St George flag. It was only after the match when I heard her slurring that I realised she was American.

The rest of the match seemed to be played out in a split second as England fans sat thanking their lucky stars, but one final drama awaited them. When the board came out showing how much extra time was needed, a ball was looped over behind Le Saux. His Chelsea team mate, Petrescu, had got goal-side but the angle was tight. Le Saux got back then seemed to hesitate. NO! In a second, the Romanian bench were running on to the pitch and the Romanians to our right were going berserk. English fans sat with their heads slumped forward unable to believe they had seen it all thrown away with a mistake. Later the Spurs General Manager, David Pleat, remarked that he thought Le Saux had bottled it, allowed his Chelsea team mate to muscle him out and then lost his nerve to go for the ball. Seaman in goal wasn't blameless either because he could have attacked the ball instead of letting it drift limply through his legs. In one last-ditch attempt in injury time, Owen hit the post but the irony of this just made the bitter pill of defeat even harder to swallow. The final whistle saw the Romanian fans dancing as joyfully as the Romanian bench who charged around the pitch as though they had won the World Cup itself. The England players were being hugged and cuddled by Ray Clemence, one of the England coaches.

'That's what's wrong with England. Look at him treating men like they were poofy schoolboys,' spat Terry angrily.

Terry and I left the ground along with thousands of other England fans. I needed distance between me and that stadium, between me and that terrible emptiness that had descended. Nobody spoke. It was like the march of the living dead – every face had that same zombie-like expression of bewilderment. David Pleat, on a flight out of Toulouse, remarked that he couldn't believe England had succumbed to a middle-ranking side. England hadn't played well, but the fact that the Romanian touch looked better and hit crisper passes didn't look good. Colombia were our last opponents and now that they had beaten Tunisia, they could qualify by beating England in Lens.

As the England fans filed quietly across the bridge, a German cameraman turned to his friend.

'What time do the English fans come out of the stadium?'

For five minutes they had been walking past him and he hadn't realised it because of the complete silence. Terry and I walked slowly back to the station surrounded by a city which had completely shut down. Shutters were down, lights were off. All that moved was the shuffling mass of sadness that was the England fans. Limbs ached, mouths were dry and there was a pain and terrible sadness in the pit of the stomach. Two England fans were in front of us. One was wearing a Shearer Newcastle shirt. I patted him on the back.

'Yer man [Shearer] had a poor one tonight.' He nodded glumly.

'Batty had a poor game,' added Terry to the other one.

'If you're going to slag off Newcastle then you can fuck off now, you cockney wankers. What about that drunken shithouse Sheringham? He was a disgrace,' hissed his friend wearing an England shirt. Our remarks were not meant for Newcastle but I could empathise with them. They didn't want to talk to us; they just wanted to be left alone with their thoughts.

'You don't slag off someone who's just died, do you? You cockney shits . . .' our aggressive Geordie shouted as we walked away. We continued to walk and left them in their silence. Terry and I had crossed the spoken rubicon. Time to shut up and keep shuffling like the wretched inmates of Papillon's Devil's Island – doomed to serve their sentences in the silence of defeat.

As we crossed the Place du Capitol, we were confronted by

television lights from cameramen from every country around the world. Frantically they ran around, thrusting a camera in the face of any and every England fan. We had just seen our team beaten and wanted to be left alone to understand how and why England came to perform so badly, and here we were being treated like a performing circus monkeys.

'What have you got to say about what has happened tonight? Do you think there will be any more violence?'

'There bloody well will be if you don't get that poxy camera out of my face.'

Then the reporter would look into the screen and report back: 'There you have it. Whilst there is no violence at the moment the threat of violence simmers just beneath the surface. These fans are on a knife edge and it could turn any way. The city itself is shuttered up waiting for dawn to arrive so the peaceful inhabitants of this sleepy city can lead a normal life again when the English fans move on in the morning.'

Lurking in the background were the stills cameramen, checking their cameras in the way infantrymen check their rifles before a firefight, making sure they would be ready to snap away a whole reel of film.

One journalist thrust a microphone under an England fan's nose.

'How long have you been in Toulouse?'

'All fuckin' night,' he replied, then walked on.

People started milling around at the street corner where McDonalds was. The tension level rose. It seemed as if something was brewing. One smashed window at this point could have released a fury. The policemen realised this and frantically called for reinforcements. In the distance, sirens wailed and lights flashed but they need not have worried, it was just a group of fans arguing as to which place was best to try and get a taxi. I didn't fancy their chances in this ghost town. Terry and I were stopped by a local.

'English very tough. Lots of fighting tonight. I have come down here to watch the action. English love to fight.'

Terry and I looked at him and laughed. He'd watched the football at home then come out to see the English riot. Entertainment indeed. On the forecourt of the station the task of getting a taxi looked impossible. Already the queue was 50-strong and growing by the second. Soon, over 500 lost souls stretched the length of the station forecourt. Fans were jumping on board trains as friends shouted. It was like the scene of the last day in Vietnam when people clambered over the American Embassy walls to get out. People wanted to get on the move and out of a city which had taken their money and turned its back when, in defeat, all the fans wanted was a can of drink and something to eat.

'Come on let's get moving – out of this toilet,' was heard frequently. Toulouse was a beautiful city which fans needed to escape to leave their bad memories behind.

One shop was open selling bread rolls. People clamoured to buy bottles of water and baguettes like starving refugees. Nothing else was open. Suddenly one taxi appeared in the taxi rank. The chant went up.

'One bleedin' taxi,

'There's only one bleedin' taxi.'

It was sung with a black humour which only football fans can bring to the party. Many years previously, after Arsenal had lost to Sunderland in a cup semi-final, I snapped at an older Arsenal fan who dared to laugh at the bitter bile of defeat. Now the whole taxi queue was laughing because England had lost and they couldn't get a taxi. I laughed along with them – not the throaty laugh that you have when you have dinner with friends over fine wine, but the laugh you have at a funeral of a good friend when humour comes hard from inside as though you shouldn't really be laughing at all.

As the taxi stopped there was a brief scuffle before four lads jumped in. Romanian fans walked past the queue to their hotel which was next to the station. England fans shook their hands and struck up conversations while cameramen hovered in the background waiting for the fisticuffs. When opposing fans from other countries embrace, pictures of it are gleefully reproduced yet when the self-same thing happens after an England defeat, it's not considered newsworthy. There is almost some form of denial from the news people that it is actually happening: obviously people back in Cool Britannia and civilised DIY-garden-centre-attending England cannot be informed that England fans are polite after all. Unless the description is suffixed with 'drunken moron' then there's no point telling the story.

In common with every other England fan in Toulouse the total shutdown had come as a complete surprise to me. Normally there was always a restaurant or some other bolthole where refuge could be found, but this was like London in the blackout. Taxis sped past with their green pre-booked light showing. The CRS stood watching the taxi queue, both looking impassively at each other. 'Inert' was how the scene could be described. Normally taxi drivers never pass up the chance to earn some money but the propaganda machine had been so powerful that even taxi drivers had decided it was too risky to chance picking up England fans. While England fans stood waiting, thousands of francs in fares went begging. On the station forecourt bodies were sprawled out snatching sleep as people realised that they were going nowhere. Although we were staying only 14 km out of town, we might as well have been on the moon. Getting to Paris on the night train looked easier.

We headed back into the town when an African prostitute stopped us. 'Taxi,' said Terry. She pointed to the taxi rank where over 500 people stood more in hope than expectation.

As we headed back towards the main square we spotted a middle-aged man. When we got close, we realised that he was a pimp. With his tough look, slightly greying hair and moustache, he epitomised the pimps from the films.

'Can you get us a taxi?' I asked.

He passed us a card from a local taxi firm. I dialled the number and when it answered I passed the telephone back to my new friend.

'You talk to them. They put the phone down on an English voice.'

He chattered away then passed the phone back.

'Taxi will be here in five minutes.'

While we waited, he berated English fans for shutting the city down.

'You English – you are bad for business. All you do is drink beer and talk about football. I have taken less money tonight than I have taken on any other evening so far in the World Cup. Austrians and Japanese are good for business.'

After ten minutes he asked for my phone again and dialled another number. No answer. He tried four different numbers before giving up and informing me that every taxi in Toulouse was fully booked for the next hour.

Terry and I walked over the road and cut through a dark alley. At the end of the alley a car advanced slowly. A blonde prostitute beckoned this kerb crawler. Just as he was about to pick her up Terry leaned in through the window.

'I'll give you 5,000 francs if you run us back to our hotel. That will give you the money for Madonna over there.'

Our French friend looked at us. He stank of drink and was obviously over the drink-driving limit; for one moment he thought we were the police. He thought about it then declined our offer but we had alarmed him and he sped off. The prostitute, who at closer range looked more like Maradona with no teeth than Madonna, glared at us for having frightened her client away. The next evening I walked down the same street to get to the Melting Pot English pub and she catcalled me in front of her friends with the words.

'Bonjour, Joe le Taxi.'

Seeing her smile at me with her missing front teeth was one of the more frightening scenes of Toulouse.

Later in the evening, close to where Terry and I had cut through, an England fan wearing an England shirt wandered along on his own. A car with four French men pulled up. One jumped out and stabbed the English fan in the back. It rated only four columns in the papers, and nobody in England gave it a second thought.

Suddenly Terry bumped into a pretty young lady leaving a club. Inside were dozens of pretty women.

'This'll do; in here, Colin.'

'No. You cannot go in,' the girl said.

'It's okay,' replied Terry, 'We're well behaved.'

'No, you don't understand. It's a ladies' bar.'

'No problem. We're broad minded.'

Try as he might, Terry could not negotiate entry. The only bar open in Toulouse was a lesbian bar and we were denied access.

Terry and I trotted across the road to another taxi rank where around ten England fans were congregated. For an hour we whiled away the time. All around us were blacked-out pubs and bars which should have been open, giving us the chance to have a drink while our taxi arrived. There is no more depressing sight to a thirsty England fan abroad than that of hundreds of blacked-out neon lights. An armed security guard with a dog looked at us warily. Taxis sped past. 'TAXI!' we shouted, and threw our arms out, but none dared to stop. Eight of the lads were staying five miles out of town so they decided to walk. After all they had nothing better to do until next Friday when England were due to play Colombia in Lens. I had a brainwave. If we went to the Holiday Inn, we could get them to phone us a taxi. Two lads who had seen the light shine above my head, tagged along. As we walked along the empty, echoing streets, a terrible thought came into my head. Were England actually to *win* the World Cup, it would be a tragedy because everywhere would be shut down and there would be nowhere to celebrate. Perhaps it would be better for the French if England got knocked out, if this was their reaction to our fans.

We walked into the square to find a huge impromptu game of football being played. The gigantic black doors of the Capitolium were one goal and two coats the other side of the square were the other. Some of the lads had bottles of beer and sat out taking a couple of swigs before joining in. Some French lads were exhibiting some silky skills while the English lad guarding the goal had a bottle of beer in each hand. His style was unorthodox yet effective. The elegant flag-bedecked frontage had never been used as a goal before. Camera crews were packing up. The England fans playing football or sitting around paid them scant attention.

The glass front doors of the Holiday Inn were shut and could only be opened by the receptionist from the inside. On the other side stood a smart doorman. We looked smart enough to get in even if the two lads with us were wearing shorts. Once inside, the male receptionist was reluctant to order us a taxi, but he agreed. After he had made the call he told us it would be one hour.

'That's okay, we'll order a coffee – if that's OK with you,' smiled Terry.

We walked into the bar to be met by the sight of the English Press enjoying a convivial drink at the bar. Why hadn't I thought of this before? If anybody could ensure they got a drink, it was the English Press. Standing at the bar among other journalists was Andy Gray, the Sky TV football commentator. We took our drinks and retired to a courtyard which was inside the hotel but in the open air. As we sat down at our table, there at the next table, was my Polish bête noire, Roy Collins, once of the *People*, now writing for *The Guardian,* sitting with three fellow journalists. He recognised me, as did other journalists sitting outside. I walked over to him and I saw him look up nervously. I had arranged to meet the *Daily Telegraph* writer, Paul Hayward, but had been unable to pin him down.

'Is Paul Hayward with you?' I asked, looking him straight in the eye. Roy stammered out his reply.

'No. He has travelled off with another group.' I smiled and walked away. Then we sat down and talked football. The realisation now dawned upon us that we would be in the same half of the draw as Argentina and Brazil, and would need to get past Argentina should we draw with or beat Colombia. Argentina had recently beaten Brazil with something to spare in the Brazilian fortress of the Maracana and looked a class outfit. The two lads with us were from Rotherham and Bolton and had just travelled out to France on their own for the fun of a World Cup. That's all the average fan was looking for. Within 20 minutes we were informed that our taxi had arrived. As we left, the lad from Rotherham made a remark.

'Why are we getting so many dirty looks from all these people?'

'Because we are England fans and they are frightened of us; and they don't like me.'

Despite having arrived home at 3.30 a.m., I still got up early for breakfast. I desperately wanted to get a flight home because my love affair with France had suddenly soured. The delights of rural France now took on the appeal of a warm, flat beer. As I walked into the breakfast room, I bumped in Bobby Charlton. I had meant to ask him for an interview but my mind was elsewhere. As I dunked my teabag in a cup of warm water in a vain attempt to make myself a cup of tea (what is it about the French that they claim to understand the delights of food yet cannot give you a cup of tea?), I heard Bobby Charlton talking about England, ' . . . that was a poor performance, very poor.'

He continued: ' . . . as for Teddy Sheringham, well he should be ashamed of his performance, it was terrible. As far as I'm concerned he shouldn't be on the pitch; he shouldn't even be out here after his disgusting antics in that night-club. How can a player expect to be fit for the biggest tournament he will ever compete in by spending his time in a smoky night-club?'

Teddy Sheringham played for Manchester United where Bobby Charlton was a director, a fact which made Bobby's candidness very revealing. Had I asked for an interview, he would never have said that, but this attack was nevertheless spoken from the heart, and as a true fan. Every fan in that hotel felt cheated. Why shouldn't Bobby vent his spleen against a player who had played badly after abusing his talent in a night-club?

I sat in a corner feeling sorry for myself. A large German came and joined me. I must have looked glum.

'Can I join a condemned man for a hearty breakfast?' he asked jokingly.

After breakfast I went and sat by the pool. The terrible events which had taken place in Lens the previous Saturday started to become apparent as people came in with English newspapers. A 43-year-old French policeman with young children had been declared brain-dead after German fans had run riot in Lens before their match against Yugoslavia. One 17-year-old told the *Bild*: 'I saw one of us break his weapon in two pieces then smash the cop over the head with the butt.

They kicked him and beat him. They went at him like animals. Then I got out of there. Somehow I felt sorry for the guy.

'There were 50 of us, the hard core, marching through the city centre, shouting "We are Germans; we're scared of nothing. Let's get the cops."

'Anybody who wasn't German got thumped. There were three cops by themselves. "Police pigs, we'll get you all," we shouted. The police yelled back . . . then they got scared. Two ran away. The third . . . we grabbed him.'

The German Soccer Federation had offered to withdraw from the World Cup while the German people donated over £1 million towards the man's family. The large German who had joined me for breakfast felt terrible about what had happened. He made no attempt to compare the English and German fans.

'English fans just drink and shout aggressively. These people were not even drunk: they came to fight. They were organised; they had mobile phones and were organised like a small military unit. Now someone is as good as dead. There is something wrong somewhere.'

The German did, however, make a valid point about English football fans which made us sit up because it's always interesting to hear it through someone else's eyes.

'There is something that surrounds the English, a sort of tension, a form of brutality in their spirit which doesn't accompany the other fans we have filmed. Even the Germans with their loud shouting when they drink do not bring that intense confrontation which the English bring to the matches. The other night in the square the tension was tangible. Only the appearance of a couple of English police brought down the tension levels. They just walked over and said, "Calm down lads; chill out", and the tension level dropped by about 20 per cent. The English don't drink to enjoy the conviviality – they seem to drink to get drunk to take them to a different level of feeling.'

The German crew were off to the next German match at Montpelier. He doubted whether they would be asked to attend the match at Lens involving England, as it was easier for them to stay in the south and send a crew in from Germany. Already the Press were printing stories that the German hooligans would be travelling the short distance across the border for a big hooligan showdown with the English. I always take these stories with a pinch of salt because historically the Germans have never fought with English hooligans outside Germany.

I booked the first flight out on Wednesday at 7.10 a.m. and checked in to the Toulouse Ibis next to the airport so as not to have to travel too far in the morning. As we entered the lobby four England fans were sitting watching the Chile *v* Cameroon match. It never ceases to amaze me how some people can sit and watch match after match. When England lose I never want to see another football match for at least a year. The England lads were surprised by our demeanour and criticism of England.

'You've got to support the team, whatever. We'll be back at the next match and if we lose that then we'll be saving for the next European Championship qualifier.'

I admired their patriotism even if I felt there should be a law against people so dumb they didn't have the intellect to notice that England had played so incredibly badly.

We shared a taxi into town with a couple who we assumed were together, yet nothing could have been further from the truth. Wendy cut the unlikeliest dash as an England fan. She was short and plump with track suit bottoms and never stopped smiling. She had flown into Toulouse alone just before the match against Romania, because her boyfriend was not interested in football – but she found herself inundated with offers of help from genuine England fans. She had not booked into a hotel beforehand, and therefore had to take her bag to the match. Nobody had let her carry it, not because they fancied her but because she was an England fan and she'd joined an exclusive club where she'd never feel lonely again on her travels. Arriving in any city is daunting for anybody, never mind a lone female traveller. The fact that she not only survived but prospered, only served to reinforce my faith in English football fans. For every arsehole story there are thousands like that one, but if I were a journalist and wrote about them I would soon be drawing my dole cheque. The plain fact of the matter is that editors don't want to hear about the good side of English fans; only the dark side.

Travelling in the taxi alongside her was Enrique. He claimed to be in town for the Paraguay match on the 24th and was the unlikely product of a liaison between a Scottish sailor and a Paraguayan mother who lived in Argentina. He told us about Paraguayan football and how despite only one of their clubs having a stadium with floodlights, they had nevertheless managed to produce the World club champions Olympia in 1979. He was a typical Scotsman in that he knew the name of the oldest club in South America, which happened to be in Paraguay, and the Scots people associated with that club. Every time I meet a Scotsman he can always reel off the list of every piece of Scots engineering around the world, the year the Scots fellow built it and how many English labourers he had working underneath him. Spooky that. His favourite story was about the '86 qualifiers.

'In 1986, Paraguay had to play Chile home and away to qualify. We won 3–0 in Paraguay then played the second leg in Chile. It was a 2–2 draw and after the match, 5,000 Paraguay fans refused to leave the stadium and stood singing defiantly before General Pinochet's troops.'

Knowing how little value Pinochet attached to life, it made me take notice. By now he was in full flow.

'Paraguayans are the toughest players in South America. If you ever get a chance to talk to Gary Lineker, you ask him who was the hardest defender he ever faced and he will tell you it was against Paraguay in 1986 in Mexico.'

He also cracked the funniest one-liner of the trip so far. We were talking about the England team selection and the decision to bring Rob Lee instead of Gascoigne or even Ray Parlour of Arsenal.

'Rob Lee. I'd rather have brought Bruce Lee in his coffin.'

However, as the evening wore on some of his stories took on a bit of an exaggerated feel. He had been a professional footballer in Paraguay, yet he had not continued to play upon his return to Scotland because he had nearly killed someone with a tackle. One thing was for sure, he was definitely Scottish because he never put his hand in his pocket once to buy any beer.

Every city always has one watering hole which becomes the focal point for all England fans. In the case of Toulouse, it was the Melting Pot pub, situated on the edge of the red light district opposite the taxi rank Terry and I had been standing at that fateful night. We paid it a visit on Tuesday evening. We had only intended to stay out for an hour but needless to say we finally staggered out of the pub at 2 a.m. Inside the pub were many different characters, all with their own stories of travel and harassment and unlikely ways of getting tickets. English fans sat around swapping jokes and stories. One thing was agreed by everybody: the French people had been absolutely magnificent. Unlike in Rome, not one price had gone up and even if some of the hotels were slightly more expensive, they were still a damn sight cheaper than when they went to Italia '90. French people had gone out of their way to make the English feel at home, despite the hard line taken by the authorities.

Inside, the pub had round tables and booths as well as bar stools. All were filled with the chattering classes of England fans, every one an expert in their own right about all things tactical and everybody convinced that the Press had done England fans no favours. As we sat in the pub the TV showed the match between Norway and Brazil. Brazil scored late and then Norway scored. Eventually, Norway were awarded a late dubious penalty and ran out late winners on 2–1. That meant curtains for Scotland who, even if they beat Morocco, would not now qualify. Once again, they got their wish to be glorious failures. As it turned out, however, Scotland lost 3–0 to Morocco so the term 'abject failures' is probably more appropriate. As the third goal went in, a chant went up to the tune of 'Football's Coming Home'.

> '*YOU'RE GOING HOME*
> '*YOU'RE GOING HOME*
> '*JOCKY'S GOING HOME!*'

Not everybody sang because not all English fans felt the same. Whereas Scots fans nearly all cheer for the opposition when England play, that isn't true of the English fans, many of whom always support the home nations unless they are competing against England. This fact underlined the inferiority complex which accompanied the Scots around France.

It had become obvious that the match in Lens was now taking on a completely different focus. While Toulouse had enjoyed our daytime bonhomie and shut down under fear of prosecution by the authorities (insurance companies said that any bar owner who dared open would not be covered), it was soon very evident that Lens would simply become a ghost town. There was even talk of the whole Pas de Calais region shutting down and the whole population moving to Normandy until the infidels returned to England. In 1944, when the Allies were planning to launch an invasion of France, they sent over propaganda telling the Germans that the invasion force would land on the Pas de Calais. The propaganda war that preceded the arrival of a few thousand England fans was just as powerful in its delivery. That time the Germans moved all their armour up from Normandy. Now the French were installing divisions of riot police. What were they expecting?

On Sunday evening the Melting Pot had been the hub of events in the town. The media reported that there had been trouble with England fans outside a bar. Hearing the story from John, an Australian, put it into a different perspective. John had wanted to see Australia in the World Cup more than anything. He had been there that fateful day along with 100,000 other fans when Australia were 2–0 up at home to Iran in Melbourne Cricket Ground. Fate, however, had conspired to let the Iranians score twice in the short spell after that, but as John had been saving for four years, he decided to come to Europe anyway and support the mother country. His view of England fans was that they were boisterous, hard drinkers but greatly misunderstood.

'Australian football is played mostly by the ethnics [Aussie word for Greek-Italian immigrants] but for the World Cup, the majority of support comes from the rugby league/cricket crowd so it's all hard drinking, Aussie-style fun, the way you guys do it. I'd already booked my ticket to France so I just changed my itinerary to follow England. I was in Marseilles, and being white down by the port area I was pretty frightened, but the atmosphere in the ground was second to none. I was surprised by the reaction to the punch-ups because I've seen worse.

'Three guys gave me a lift up here then moved on somewhere else. I've been here for three days and I've watched the atmosphere change during that time. The other fans make more noise and jump about in the streets while the English seem to congregate together and talk. The English guys have an incredible knowledge of the matches and can tell you about a penalty which so-and-so scored ten years ago even when they've been drinking for five hours. Some of those guys could get a PhD in football knowledge. It's uncanny.'

He then went on to tell me about Sunday night: 'All the England lads were in the pub and it got so busy that everybody spilled out on to the pavement. It was good-natured and some of the lads were singing. Around midnight, the riot police turned up and started kitting up opposite. They then started to push everybody back into the pub even though it was too crowded. Then the cameramen turned up and started flashing away which seemed to start off the riot police who acted as if they wanted to pose for the cameras. The riot police did a sweep to show who was the boss and the flashes really started snapping. This incensed some of the England fans who tried to attack the cameras and it got silly for a short while, but all the anger was against the cameras.'

John left the pub around 10.30 p.m. to get a train up to Lens. Terry and I stayed in the pub until the early morning and spent only three hours in our beds in the Hôtel Ibis, emerging bleary-eyed for our 7.10 a.m. BA flight back to Gatwick. I went home and slept for 12 hours straight through.

11

Laughing in Lens

It soon became obvious that the match in Lens was taking on the aspect of a military assault. With talk of 50,000 fans turning up without tickets, high on drink and in a mood for smashing things up, it was hardly surprising. Perhaps it was because it was close to the battlefields of the Somme and had been the front line for the British and Commonwealth armies, or perhaps paranoia had become fashionable, but some of the utterances about the England fans defied belief. Estimates of fans travelling for the match varied from 15,000 to 50,000. Scenes reminiscent of the destructive armies of vandals and Goths who sacked Rome were being portrayed to the public of both England and France, while the poor people of Lens who were originally looking forward to 20,000 English people adding £1.5 million to their local economy, now found themselves under siege from reporters who asked if they feared for their daughters' safety and how they viewed having their homes smashed and 20,000 drunks pissing in their front gardens.

At the travel agent's on Thursday morning it became clear that a large number of people were intending to cross the Channel on Friday morning. The earliest I could get my car on the shuttle was 2.15 p.m. and the earliest ferry was not until 4 p.m. However, I finally managed to get a place on the Dover Seacat at 8 a.m. on Friday, returning the next day from Boulogne at 2 p.m. Three of us had tickets for the match from my French friend, Monsieur Desereviges, which was no problem because all the talk of the French police checking tickets against names was complete balony. It would have served the British Government better to spend the £1million on maps and phrase books for the travelling England fans and set up liaison buses like the ones operated by the Football Supporters Association.

We set off early on Friday morning. Carl, who had come with me to Rome, had decided that Lens was the one for him after he was unable to get an air ticket at the last minute for Toulouse. Also on board was Danny, who only the night before, at closing time in the pub, had made a split second decision to go. It was a question of picking him up at junction 10 on our way through to the M25. The lack of any overnight bag signified that he didn't intend to inform the wife that he wouldn't be home that evening but would be in Lens for the big match instead. Terry had decided to meet us at the departure gate at Dover as he was travelling from Cambridge. At Dover I bought a *Guardian* newspaper and read on the front page that the prefect of the Pas de Calais had imposed an alcohol prohibition corridor from Calais along to Dunkirk then in a 20-mile band down as far south as Lens, a 1,400 square mile alcohol free zone. The Mayor of Lens, André Delelis, had asked all supermarkets within a 30-mile radius to clear their shelves of alcohol. Two events – a concert by Jimmy Cliff on Monday evening and a BBC Radio 1 roadshow – had been cancelled, yet events had gone on the day after the Marseilles skirmish without any problem. It had also been decided that the big screen showing of the match in Lens was to be cancelled for this night only. On top of this, the English propaganda Stasi were telling everybody that anybody found drinking on the streets of Lens would be arrested. When one fan read this on the Seacat he asked if the Lens police had cells enough for 5,000 fans: 'Stop me having a drink before a football match? – they've got more chance of finding an Italian war hero,' he exclaimed. Our party paid extra and travelled first class, which entitled us to free drinks. The ferry we were on, as a concession to the French alcohol ban, did not sell any duty free alcohol and as the boat docked the captain made an announcement: 'Please be careful when going through customs. You must not be seen drinking any alcohol. If you have brought any drink with you please be warned that any excessive amounts of alcohol will prevent entry into France.'

As we drove through customs into France, there were indeed a large number of riot police at the gate but they took one look at us and waved us straight through. The previous day four lads had been turned around on entry for possession of 168 cans of beer and 6 bottles of vodka. 'Just going for a quiet picnic in the countryside, officer' cut no ice and home they went, no doubt to return on a later ferry. Calais had been shut down the previous evening, so a group of lads went to Ostend, got plastered and went on a smashing spree in the town. People who associate these sort of people with football make me laugh – because smashing up a town 100 miles away from a match in a different country has nothing to do with football, but still the fans continue to suffer guilt by association.

We drove straight out of Calais (most visitors to France usually drive only as far as the beer hypermarkets) on to the motorway, paid our toll and sped along. English cars passed us every two minutes. The landscape as we approached Lens betrayed the mining past it now hankered after. Mining wasn't glamorous as the grass-covered slag heaps showed, but mining was infinitely better than the unemployment which now blighted the town. As we sped south, we could see a giant ski run which had been created on a mound. If it was on a slag heap, then it was improvisation of the first order; if not, then it still looked good.

Danny was looking for a ticket so we decided to visit the ground to see what the situation was. The town of Lens has a population of 37,000, while the ground holds 42,000, so it was hoped that there would be spare tickets, especially if what was said by the bar owner of the Zeulon, a favourite hangout for the local Racing Lens fans, was anything to go by.

'It's better a town be dead for a day than a town be destroyed. Football is supposed to be a party. I've got tickets and was supposed to be taking my son but I won't be going. I'm taking my family to the seaside instead.'

Perhaps there were thousands more like him who would sell the England fans their tickets. Unfortunately, with the numbers travelling far exceeding tickets available, the price would have to reflect supply and demand. Once upon a time, hope and a tent was all a football fan needed to travel with, but now the World Cup had become awash with people wanting tickets for reasons other than football – in which case, a large wallet was an important part of the travelling football fan's luggage. If you were lucky, you could have bought tickets for the first two matches on the black market for £200; if you were unlucky, £500. Our fears were realised when we turned into the road leading up to the car park and saw England fans with boards written in French and English asking for tickets, like the hitch-hikers you see with town names they're trying to get to.

We pulled into a car park just behind the ground, full of cars with

English number plates. Just behind us was a large green bus off-loading CRS riot police. In the car park the England fans were sitting around drinking tins of beer. The riot police looked at us indifferently then walked on. One red builder's van had two lads sitting on the tailgate. They had a large bucket full of ice and had wine and beers enough for five people.

'Expecting company?' asked Carl.

'No, just a few aperitifs before we have a drink,' replied the man laughing.

Back in Calais, Dave West, owner of the huge cash and carry Eastenders, was bemoaning that the alcohol ban would cost him £100,000 in lost trade. Perhaps our national sport should be drinking – perhaps it already was?

As we drove through the town just after midday, the first signs of the English were apparent. Groups of fans wandered aimlessly around a town shut for business. Usually the bars and restaurants enjoyed a roaring trade but today the cash registers would not be ringing.

Just up the road was a monument to man's inhumanity to man and a lasting tribute to the courage which saw many young men in their prime run across a strip of land to be blown into thousands of tiny pieces or mown down by murderous machine-gun fire. The young Englishmen here today would never dare defile the place where thousands and thousands of their great-grandfathers are buried – more people than were visiting Lens that day. As one London fan reminded me in a bar later in Arras, 'There's more London people buried around here than is buried in the whole of London.'

Vimy Ridge was donated by the people of France shortly after the end of the First World War in perpetuity to the people of Canada in gratitude for the ultimate sacrifice which that nation's young men gave to protect their freedom. Vimy had been a classic trench battleground for many years, which had seen thousands of men charge forward to attempt to take a small piece of ground only to be cut down like harvested corn. Honour and defence of their country. The beer bellies in Marseilles charging down the road to defend the honour of England probably had the same idea but the stakes at Vimy in that terrible conflict were very much higher. Back in 1917 the Canadians had an idea which would ensure that they broke through: they dug underneath the German lines and came out on top of them to stop the carnage as they ran across no-man's-land. To do this, they needed expert miners, so they went to England to get the best. The British miners came and dug the tunnels underneath the German lines and due to a technically brilliant attack campaign, the breakthrough was made. For anybody to contemplate that the English would not show respect in Lens for this ultimate sacrifice was beyond belief. Those lads sitting on the verge in a state of boredom had no idea, probably, that they were only three miles from a piece of history that makes people who travel there proud to be English. Why the British Government did not spend money informing football fans that not only was Vimy Ridge in close proximity to Lens but also many hundreds of Commonwealth War graves I am not sure. They would obviously rather spend their money on the stupid, futile advert which said you wouldn't get in if you purchased a black market ticket. This was fast becoming the black market World Cup: so black, there were no grey areas at the edges. You either paid black or you didn't get in. It was only the thought of the earnings from the black market which stopped yet another French strike. Even members of parliament were buying tickets from the black market to see the matches.

Against this background the political decision to shut everything down was made, and on the stupidity Richter scale, it was beyond measurement. Fifty Germans attacked a policeman so they shut down Lens for England's visit while in Montpellier the day before, it had been business as usual for the Germans – because as everybody knows, you can't blame 10,000 Germans for the actions of a few hotheads but the English fans must all be made to pay for the actions of 200 Goodwood racers on the front in Marseilles.

As one Scots fan said to me in St Etienne: 'What's the difference between a Scotland fan and an England fan? About 500 Pressmen frothing at the mouth, gagging for a story.' Then he laughed and walked away after telling me a few of his mates had slapped some sooties in Paris and been congratulated by the local gendarmes.

If all arriving England fans were forced to sit around bored, they would use their ingenuity to obtain drink. These lads with 168 cans of beer and bottles of vodka were not looking to drink it, but were more likely to be looking to sell it and make a profit just like everybody else in the French nation who'd purchased tickets with the express intention of moving the tickets on the black market. And there were plenty more lads with boot-loads of booze heading south to Lens to sell the thirsty lads a beer or two. An army marches on its stomach and those England boys had plenty of stomach to fill so they could cheer with gusto inside the stadium. Football fans shouted in rage and shook their fists at the injustice of it all, but we could take it. Whatever the stupid authorities threw at us we could take it because we were the descendants of the men who dug those tunnels at Vimy, which needed to be built in complete silence and in complete darkness, because as soon as the Germans heard you digging a tunnel they would dig another one underneath and fill it full of explosives and detonate it. Boom. Good game, Tommy. Better luck next time. It was the ultimate penalty from a German, and English football fans knew how good the Germans were at a penalty.

In our car we had a plan. We would head south until we found a town which would serve us a meal and a glass of wine then travel back into Lens by taxi. We only had to go 14 km before we came to Arras. With its cobble-stoned streets and central square dominated by a church, it soon became a focal point for many England fans. As many of the lads had mobiles, the word soon spread along the bush telegraph where the alcohol was being served. Lille and Arras were serving, as were other towns in transit. As drinks bans go this one hadn't really got started. We pulled up outside the Café de Picardie and were immediately greeted by a sign which read 'Picardie welcomes English people' and the friendliest bar owner I have ever met, until I met the next French bar owner.

'You have no tickets. *Mon Dieu*. I must try and get some for you.' With that he picked up the phone.

Carl and I went over to the Office de Tourisme to try and find a hotel. The lady behind the desk informed me and other English fans that there were no rooms available in or around Arras, that they were all full. Then she informed us that there had been trouble last night in Ostend as well as Calais. Why that should make the hotels fill up in Arras was beyond me.

'Have all the people from Ostend and Calais been evacuated to Arras, then?' asked one of the other England fans, but his dry humour got lost in the translation to French. Arras sees thousands of visitors every year and was full of hotels. Finding them full on the night of an England match was an unfortunate or spiteful coincidence, depending on which school of cynicism you frequented. Eventually the lady suggested Amiens. The lady offered us a hotel in Amiens. That was 50 miles away. While other England fans worked out whether or not they would accept, we walked out to our friendly bar. An hour later we found a small chambre de l'hôte gîte in Agny, only four miles from Arras, charging only £8 each for a bed. The owner was apologetic about taking a £50 deposit from us but there were a number of keys to the front gate and rooms which would need to be replaced if we lost them.

The local bar owner in Agny welcomed our presence. Pride of place above the bar was a Danish flag which had been left there by some Danish fans visiting for their match against Saudi Arabia. When he saw Carl's flag of St George, he asked if he could have it when England won. Much to Carl's dismay, I promised it to the owner when that happened. As far as we were concerned, the victory was a foregone conclusion. More to the fore was the fact that we would probably be playing Argentina in the last 16 and that would be a tough match. Colombia had sent their best player, Asprilla, home because he had criticised the manager's selection policy and had been subjected to the usual death threats from the drug cartels who were betting on the matches, so their minds would be somewhere else. Anyway, Colombia had shown nothing in the previous matches which made anybody think they would be difficult to beat.

The bar owner called us a taxi to take us back to our Bar Picardie in Arras. We booked the taxi for a collection from the bar at 7 p.m. then a further collection in Lens at 11.30 p.m. Our driver spoke perfect English and was pleased that the English were in town.

'I work all night tonight earning lots of money,' he told us proudly. 'Big taxi users, the English. They like to drink and get in cabs. The French drink and drive, but not the English,' he stated.

At least we were law-abiding in one way: we had respect for human life – although looking at the centre of Lens with its total shutdown, one might have thought differently.

We sat down outside the bar around 3 p.m. as more English people arrived in the square and settled down in the pleasant pavement cafés. The owner came outside and asked us if we still needed a ticket and gave us the address of a hotel where tickets were on sale. Danny and Terry shot off to get one while Carl and I relaxed over a cold beer.

The mobile rang. It was Barry direct from the centre of Lens:

'Colin, it's full of boneheads here just hanging around getting more and more drunk. We're looking for one ticket but things are looking tight here.'

I explained to Barry that there might be tickets here. Twenty minutes later, Barry phoned back and said that beer had been sprayed over passers-by and that the sheer volume of people milling around had spilled into the road stopping cars, the CRS had baton-charged and people had been running over cars to escape. The tension levels were rising. With that early baton charge, the cameramen had come out of the shadows as woodlice emerge when you move a piece of rotten wood. Cue the tension levels due to rise off the Richter scale.

The Worthing Mafia arrived in the square in Arras around 4 p.m. in their mobile homes. As the lads emerged, we could see they all had blonde hair, an act done in one of those mad beer-induced moments that people live to regret. It must have been a trend because the Romanian team did the same thing. All it elicited was wolf whistles and laughter from the assembled throng. One of the vans had been broken into the previous evening and had everything stolen: money, credit cards and passports. Not the end of the world, not even close to the end of the world, especially as they didn't get the gold dust that was the England match tickets; unless you were a steward on Virgin Atlantic and had taken two days' sick leave to see the match and were due to be on the Friday flight to New York. It reminded me of the story of the guy who took a sick day to go to the Oval and sat in the front row in an Arsenal shirt. Every time the ball went to boundary the camera closed in on him. His boss, a big cricket fan, used to sit in his office with a portable TV. When he went in the following Monday, his P45 was on his desk with a note. 'Go back to the Oval again today – you will now have plenty of time to watch cricket.'

Generally, however, the loss of their money was not causing them too many concerns, as the lack of tickets and the prices being bandied about were a bigger worry. The black market price had now risen to £350 with some fans being asked for, and coughing up, £500. Only those people who've never experienced the thrill of actually being there wonder why fans break the bank to see a match. Being at the stadium is like nothing else on earth. Not only that, but to sit outside and be so close while not actually going inside and seeing any of the action leaves you with a feeling of emptiness and no matter how much you try, you cannot share in the emotions that go on after the match. You are always outside the conversation. With huge English TV audiences, everybody has an opinion, but only the 20,000 inside the ground can speak with any authority.

No passport, no money, no credit card, perhaps no job; the only thing to do is scrounge some dosh from the lads who have got these minor trivialities then order some beers up. Later on, to the tune of 'I ain't got nothing, I got life' by Nina Simone, the lads did a brief rendition.

'I got no dosh,
Got no cards,
Got no passport,
No respect,
Got bad breath,
Been bashed up,
Here in France,
But what have I got,
Got a ticket, Got a ticket, Got a ticket, Got a ticket,
What have I got? (holding tickets aloft)
I GOT LIFE!'

The female bar owner in our little corner of England thought we were smashing and applauded us. Not only was our establishment a bar but it was also a restaurant and bakery selling cakes, baguettes and pastries. England fans, from time to time, staggered in and purchased some solids (as they put it) then gulped them down as they staggered back down the road. Further down the road in the far corner of the square was an Irish bar. The noisier elements of the England fans in Arras had situated themselves inside and outside of it. Every time the chant of 'England' went up they echoed around the square, and each time the faces of the French people grimaced with palpable nervousness. Two doors down from us was another bar. At around 6.30 p.m. a coach-load of lads turned up wearing identical red T-shirts. On the front was the name of their Sunday football team, which was so distinctly forgettable that I forgot it as soon as I left the square, and on the back, a flag of St George.

Suddenly, from nowhere, the flag of St George has replaced the Union Jack for England fans. Only a few years ago everybody had a Union Jack with only a few sporting the flag of St George; now it was the other way round. I had yet to see a match in France on the TV which didn't sport at least one St George flag pinned up. English fans might not be the most colourful but they were kings at adorning the stadium with flags, many of which showed which area they came from or which team they represented back in England. It's something to be proud of when you get back and people tell you they saw your flag with your town's name on the TV.

By now, Danny had given up all hope of finding a ticket. He had gone up to the hotel near the station, but had been greeted by a huge mob of drunken English fans. He was told: 'Yes – tickets were on sale here last night for around £150 but the English fans started fighting so the ticket sellers moved on somewhere else today.'

So Danny, along with around 1,000 other fans, settled down to watch the match in a bar in the square. Unfortunately, as the crowd numbers rose along with the decibel level, the bar owners started getting nervous. After one chant by the red shirts next door, the bar owner emerged into the sunlight looking decidedly white around the gills.

'Please, gentlemen, you must keep the singing down or else the police will come and extend the shutdown zone.'

Every time a chant went up after that he came out, wildly gesticulating to indicate to keep it down.

In our group, the beer and banter flowed in equal amounts. It was a scene being repeated outside every pavement café which England fans had managed to frequent. It would have been repeated in Lens had the stupid politicians not over-reacted. By now, the CRS were baton-charging England fans who retaliated with bottles then ran. Barriers had been set up in the main street to prevent ticketless fans getting near the ground.

Our cab turned up dead on time at 7 p.m. Terry, Carl and I, along with one of the Worthing lads, drove into town. As we left, the female owner of the bar brought free drinks out for the English. Halfway along the road, a cavalcade of cars with motorcycle outriders shot past us all lights and sirens. We arrived in Lens and the cab driver dropped us off, informing us that he would collect us from the same spot at 11.30 p.m. After our problems in Toulouse, I needed to hear that. All along the main street were banners welcoming, in that country's language, all the countries who would be playing in Lens during the World Cup. Ironically, the two banners next to each other were England and Germany. One had caused problems, making us unwelcome. As we alighted from our taxi, a lad was sitting on a concrete obelisk. He looked downcast, the look that accompanies the awful realisation that you will not get a ticket and will not be inside that ground. It is a hollow empty feeling, as if the whole trip were a complete waste.

'What's been happening?'

'Nothing much on this street here, but the police have made a few baton charges down by the station.'

Carl and I walked down past the station amongst the milling fans. There was a strange atmosphere, unlike any I have experienced before.

There was tension from the expectancy of the match, but the quiet shops and general listlessness of the spirits amongst the waiting England fans made it almost supernatural, like the opening credits to the *X Files*. People were walking around with nowhere to go, no direction and nothing to fall back on if they couldn't buy a ticket. It was strangely like a river which flows quickly near a weir but one part always has a zone where the water just sits and swills slowly, unable to get back into the flow. Fans with tickets moved towards the barriers while those without were gripped by inertia. Would they be able to find a bar? Would they be able to get a train to a town with a bar? Could they take a chance and try and get to the ground once kick-off started? Johnny Nash had been due to play a concert here last night. It was definitely like one of his songs: 'There are More Questions than Answers'.

There were about 3,000 England fans standing in and around the roads leading to the barriered-off streets. The wild estimates of 50,000 travelling to Lens were hopelessly wrong. As the fans milled around a feeling was in the air which only seems to surround England fans. Fun for fun's sake and pure joy are never on board with England fans.

There was something violent inside the England fans, a sort of lingering darkness which gives the English fans a pre-match, brooding menace. Perhaps it is their approach to life and football, for in their hearts there is a dark side which seems absent in other fans. Darth Vader would have been an England fan. England fans mass together and sing with an aggression which frightens. The same mentality which was needed to conquer and control the Empire which the sun never set upon could not be bred out in four generations. This menace cannot be portrayed by a news camera because the thing that makes the England fan is the same thing that built the Empire and gave Europe breathing space in 1940 when Britain stood alone against the terrible evil of Hitler. Newspaper reporters chased this enigma like fools chasing the end of a rainbow. They would all chase in vain. If one camera ever captures that on film, they will realise riches beyond the dreams of avarice.

When we got to the barriers, we inched our way through the England fans who had no tickets but were standing three deep in front of the CRS. We showed our tickets and were let through. I got the feeling that the riot police felt uneasy about their role; that they were unsure why English fans were being treated like this – after all, this was the French who have a most healthy disrespect for all things authoritarian. There was no aggression from the CRS. Only politeness to ensure they did what they had to do.

As I walked through, I was met by a photographer. One fan the other side of the barrier walked right up to the line of CRS, poked his head through and asked the photographer:

'Why do you hate England fans?'

He tried to look away but the England fan followed his eyes.

'Why?' he persisted. 'Why?'

'It is my job,' he finally replied, with a foreign accent.

'Funny,' mused the England fan. 'You were only doing your job when you were snapping Lady Di the night she died yet that wasn't considered a defence – nor was it a defence in Nuremberg or Serbia when people stated that they were only doing their job. You're malicious, you lot: vultures, scavengers with no dignity.'

The photographer looked embarrassed and walked further down the line to get away from someone who had touched a chord.

What do you call it when a photographer takes a picture of three fans beating up one person but does not go to his aid? Would that photographer have taken a picture of the England fan who had his throat cut in Marseilles or the one who was stabbed in Toulouse? They took pictures of the policeman when the Germans clubbed him senseless, the policeman who now lay not far from there in a hospital, brain-dead. Yet all around the photographers hovered like vultures, waiting for the violence which would earn them money selling pictures. More than anything, England fans wanted to see the police baton-charge this vile filth and give them a chance to snap away on their throwaway cameras.

At the other side of the barriers there was a carnival. It was like entering a joyous oasis in a desert full of tension as England fans sang and danced. In the centre was a roundabout with a giant obelisk with a football on top. It was the fun centre point. Fans had a football which was being kicked high in the air and every kick elicited a cheer from the fans. French people were standing around on the balconies watching the England fans with smiles on their faces. Can these happy people be the savages of popular myth? The biggest cheer was reserved for when the football went over a balcony and into a French family's front room. The lady retrieved it and sent it back down with a smile.

Terry, Carl and I headed towards the ground. The Felix Bollaert Stadium is situated alongside a railway line so the police had a natural barrier to enable them to direct the crowd and control any disturbances. As we walked to the ground, the police had set up another control barrier. In the middle of this mass of people trying to get in was a huge black man and another in a red shirt checking tickets. Standing behind them was a row of riot police looking on impassively, doing and saying nothing. As this was also the entrance for the car park then the only way to describe it was organised confusion. Surveying the scene was like watching a farce, only we were also the participants. Just as we approached the barrier, two cars drove past with a female journalist frantically asking the male driver questions, while the cameraman ran alongside recording it. As the driver put up his electric windows, I spoke to the journalist.

'Who was that?'

'It was the Mayor of Lens.'

'What did he say?'

'He said that there have been no problems and he is very happy with everything that has gone on so far.'

'So he's happy with the behaviour of the England fans?' I said.

'Yes,' she replied, breaking into a run, but she didn't hear because like all journalists who were looking for a violence angle it wasn't happening. I ran after her and stopped her.

'He must have said something else.'

'No, that was it,' she panted and went to run.

I caught hold of her arm: 'Are you going to report that?'

I looked her in the eye but she averted her gaze because she knew that that interview had suddenly become aged. That interview was old news as soon as she realised that the Mayor had no new angle on violence. The only punch-up story of this World Cup had happened 12 days ago in Marseilles; the only real violence had been a one-off by some nasty Germans. Never before had so many chased so little with such determination in forlorn hope. In truth, they had a better chance of bottling the wind than finding more violence but this chase had long since overtaken reason and left it sitting puffed out and deserted – not unlike the puffing beer bellies in Marseilles – completely out of breath and ideas.

This was the ritual for a xenophobic moron:

1. Find bar 2. Order drink 3. Abuse bar owner 4. Go for piss 5. Repeat all over town

This was the ritual for a decent England fan:

All of the above except 3, which becomes 'talk amicably to bar owner in between chanting loudly'.

It's no wonder that journalists cannot tell the difference, but who was going to tell them? By now, the news boys or the Rotters (as they loved to call themselves) were rampaging across France behind the England fans, like blood and guts General Patton, desperately trying to find violent stories for those back home who needed it in writing as a junkie needs his fix. And, if it didn't happen as in Stockholm nine long years ago, who was going to contradict them? None of them would get the sack for increasing their newspaper circulation by telling lies about a few football fans and inventing violence stories.

As we approached the barrier, the railway embankment was lined with photographers, at least 30 strong, who had climbed over the fences – to get a better shot of the England fans squeezing through the barriers – like a pack of wolves waiting to attack, their teeth the buttons on their cameras. The Mayor's car was just in front of me, by now surrounded by football fans. It was part of a two-car convoy. The car in front inched forward, angering fans who were trying to get through a small gap. Shouts of 'Back off, arsehole!' and bangs on the roof could be heard. 'We've got as much right to get in as you.' The first car got through but the second containing the Mayor was stuck fast. Just in front of the barrier was a man giving out white plastic hats with the red cross of St George on the top. Also on the side of the hats was the brand name, Snickers. I took one and put it on for fun, as did other England fans. As I stood alongside the car with the Mayor in the driving seat, I noticed an elegantly dressed woman in the front and a man and woman in the back. The other England fans in the car noticed the woman in the front.

> *'Get your tits out,*
> *Get your tits out,*
> *Get your tits out for the lads'*

The crowd pushed forward while the car was stuck fast. As I stood alongside the car, I looked behind me. Standing there dressed in official England shirts and black shorts were two undercover police officers. One had longer black hair, but the way they surveyed the crowd with steely eyes, never letting their gaze be averted from the funny people and situations happening around them, made it so obvious that they would have done better had they been dressed in full English Bobby uniform. I walked back towards them.

'Spotted anybody who shouldn't be here yet, lads?' I asked.

They looked bewildered, as though surprised that I had noticed them, but they stuck out like sore thumbs, making their dressing up as England fans even more ridiculous. I half-expected them to whisper at me asking me not to blow their cover. No wonder there had been trouble in Marseilles if this was our finest in action. I called Carl and Terry over.

'Look at these two. The Mayor is stuck in traffic, the lads are asking his wife for a quick flash of her boobs and they stand here like Eros because their job is defined as spotting. But spotting what?'

'They probably had spotted dick for dinner,' laughed Carl.

I walked over and tapped on the Mayor's car window. He wound it down slightly so he could hear me but not too much.

'Don't worry Mr Mayor, if anything happens, our finest undercover police next to us will be able to state quite categorically that the attackers weren't category C because they didn't recognise them.'

In terms of organisation, you couldn't have described the chaos theory any better. Overhead a helicopter hovered, shining a spotlight down. The chopping sound of the blades competed against the cheering crowd and people shouting and singing for the Mayor's wife to get her tits out.

As we got to the barrier, my ticket was checked while another man in a red T-shirt snatched the white hats from the heads of England fans including myself. If it was against the rules to wear a plastic hat he could have had it, but I didn't see the point in his snatching it roughly from my head. He took them, screwed them up and threw them up on the floor.

I walked through the CRS and stood in front of him: 'Pourquoi?' I said to him. He mumbled something in French and stopped snatching hats for a couple of seconds. The CRS looked at me apologetically. I could only think that the word 'Snickers' meant that a TV camera might focus on one of the hats and a comment might be made by a TV cameraman, so giving Snickers about £10 million worth of free publicity. In a World Cup which was underpinned by corporate greed, this was inexcusable. So the answer was to snatch hats off heads in an undignified manner – although it was naïve of me to think that dignity and big business could ever go hand in hand. It didn't matter that cars and fans were going through the same gate and it was a jumbled mess: get the priorities right by snatching free plastic hats and jumping on them. The humorous self-restraint shown by the England fans during that five-minute period was immense, especially when a 52-seater coach came through.

As we went through, Terry went up to the senior officer and explained that the Mayor was stuck outside. The officer thanked Terry and went and cleared a path for him.

As I went through I stood on the wall facing the cameramen.

'Vultures!' I shouted.

Other fans joined me until we were about 10-strong.

'Vultures, Vultures, Vultures,' we chanted.

Then one fan started the sound.

'Baa Baa Baa Baa Baa,' like a sheep. The sound echoed around the tree-lined road for about 20 seconds as other fans picked up the refrain. The cameramen would not look us in the eye. 'Cowards,' shouted a fan. But we had a place in destiny to look forward to while all they had was the implicit knowledge that we knew they were vermin. We were going to watch a football match, watch our beloved England and secure our place in the folklore of English support. Why waste valuable time and breath on that lot? Nevertheless, we had made our non-violent point. Many years previously during a push on the Somme, the soldiers of Australia had marched past rows of English officers and had made the same baaing sound because of the stupidity of the actions which they were being subjected to. Now, surrounded by their graves in the immediate area we had done the same thing.

I had arranged to have a meeting with Paul Hayward of the *Daily Telegraph* and while I waited outside the press area, I marvelled at the relaxed attitude the French had managed to foster despite the intense pressure to do otherwise. England fans went up to the gate to get to the other side of the ground and walked past the man who politely informed them that they had to go around the outside.

As I waited, Arsene Wenger, the Arsenal manager, walked through. Before he could go beyond the press barrier I was shaking his hand telling him I was Arsenal's number one fan. As an Arsenal fan it was a big moment for me. Along with the French people in Lens that day he looked bemused and worried in case I was one of these thuggish England fans. When I looked at him I suddenly realised that he was actually petrified. He managed to free his hand from mine and shot through the barrier.

'I think you've eaten too much garlic,' chortled Carl.

Paul Hayward emerged from the press area with his accreditation badge hanging round his neck. With his blue designer shirt and jacket it somehow looked out of place. Maggie Thatcher had once berated a political journalist, saying that it wasn't a proper job. That would have described this man to a tee. Even the other sports journalists looked at him with envy, saying that he's a nothing writer, going around the world writing about sport. Every child who loves sport has a dream when they are at school: footballer, racing driver, tennis player, golfer. But imagine you could do none of these but were paid instead to go around the world and write about the grace and beauty of these sports; imagine you could get close enough to touch the athleticism, smell the sweat, feel the aura of athletes then have the talent to transcribe this beauty on to a blank page. That's a sexy thought (without any sexual connotation). With his good looks and talent, it is no wonder that some of the scribes in the press box wanted to rip his heart out. He'd already won the Sports Writer of the Year award as a young writer with the *Daily Telegraph*, when he was poached by *The Guardian* and then reclaimed by the *Daily Telegraph*. Enough golden hellos to buy him Paul Smith jackets for a few years yet, thank you very much. Just before the World Cup, I phoned him at the *Telegraph* and a sub-editor told me that he hardly ever came into the office. He worked from home. Sure I was jealous. I was out there swapping banter with undercover jerks while he was guaranteed to be at every football match that counted during the whole of the World Cup. I first met Paul in Poland and he asked about my book, offering me help, so I took him up on the offer. The fans might generalise about the shits in the press box but the Press, like the fans, have their share of good and bad. Paul was one of the good guys.

I asked about the mood in the press camp in relation to England's chances.

'The general consensus is that England will probably win tonight but will meet their nemesis against Argentina.'

I had to admit that this was pretty much the view of the fans except for those who never believed England would ever lose. Most of the veteran fans had memories of travelling out with hope alongside long, stagnant, empty-handed return journeys; and there were more memories of this kind than we cared to admit so we tended to face reality as it arrived. Yet no disaster or débâcle had ever stopped an England fan travelling the next time with the same high expectation level, unlike the Press who always weighed previous failure against future hope.

The Press view of Hoddle was most illuminating.

'The Press are really spitting blood about Hoddle. He was always viewed as a man with his own opinion but as soon as England qualified by drawing with such style in Rome, then he became arrogant and completely convinced of his own superiority. You must balance this with Hoddle's view that the Press have absolutely no part to play in England's ability to win the World Cup. The Press cannot help us win, is his view. He said that in Cannes when we were excluded from the pre-tournament friendly. Respected Pressmen were reduced to asking one of the locals who was inside what the team were and any other titbits. The big writers, the number ones, were reduced to feeding off crumbs in the street.'

I picked up on the phrase 'number ones'.

'Up there in the Press box there is a huge pecking order and the number ones are really where it's at. Nothing is allowed to be written which contradicts the number ones' view. That is why so many papers print the same thing. You [Colin] wouldn't last two minutes up there with your differing view of things. That is why you frightened them so much in Poland. The Rotters are currently up there causing even more consternation because they are fidgety, looking for trouble, filing story after story and charging around like whirling dervishes. But the feeling is that Hoddle has overstepped the mark since he has been here. His belief is that the players should isolate themselves, "cocoon ourselves", to quote him. I mean, we have no divine right to be able to speak to the players but some of the Press have an immense history of friendship. They [Press boys] spend three months ghosting the players' autobiographies or speak to them on the phone for hours doing their columns, listening to their gripes and their wives moaning when their husbands are out late at night; then they are told they can't talk to them. The first thing the players do when they get a paper is look for the transfer news. If they get an inkling that there might be something in it, they phone their favourite journalist who phones around for them, getting confirmation one way or the other. Some players even phone their Press mates for a chat, when things are going badly at their clubs or they have had a big fall-out with their manager.

'I had heard the story that some players have clauses in their contracts which states that if a player comes in on more money than them, the club will match his money – so when it looks as if a highly paid foreign player is being signed, it means a huge pay rise for them too.

'So, holed up in Hotel Hoddle, they phone their agents who pass out the gossip for money or just for badness. Look at the *Sun* today printing tonight's match team. That's the second time they have done it and it came directly from inside the camp via one of the players' agents. Hoddle went ballistic about that. He went around the camp threatening dire consequences if he found out but the players are all in on it. You can only treat grown men like children at a boarding school for so long. The word is that the players have really become close, are a really tight-knit team and that Hoddle's actions are beginning to grate with some of them. The treatment of Beckham is a case in point: he was dropped, then the Press were fed the line that he wasn't focused, then he had to come in front of the cameras and bare his soul as though he were some recovering drug addict in therapy. That caused a rift. There is even talk that John Gorman has had a slight fall-out with Hoddle about the refusal to start with Owen and his treatment of Beckham. The Press have nicknamed the training camp at La Baule, Camp Paranoia; backs against the wall; backs against the sea; razor-wire to the front.'

I asked about Paul Gascoigne. The fans were split 50–50 about Gazza until Toulouse when the Romanian débâcle had changed a lot of minds. The words that Hoddle might have made a mistake regarding Gazza's omission had surfaced since the Toulouse defeat.

'Just before the World Cup started, it looked as if there was going to be a truce and that Hoddle was going to give some access, because of the way he spoke to the Press about Gazza, instead of locking us all out. When Hoddle made the decision to leave Gascoigne at home, he called in the number ones and asked them to sit down and have a chat over a cup of tea. Inside that room with the door shut on the rest of the media, Hoddle opened up to them. He wanted to tell them first so that they would have first bite at the facts of the story. Hoddle explained that in his opinion, Gascoigne had serious fitness problems which he couldn't reconcile or risk. The man was desperately unfit both physically and mentally. True, he had authorised a drinks party the evening before but Gascoigne had gone right over the top. The next morning he went down to the bar, pestering the barman for tins, filling his golf bag up with tins of lager to enable himself to top up on the golf course. He then went out on to the golf course and drank the lager during the round. The England coaching staff all know that Gascoigne is desperately unfit and cannot get himself into the right sort of shape for a tournament such as this. If Gascoigne isn't an alcoholic then he's close to it. At the very least, he is drink-dependant. His choice of advisers and friends like Danny Baker and Chris Evans is, in Hoddle's opinion, a mistake. He wasn't asking for Gascoigne to be a monk – just to get himself fit for the World Cup. It was his last chance on the biggest stage of all yet he had had months to get fit and squandered them.'

The words of Graham Taylor and the refuelling habits alongside Walter Smith's words about Gascoigne having yo-yo weight problems, made me think. I had been a vociferous supporter of the 'take the risk and bring Gazza' school, but now I saw it in a different light. It explained to me why all journalists focused on the fitness side of the story when it broke because that's the way the number ones had decided to write it and nobody was about to criticise that decision when the number ones were all coming out on the side of Hoddle's judgement. But if the number ones thought that it was the start of a new Hoddle era of co-operation, then they were in for a rude awakening.

'Now Hoddle is out here he has cut off access to everybody, even the number ones. No more cosy tea-and-biscuit chats with the number ones. No special briefing. Everybody is reduced to feeding on scraps. He brings in Tony Adams every other day and all he ever does is talk in therapy speak. Especially upset is David Lacey of *The Guardian* who stated that it was like being supplied with one bromide after another. If the England fans had stayed calm in Marseilles then we would have had blank pages.'

I meant to ask him who the six number ones were but I assumed that Lacey was one of them as I remember that Bobby Robson always held a particular regard for Lacey when he was England manager. Then we shook hands and Paul went back to his world while I went for yet another body search and ticket check in my world. To get into my world you just needed a belief in England and a desire to see your emotions put through the wringer at regular intervals. It was nothing complicated because everybody took you at face value and when the whistle went you were the same as the person next to you, united in one aim. One person, one thought, like the Borg in *Star Trek*. I have no idea what it takes to get into Paul's world. Once I wanted to know because I wanted to be there. Every novelist or aspiring football writer like myself wants to be Paul, just as every young player wants to be Gazza or Beckham. I doubt whether I have the self-control needed to make the prodigious step into Paul's world.

Following more chaotic scenes as I was checked and searched again, I walked up the steps and into the stadium at Lens, notwithstanding that this wasn't a football stadium but a simmering furnace where the hopes of a whole nation were as hot as molten steel, bubbling and spitting its white-hot liquid over the top. Inside was a passion I had never experienced before. People talked about the feeling and atmosphere which pervaded Wembley during the European Championships and the night England thrashed Holland 4–1, but this atmosphere was above that, burning with an extraordinary intensity.

Our seats were just behind the England dugout, close enough for the substitutes to hear our comments and close enough for us to hear theirs. The national anthems were played and for the first time, I noticed that the players were subjected to a trial-by-camera as a mobile camera was thrust in their face while they sang or stood to attention. The players only had that for a couple of minutes, however: England fans had put up with it for over a week since Marseilles. A few days later, when Chile played Brazil, the Chilean striker sang his national anthem with such fervour that the cameraman stood there and ignored the other players.

Tonight the overriding feeling for the England team was one of steely concentration. The dream team of England at last included Beckham and young Michael Owen in the starting line-up. If ever two footballers epitomised England, then these two were it. As a nation, we always seem to say that so-and-so will be a great player when they are older while other countries play their best players regardless of age. Now the world would see young Michael Owen from the start. Inside the stadium there was a small knot of Colombians but they were vastly outnumbered by the England fans who amounted to at least 20,000. The singing started from the first minute and continued with a steady beat like a military march.

As I sat down, I remembered the description of Lens Stadium from my guide book. It was like an English ground. When I sat down and saw that I couldn't get my legs behind the plastic seat in front, I realised what the book meant. Like many grounds in England where they have tried to bolt seats on to old terraces, they have failed to give enough leg room for the average adult. The same people had designed the seating layout on nearly every charter flight I have ever travelled on.

From the kick-off, England imposed their rhythm on the match and possessed the better movement. Beckham sprayed the ball around more or less at will with an accuracy which must have frightened any watching Argentinian.

From the packed seats the white army sang.

'It's coming home, It's coming home,
Football's coming home,
Three lions on a shirt.'

Back in England, roads were deserted as the whole nation watched with bated breath. After five minutes the Colombians looked as if they had nothing in the locker which would trouble England except for one shire horse called Freddie Rincón patrolling the midfield: the Colombian brushed Le Saux aside as though he were swatting a fly. Whenever he ran forward it was like an express train on steroids, until, that is, Ince hit the train at full tilt. An unstoppable force met an immovable object. Ince got up, faced him eyeball to eyeball and I think the other fellow blinked. Tension does funny things to people inside a football stadium. It makes me concentrate completely on the match, while it makes others want to sing and shout. Most of my shouts are at players moving around and I have no doubt that Glenn Hoddle does the same. Whilst, like many football fans, I will never have Glenn's tactical nous, I can shout my tactics along with the best of them. Glenn was up doing his arm movements at every turn, twitching his facial muscles, hands on hips, saying the odd word to his coaching staff. On the pitch, Le Saux, coming in from the left side, showed how much tension there was when he hit his shot too wide, creating a whale-call of a groan as it went agonisingly close. A couple of minutes later, with the stadium clock showing 21.20, Owen made a darting run and crossed. From the defensive header the ball came out to Anderton who from my angle seemed to control it and shoot in one moment – it was an exquisite piece of skill. As the ball left his boot the stadium rose half-way then took off into the air as the ball rippled the net. It was as if the lid had been lifted off a pressure cooker. Players ran around jumping and whooping, while the fans responded with a surge of cheering and singing. Now the calypso rhythms could start. Along from me, the man with the giant red rose and World Cup did his own particular war dance which involved running along the stand doing a hop, skip and jump. As an England fan I have to say that the next few minutes were a complete blur as I was up on my feet doing a dance like nearly everybody else. Opposite us, a group danced along the front of the stands in unconfined joy. Then Ince was fouled. Perhaps it was the revenge for the bone-cruncher he'd dished out to Rincón earlier. Up stepped Beckham. It was 30 yards out. A four-man wall lined up.

'Give 'em a special, David,' shouted a man behind me.

The goalie waited. I turned to Terry and remarked that the goalie had given him an awful lot of goal to aim at if he got it up and over, but you still had to have enough talent to be able to do it. The ball left Beckham's boot and the whole stadium was on its feet. The England fans were delirious as a perfect trajectory found the net. Beckham ran towards the England fans. His earnings in the last year had been over £8 million yet in that moment after the goal he was just one of us, shouting and cheering, sharing our thoughts – but he wouldn't risk injury doing the mad dances we were doing. Then, in the stands behind the goal, the conga started spontaneously. Up and down it weaved with a snake-like meander which only those drunk on the drug of football could achieve. Just at that moment, the world through English eyes looked a better place. Those old politicians who send young men to war should become football fans because moments like this might help to prevent people feeling so bitter that they have to send men and women off to kill each other. Whilst the dream is for everybody to speak one language, the language of football *is* universal and Beckham's joy was there for everybody to see. Beckham never spoke one word but for an instant, a whole nation thought the same thought as him, like a giant Uri Geller telepathy experiment. One day big business will try to bottle that moment and sell it back to us like the water which falls from the sky for free, but for now the fans still owned the patent on it. Half-time came and went in a surreal atmosphere, especially when the news came through that Tunisia were leading Romania 1–0.

Perhaps the atmosphere had made me forget the reality of corporate Coupe du Monde which was France '98. The corporate raiders sitting around me had more important things on their minds than the beautiful game, as they all compared betting slips to see how much they had won in their syndicates. Sitting next to me in the stadium was a middle-aged couple from Middlesbrough. The lady looked very smart, almost out of place, in her red dress. She had never been to a match before but her husband had got two tickets and brought her. They must have been the only couple in the stadium who had not had a drink before the match. They had obviously not bothered trying since they had read the paper which said the whole region was a temperance zone.

'That's the difference between the new football fans and veterans. A vet will always find a drink and believes nothing the authorities tell them,' I stated cynically.

She laughed at my stoicism.

In the second half, Colombia made several changes yet England could have scored four more goals. The substitutes had been warming up during the first half and every time they ran past to go behind the goal the fans clapped them and they applauded us back. One Liverpool fan kept shouting at Glenn to get Macca (Steve McManaman) on. Suddenly Macca was stripped down and on the pitch. After five minutes he made a run and lost the ball which came out of play just in front of us. As he ran past the dugout the other subs with whom he had spent the last three matches sitting, made a comment about his run.

'High skill factor,' replied Macca to the subs who jeered him mockingly and, as he ran away grinning, he turned and made a face at them. For me, that showed the strength of spirit in the England camp when players were behaving like mates in a Sunday team having a bit of fun. It was the type of spirit which teams need if they are to win World Cups. I have never felt so confident as I felt at that moment. Later in the second half, Anderton showed the pace and power which exists at this level. He passed to Beckham who chipped it over the full-back. Anderton put five yards in to the full-back at a pace which took your breath away.

Meanwhile, the band behind the goal went through the full repertoire.

The Great Escape with 20,000 fans going 'De Da Da De Da De Da Da Da Da.' Andrew Lloyd Webber would have been appalled at the key and tempo but nobody cared. The band played on in between shouts from England.

> '*Boom Boom Boom Boom INCE.*
> *We're on the ball,*
> *We're on the ball,*
> *We're on the ball.*'

The drumbeat pounded away. This was a drumbeat-led song, not the trumpet-led *Great Escape*.

It was a relentless, monotonous marching tune in an area where just over 80 years ago, young men marched away gloriously to an ignominious end. Now young Englishmen were marching forward to a glorious future.

Then it was time again for the Mexican wave and every other party trick in the fans' repertoire. The band played on; the fans cheered. Late in the game, Sol Campbell went on a mazy dribble, running 70 yards and only being denied by one last-ditch tackle. Had he got past the defender, it would have been one of the great goals. Yet still people looked at English football and reckoned that it lacked technique compared to that of the Continentals. At the final whistle the England fans were still singing. This was about as good as it gets. It would be the springboard into the World Cup proper which would start the following Tuesday with the sudden-death knockout phase. It might have been Croatia in Bordeaux but the Romanians had equalised, so it was confirmed as Argentina in St Etienne.

Carl forgot that he had put his flag on top of the substitutes dugout and went back to retrieve it. The lads sitting at the front had wasted no time in tucking it away in their bag and apologetically got it out of the bag. I think that sitting near McManaman had given them light fingered Scouse tendencies. We streamed out of the ground still dancing and laughing. At the mini-roundabout, the England fans congregated and the TV camera lights shone while the reporters filed their stories or pointed a camera at the fans. One fan tried to shin up the pole to the top but the riot police politely stepped in and pulled him down. In a display of solidarity with the riot police the fans chanted,

'We hate Germans,' which elicited no response; so they sang:

> 'If it wasn't for the English,
> Wasn't for the English,
> Wasn't for the English,
> You'd be Krauts.'

The England fans walked on oblivious to the TV cameras. As we walked past the railway station more riot police were in attendance. I began to think there couldn't be another CRS squad left in the whole of France. TV commentators shouted and their reports while delirious fans made stupid faces at the camera as they tried to talk. Microphones which were thrust into the faces of all the England fans and all they could say was 'brilliant', 'superb' or 'what about Beckham's goal?' All the fans wanted to talk about was the match and the joy they were feeling – and I bet *that* never made the evening news bulletins.

We walked up to our rendezvous point and waited along with hundreds of other England fans. One fan who could see that we were in the know struck up a conversation with us. As we stood waiting, we heard the chant come up the road. I thought I had heard it during the match. It sickens me every time I hear it, and as far as I and many other England fans are concerned, it has no part at any England match.

> 'No *surrender*, No *surrender*,
> No *surrender* to the IRA.'

The mindless boneheads came past us chanting this pathetic refrain. As they got to me I shouted at a couple of them: 'There was a Good Friday peace agreement, so we can drop that song now.'

If they did hear me then they chose to ignore it or perhaps they did not have the intellect to argue with our little group.

Then it was quiet save for the agitated chatter which comes from excited people talking on an adrenaline high.

A girl with a banner saying MANPOWER led a corporate group who followed meekly along behind. They were dressed perfectly correctly and I'm sure they had just had a great time, yet somehow I felt that if the passionate fans who'd just paid a king's ransom for their tickets had not been there, then how much of an atmosphere would there have been in that stadium? Winning the match had been great, yet part of what people were going to talk about was the atmosphere which the fans created. It was an argument for another day; tonight we needed to celebrate. Our little bar in Agny was awaiting our arrival and five minutes later our cab turned up. As he pulled up, chasing England fans tried to get in the cab door.

'We saw it first,' they shouted aggressively.

'We *booked* it first,' Terry pointed out quite forcibly. The taxi driver promised the other waiting fans he would be back in around 20 minutes.

Dave from Southampton jumped in and offered to chip in wherever we were going. He reckoned that wherever we stopped it would be better to try and grab our taxi than take his chance waiting there. If the experience in Toulouse had been anything to go by then he was quite right.

Dave was a time-share salesman in the Czech Republic, who had married a Czech girl and now had two children with her. I had no idea that time-share had got as far as the Czech Republic. It all sounded a bit fishy to me. He told us that his mate was the one with the giant rose and World Cup but that they had lost each other. His other mate had crashed his car but he was unsure where. He had abandoned it, as he had been drinking and didn't want to get nicked before the match.

'So how will you find it?' asked Terry. He didn't answer. I began to think that perhaps he was an undercover policeman. Perhaps his mates had asked someone to tail us after I had taken the rise out of the other two outside the ground. He did seem very vague on points but we didn't really care. We were off to Arras to see if we could find Danny then on to Agny if Danny wasn't there. If Danny was there, Dave was out in the square at Arras because this taxi only carried four passengers.

When we got to Arras there were riot police everywhere with some roads shut. The Irish bar was closed as was every other pub except the okay one. As we pulled up outside the bar in Agny, the locals all started cheering us. The young girls kissed us as we entered the bar as did the bar owner's wife who looked like Pat Butcher in *Eastenders*.

'Bloody hell – if this is what it's like when we win a football match, what must it have been like when we liberated them in the last war?' exclaimed Carl.

Danny was in full flow in the pub and had become a big favourite with the young French girls; too much of a hit, in fact, as the local boyfriends looked all set on filling him in. Thankfully when we arrived he started talking about the football. Danny explained that everything had been fine in Arras until a group of West Ham fans turned up. They had gone into the Okay Pub and in the second half started a fight with some Nottingham Forest fans. That was the signal for bars to shut down and the CRS to turn up in big numbers. I wondered if it was Matty's friends from Toulouse. I thought back to the words of the woman in the tourist shop in the morning and realised why Arras didn't want English football fans staying.

As we sped towards Agny, English words came over the taxi radio.

'Hello, I am standing in the Place de la République. I was promised a taxi in 20 minutes over 40 minutes ago. Where is it?'

'Oui,' came the reply.

The English voice got more exasperated.

'No, I am trying to tell you that I have been waiting here for over 40 minutes and can you tell me when the taxi is going to get here?'

'Oui, oui, oui, monsieur, oui, oui.'

As the English voice got more and more irate the number of 'Ouis' became torrential and the taxi radio controller added more tone to the 'Ouis' extending the last 'Oui' with a flatter tone of delivery. The English voice couldn't discern that he was just having a bit of fun and that he was doing his best to get him a cab as fast as he could. Eventually the English voice lost control.

'I'll give you 'Oui'! I'll wee all over your effin' car and driver when he arrives.'

'Oui, oui, oui, oui oui, oui, oui.'

Despite remembering how desperate we ourselves had become in Toulouse looking for a taxi, we split our sides laughing. Our taxi driver turned to us.

'The Englishman is very unhappy, eh?' He said it with such a straight face that he evidently didn't understand why we laughed so much our sides hurt.

We presented the Agny bar owner with our flag of St George and it took pride of place above his bar along with our two ticket stubs. He was genuinely pleased to see us and even the obligatory French drunk who talks you to death was in attendance. On and on they go, while you stand there and smile and nod your head waiting for them to run out of breath. Yet they never do. They talk to you about an inch from your nose, too, after they've eaten the whole contents of the local garlic factory. They think you are smiling when you're actually grimacing at their breath. At 1 a.m. our friendly bar owner told me he had to shut because the police would be calling round that night.

Back at our gîte, we arrived to find that the group staying opposite us were also England fans and were having a mammoth party. We joined in but were bushwhacked and soon retired, leaving them to it. When I went down in the morning at 9 o'clock one of the fans was fast asleep on the sofa with a beer in one hand and a half-eaten bacon roll in the other. I woke him and he started where he left off by downing his flat beer in one go and munching on the congealed, greasy-bacon sandwich. Some people really know how to celebrate an England win in style . . .

12

Folly and Despair

'When Brazil lose a match the fans are only unhappy for a while because we know we are the best and think we will win next time – but when Argentina lose, it's the end of the world for them because football isn't about joy like it is for us; it's only about winning. So when they lose they have nothing.' – Brazil fan.

'When England lose it's always to the bloody Germans and always on penalties.' – England fan.

'Those people who say that big matches do not revolve around one critical moment are idiots.' – John McEnroe.

On Saturday morning our foursome returned to England while the Worthing Mafia left for St Etienne without Barry and Motty who needed to fly back to see how the renovations were going in their restaurant in Worthing. As businessmen go, they were great football fans. I can't imagine Rupert Murdoch stopping a big takeover because of the World Cup, but then again, he'll never dance the conga in Lens after Beckham scores, will he? The Press, while delighted that England had overcome the group stage, still centred on trouble. *The Times* saw it like this:
'England win marred by 489 arrests.'
It also reported that Paul Dodd had been arrested at Dover after a theft from a ferry. As the man said, 'Loose upstairs'. I remember the Carlisle lads stealing some Burberry hats in Stockholm 18 years previously. 'I bet he never done nuffink.' If he had another brain he'd

still be a half-wit. How *The Times* could equate the dimwits perpetrating these Doddyisms with all England fans continues to remain a mystery.

The early rounds had been pleasant rather than exciting. FIFA, in their obsession to make football a non-contact match, had ensured that there would be goals aplenty as players became frightened to tackle. No match really had you on the edge of your seat although one or two flashes of brilliance had whetted the appetite, but the real World Cup of passion, drama and heartbreak started now.

The second round looked like this:

Sat 27 June	Marseilles 4.30 p.m.	Italy *v* Norway
Sat 27 June	Paris 9 p.m.	Brazil *v* Chile
Sun 28 June	Lens 4.30 p.m.	France *v* Paraguay
Sun 28 June	St Denis 9 p.m.	Nigeria *v* Denmark
Mon 29 June	Montpellier 4.30 p.m.	Germany *v* Mexico
Mon 29 June	Toulouse 9 p.m.	Holland *v* Yugoslavia
Tues 30 June	Bordeaux 4.30 p.m.	Romania *v* Croatia
Tues 30 June	St Etienne 9 p.m.	Argentina *v* England

Along the way, the minnows who had been knocked out had nearly all sacked their managers. In this win-only World Cup it was the only corollary for a national team manager. The only certainty in football management is the sack. The England fans started to watch the second round matches with dedication because they wanted to know who they would be playing. English football fans are a knowledgeable bunch; even when they have consumed the entire contents of a brewery they can still tell you the pertinent facts. Now, to try and prevent stalemate, FIFA had introduced the golden goal. As soon as one team scored in extra time, that was it. It was yet another way to test the frazzled fans' nerve ends.

Brazil impetuously shrugged Chile aside while Italy were just Italy and won 1–0 in the usual flair they bring to World Cups.

France made history of a sort when they won in extra time with a Laurent Blanc golden goal. Their fluid movement in midfield only showed up the problems they were suffering up front without a recognised striker. The French had no passion for the game, for it was the head of the organising committee, Michel Platini, who stated that the French still think a tour by the Bolshoi Ballet is a bigger event than the World Cup. After this win something started stirring in France.

Walter Winterbottom, the first England manager, once said that an African team would one day win the World Cup. At the time it was quite a revolutionary statement, yet when Nigeria won the 1996 Olympic tournament, beating Argentina in the semi-final and coming back from a two-goal deficit against a Brazil side containing Ronaldo and other star players, it didn't look so far-fetched. Lined up against the Nigerians were the Danes, a team that had shocked Europe in 1992 when in the European Championships, they had been recalled from their beach holidays due to the political expulsion of Yugoslavia and carried all before them.

Denmark tore into Nigeria from the start and Nigeria, playing with the ego of Gazza, the technique of a gazelle and the mentality of a Sunday park team, were thrashed 4–1. That was the end of Africa for another four years.

Holland or Yugoslavia would provide the quarter-final opposition to the winners of England's match so the England fans watched for pointers. Yugoslavia looked like a team who started the match with no ambition then downgraded their expectations. The Dutch, on the other hand, are different. The Dutch fans who attend matches dressed in orange from head to toe add colour which provides a spectacular backdrop to the silky first touch which all Dutch players have – especially the Dutch master Bergkamp, who plies his trade with Arsenal. When Holland scored, it looked like a foregone conclusion, but you write off Yugoslavia at your own peril. Holland scored a goal in the last minute but the racial divisions within the team surfaced at the end. As the Dutch goalkeeper ran to congratulate the black goalscorer, Davids, he was told that this was a black celebration only. There then followed the undignified sight of two Dutch players swapping punches. With that sort of team spirit, English fans saw no problems.

Germany were just Germany. Though they were a goal down to Mexico just after half-time and seemingly going nowhere, they surged back to win 2–1. The winner came from their top marksman, Oliver Bierhoff, a man who had outscored Ronaldo in Italy's Premier League, Serie A. When England fans remembered that Ian Rush could go to Italy and muster up only three goals in one season, the Bierhoff tally of 19 looked frightening. The winning goal against Mexico scored by Bierhoff was headed with such power that you felt that the fiendish

Germans might have discovered some special neck exercises when they reunified Germany and opened the vaults to the East German athletics factories which churned out to so many perfect athletes in the days of the Cold War.

The blonde-rinse clones of Romania met their nemesis in Croatia who won 1–0 with a disputed penalty. In truth, Croatia were not troubled by a Romanian team which seemed to have had their Cup Final against the English. None of the previous matches had really set the World Cup alight and apart from the incredible performance by the Danes, nothing really left an indelible memory. Argentina would provide England with a true test of how good we were. In return, England would give the World Cup the best match so far of France '98, one which would make the world talk about English spirit. In the back of everybody's mind was the fateful meeting in 1986 when Maradona famously cheated, yet talk of revenge masked something deeper within the English psyche which seems to make us good losers. Only Hoddle knew how he approached that game in 1986, what his attitude was when he walked on the pitch. His room-mate, Kenny Sansom, certainly knew what the team attitude was: they were frightened before they went out there. Hoddle was at his peak in 1986 and he had the chance to impose his name on the world. Yet his room-mate with whom he had spent three weeks went out to that match with a negative attitude. If you live with someone for three weeks and they are super-confident, that confidence rubs off on you. Here's how Kenny saw it in 1986.

'In the first half we were frightened of them . . . it was we who seemed to be reacting badly . . . had Maradona not been on their side our attitude would have been different; we would have played better and probably won. Amazingly, we played our best football when 2–0 down. The English spirit came pumping through . . . they became frightened of us. Why does it go wrong when it really matters?'

Football at this level is 10 per cent perspiration and 90 per cent inspiration. Now England had the players even if Arsene Wenger, Arsenal manager, thought that England were good at the back and front yet lacking in the middle. Wasn't it the great Johan Cruyff, Mr Football himself, who had stated that England could not win the World Cup because they gave the ball away too much? If Hoddle believed that or still harboured the doubts of '86, then he didn't show it. His press conferences became more about the way England would play and less about Argentina.

The Mayor of St Etienne also brought some common sense into play when he refused to sanction a complete pre-match shutdown of the town. When asked about it he waved journalists away:

'Do you think they will shut down the whole of Paris if England get to the World Cup Final?'

England fans looked at the fixtures. Now the way was clear through to the final. They'd play Holland in the semis on Saturday in Marseilles; Brazil a few days later in an evening semi-final; then on to Paris. All they had to do was beat the Argies. The word *revenge* cropped up quite frequently, although Batistuta, Argentine centre-forward, played it down by stating that politicians started the Falklands War. All footballers saw was the same as everybody else: the return of the coffins.

The first England fans arrived in St Etienne late the next day then spent an enjoyable few days watching the other matches on the big screen, only to learn that when England played the big screen would be switched off.

'If it wasn't so stupid it would be ludicrous. England are considered responsible enough to watch other teams but not England,' wailed the spokesman for the FSA to no avail.

The next morning, Harry emerged from the bus, bleary-eyed. Surveying him was an elderly Frenchman. Harry gave him the thumbs up. One or two French people stood and looked at his bare, tattooed, upper arms. Harry cracked open a bottle of beer. He then gave them a rendition of his latest song. This a cappella karaoke was sung to the tune of 'All Shook Up'.

> *'Well bless my soul what's the matter with me,*
> *I've been drinking lager till a quarter to three,*
> *I've fallen down and I can't get up,*
> *I'm pissed up,*
> *I'm all frogged up.'*

If the English lads thought that tickets were difficult to obtain for the previous matches then it was nothing compared with getting tickets for the match in St Etienne. By the time the morning of the match arrived, prices had reached £350 and were rising. In *The Guardian*, Jim White wrote that the English were on a par with the Japanese when it came to negotiating ticket prices, even if five England fans were chasing every spare ticket. Dave from Southampton summed it all up.

'When you set out you have a limit on how much you want to pay. Once you get here, your resolve goes after about ten minutes. You just want to get inside that ground or else being here counts for nothing – you might as well have stayed at home and cheered in the pub. It gets to the point where you just don't care how much you pay. When that tout shows you the ticket then all your savings for the family holiday go out of the window. That can wait because you've got to have that ticket to make sure you're part of it. Getting that ticket makes it all worthwhile; that's paper sex, that is.'

England shut down early on Tuesday as the whole country waited with bated breath for this match. Hoddle, it seemed, had exorcised his demons and people really began to believe that we could beat Argentina and go on and win it. I had made my decision to go to work then watch it on the TV down the pub. I would be in Marseilles on Saturday for the match versus Holland.

Barry and the lads cruised around St Etienne looking for tickets. Matty and the others had decided that – win or lose – they were going home as they'd had enough of chasing tickets. They were never sure if they would get in and so were unable to enjoy anything in between matches. After two fruitless hours in and around the ground and town, they decided to head out to find a little bar where the two lads among them without tickets would have to watch it. Barry, at last, had lost his nickname 'Lucky Barry'. Never in the history of following football had Barry been unlucky. It was a bad omen. Hadn't Barry booked into a Nice hotel on spec and bumped into Ruud Gullit? Hadn't he cadged tickets for games in Toulouse and Lens? Yet here he was in St Etienne, beaten for the first time. He took a wrong turning down a narrow side street. Coming in the opposite direction was a jeep which pulled right up against the wall to let Barry past. The driver hung his head out of the window.

'Oy, mate, you got any tickets?' asked Barry. The man looked up with a look which said he might have, or at least knew where to go.

Barry shouted back into the bus.

'Lads, quick, jump out, this geezer's got tickets.'

'I'll give you £100 each for them,' shouted Barry animatedly. In a city where the price of a £30 ticket was now closing in on £500, this was akin to unarmed robbery but the French guy opened his glove compartment to present two £50 tickets. At twice face value, that was the bargain of the tournament so far. As they sped off, the bus rocked with joyous laughter. Anybody who has been that close to the edge of despair knows the feeling of sheer joy when against all the odds you get that ticket. Seeing a 100–1 horse romp in doesn't even get close.

By now the value of the Sheffield Wednesday four-piece band was being felt. They were becoming celebrities in their own right. The Football Association saw them as a 12th man and helped them with tickets, which must have been a first for the FA.

The Queen on walkabout the same day was stopped in her tracks by a journalist's question.

'Will you be watching the match tonight, Ma'am?'

'What time is it on?'

'Eight o'clock, ma'am.'

The Queen suddenly realised that she should at least know something about her subjects' passion which even her grandson is nuts about.

'Oh yes, I think one should. It will be difficult though.'

What – the match, or you sitting down to share with your people a defining moment? You and Marie-Antoinette together. Let them eat cake, eh Mrs Windsor?

As kick-off approached in St Etienne, the England band were in full swing and whilst the numbers of England fans inside the stadium would not match the dizzy heights reached in the group matches, the tightly-knit support which was producing a spirit of comradeship was felt in the passionate singing. There was joy in their voices as the song was coming to the fore. Now English song had a spring in its melody.

With close on 30 million people watching the match in England and joining in the singing of the National Anthem, a football match began. Because that's all it was: a match between 22 athletes with the utmost respect for each other. Before the match the players shook hands. The Falklands and the land disputes and the mineral rights of the South Atlantic became utterly irrelevant. If it weren't for politicians, then this is how conflicts could be sorted – in the ultimate field of combat where sportsmanship and honour come to the fore and the only deaths are deaths of dreams.

In the toilets just before the match, two lads looked around furtively. All around them were England fans. They laid out their lines of white powder on the sink. Harry watched them as they continued sniffing to make sure they had taken it up their nostrils.

'You surely don't need extra courage to watch this fixture.'

One of the lads smiled at him: 'Charlie puts a whole new perspective on the match.'

'Yeah,' said the other, 'gives us the added confidence to see it right through to the bitter end.'

Then they were gone, laughing that confident, cocaine-high laugh. 'Bloody Hell,' thought Harry, 'it'll be a sad day when I need a line of cocaine to watch England in the World Cup against Argentina.'

England started tentatively, giving too many silly balls away without getting into the tempo of the Argentinians. Suddenly the ball broke on the left and Le Saux fired it across. In came Shearer and only the width of a boot lace prevented a certain goal.

'We can win this, that was a real chance,' shouted Harry across to Barry. There was no reply as the tension mounted. Then a minute later, disaster struck as a ball was played through. Seaman misjudged the flight and as the Argentinian flicked it forward, he left his leg in and waited for the collision. Two nations held their breath and then one slumped as the referee awarded a penalty for Argentina.

Batistuta stepped up and drilled it to Seaman's right and despite Seaman getting a fist to it, he could only help it into the net. We had a mountain to climb. Nails were being bitten down to the elbow. But England made a comeback. The young hope of this new England surged forward into the box and went down under the slightest of touches. Once more, the referee pointed to the spot.

Shearer stepped up and then there was bedlam. The ball was drilled high to the left, firm and true. England was on the rampage. Cue Owen to start his fast runs. The faces of the Argentina defenders looked panic-stricken like those of people halfway down a giant rollercoaster.

After 16 minutes, people in the Geoffry Guichard stadium were able to say that they saw one of the truly great World Cup goals. It should have been the defining moment of England's World Cup game, a moment which turns good into great and inspires teams to go on and become legends, to get commentators to make statements which people repeat when they play football with their children in years to come.

Michael Owen picked the ball up and accelerated past the bewildered Charmot. Ayala stood up like all good defenders do but the sheer pace meant that Owen was past while his tendons were receiving the brain signal that they needed to respond to the muscle twitch. The goalie moved out a yard to cover the angle, and as he did Owen drilled the ball past him then turned and ran away while the world stood up and applauded. The referee should have stopped the match then to enable the English to catch their breath. They should have awarded the match to England because we had them on the ropes and they were offering no resistance. But football isn't a boxing match; more's the pity. What unfolded then was a superb game of cut and thrust as Argentina strove to claw their way back into the match.

Five minutes before half-time came one of those incidents on which matches are lost, where a two-goal lead takes the heart from certain players, where they cannot raise their game because they have tried their best yet still cannot stop the opposition scoring more. The ball came over and Shearer headed back the perfect ball which saw the Argentine full-back lunge for the clearance in despair. Behind him ran Paul Scholes. The keeper dived as Scholes hit it cleanly. Perhaps he was already doing his victory dance in his mind or took his eye off the ball and lost sight of the goal. Whatever happened, the ball was inches wide. Scholes sank on to the turf holding his head. It was a free shot from a perfectly flighted ball only six yards away and he'd missed. Against a team that had not conceded any goals before tonight, this blunder might prove costly because chances of that quality at this level are few and far between.

Every football fan is superstition personified and there are those who swear that things come in threes while others say you make your own luck. In the few minutes that followed, England didn't heed the words of Mr Cruyff and gave the ball away too easily. On the stroke of half-time, Argentina were awarded a free kick on the edge of the English penalty area. It was in a dangerous position but perhaps what all the English players had on their minds was simply to avoid letting the ball in and then it would be half-time. Fifteen minutes for the Argentinians to allow self-doubt to creep into their minds. England would come out stronger the way they had done in all their previous matches. Four men lined up in that wall. He would shoot, of course, or try to get one player in behind for a header. At the end of the wall was Scholes. To his left was Campbell. Batistuta ran forward, jumped over and López, behind him, put a perfectly weighted pass to Zanetti who had spun off the wall into the space. By the time Campbell reacted, the ball was winging itself past Seaman into the net. The Argentinians had been gifted a get-out-of-jail-free card. In a blur, the half-time whistle could be heard. Dejected, the England players trooped off. Instead of being almost home and dry, they now had to suppress the Argentine machismo once again. You could see by the unrestrained joy from the Argentine bench that they had enjoyed a Great Escape.

England had nothing to fear in the second half. One minute into the half came one of those moments which will live with every Englishman who saw it until the day he dies. People will talk about it the same way they talk about Hurst's '66 goal, the drought of '76 and the death of Princess Diana.

Only David Beckham knew what he was thinking when he lashed out at the Argentinian with his boot as he lay prostrate after a clumsy foul by Simeone. But what did he expect? We were playing a South American team. They weren't going to be anything other than physical and cynical whenever they could get away with it. The red card stunned everybody. With eleven against eleven you always have a chance, especially with England's flair, yet to win this game now would take resilience and a piece of set piece brilliance. No longer would the English forwards be able to set Owen running at the petrified Argentinian defenders. They would have to concentrate their energies on denial of space.

The English fans in the ground responded by putting up a constant wall of sound while the English players built a wall of steel. The Berlin Wall could never prevent people getting through but this English wall with the linchpin Adam in the centre prevented anything from passing. The English, with their backs against the wall, responded with a rearguard action in the best tradition of this country's stoicism under siege.

During the second half, the fact dawned on the English fans in the stadium as well as those at home, that Argentina were not better. We *did* have a chance. Still the England fans sang and clapped. They clapped until their hands were raw and their voices croaked and then they gave more. This was the football equivalent of Scott of the Antarctic and we were all Oates telling the world that we are just having a sing song and we may be singing for some time yet.

Then, with nine minutes to go, the injustice arose which always comes when someone or something is doomed to fail. A corner was drilled in and Shearer jumped with the keeper. It went through, hit Campbell in the face and shot into the net. England players ran from the field dancing unaware that the referee had disallowed it. How could this have happened? Then 90 minutes were up. Sudden death.

'These Argies could play all night and they won't score,' said Harry, almost unaware that it was sudden death. Somewhere in this raging inferno of 30 minutes of sudden death, an Argentinian handballed inside the penalty area, yet the referee chose to miss it or perhaps he genuinely did miss it. Still the fans sang and clapped along: it was the 'Last Night of the Proms' meets an American religious revival meeting.

'We're on the ball,
We're on the ball,
We're on the ball,
We're on the ball,

'Rule Britannia,
Britannia rules the waves,
Britons never never never,
Shall be slaves.'

Back in England giving the expert summary for ITV, Kevin Keegan made a prophetic statement: '99 per cent of these guys are brilliant. They are a credit to their country. I know them because I've met them all.'

Of course he knew them the way we all knew them because their hearts and minds were our hearts and minds. It was the same with the guys in Marseilles, the only difference being that we don't charge up the road of the Vieux Port area. Those guys in Marseilles – even those who'd ended up in prison – were cheering England, being proud of their country.

Then without any fuss the referee signalled an end to the most compelling drama anyone had seen in a long time. The only way to describe it was summed up by the Argentinian Manager, Daniel Passarella: '... but the English, what passion'. From a nation where emotion is inbred from birth and passion permeates the way they live, dance and breathe, it was the greatest compliment he could give us. After 120 minutes of gut-wrenching emotion, the fans had played their part in a democratic way which didn't reflect their own country. This was the fans' football, by the fans, for the fans.

'Oh my God: penalties,' stuttered Harry through clenched teeth, by now the frown lines on his brow slicing deep into his skin. All around him the same words were half-whispered as the fans' worries echoed around the ground. Gradually a whispering hush descended on the place.

England stared into the abyss. Twice before we had stared at this awful spectre and twice the German mentality had prevailed.

Penalties. What a terrible way to end a match. Argentina and England, two great teams, had given everything to produce a spectacle of gladiatorial intensity that left them equal on the scoresheet. Now the rules determined that they must dig deeper within themselves – only the ghosts of those who once lined the streets around Tyburn for public hangings, or today's queues to gain entry to the 'London Dungeon' for enjoyment, only these relish the thought of such encounters. For the rest of us it is Hell, although one cannot imagine that Hell would be so harsh as to raise, then lower, the expectation of the human spirit in such a short space of time.

For some players it becomes too much and they decline to participate because they know that nobody will remember their refusal to take the responsibility of a penalty, only the poor person who accepted and missed. For players and fans it touches the spirit inside, and crushes the emotions. It is so cruel that every time England loses a shootout, the whole country spends days looking at better ways to end matches. Penalties must have been invented by someone who knew about torture – they are the concentration camp of football grounds. Only the very strong, or weak in death, can escape by getting past the wire to leave and not listen to the suffering going on behind them. But even those who walk or turn away come back, drawn to see the final resolution lest events go their way and they then missed the exhilaration that penalty victory brings. I've seen watching fans racked with fear then explode into manic celebration when they've seen victory. Even those who have no passion for football cannot fail to be touched by the drama of it and the incredible pressure which the players must be feeling. One day Arnie Schwarzenegger will make a film in which a robot is produced which feels no emotion when running up to take a penalty. And no football fan will watch the film because they'll know it's an impossibility. From the moment the penalty scenario becomes reality, everybody discovers some form of god or religion, even the staunch disbelievers. Penalty shootouts test the football fan's mettle like nothing else, and especially England fans.

The fans were now powerless. They were entering the land of the lottery. Hoddle was on the pitch pointing at people, getting nods or shakes of the head from his players. The five to ten minutes before it seemed to drag on for hours. Then, as thousands of condemned people sat in silence, the players not taking the penalties sat on one side while the players taking them went into the centre circle. For England, it was Batty, Ince, Merson, Owen and Shearer. Five young men in all their human frailty epitomised by a reformed alcoholic and drug addict in their ranks, yet expected to carry the burden of 50 million lost souls of England on their shoulders. One chance, one shot, one second, death or glory.

Argentina was first to play.
BERTI scored   1–0
Alan Shearer stepped forward.
SHEARER scored   1–1
SHEARER SHEARER SHEARER
Then up stepped a nervous-looking Argentinian. Everybody looked nervous now except Seaman, who just looked focused. Now the fans chanted because we knew we had the power. Hadn't it been our noise that had kept the lads going?

SEAMAN SEAMAN SEAMAN

CRESPO missed   1–1
The England fans went wild. Victory was within our reach Everybody was silent and prayed as the next white shirt came forward. Ince stepped up took a few paces back and hit it to the keeper's left. 'NO NO NO! I don't believe it!' shouted Harry, as he held his head in his hands. The groans could be heard on the other side of the English Channel. Now it was time for the Argentinians to celebrate. England fans started walking out, unable to watch, while others hid their eyes as they sat in their seats. One penalty after another hit the net as everybody scored so the score remained at 4-3 to Argentina.

Up stepped David Batty. It was the last remaining penalty of the regulation five. If he scored, it was the miss of death stage – the death of sudden death – death without glory. He had volunteered to take a penalty because other players hadn't fancied it. The truth is that after their sterling rearguard action, the English looked dead on their feet. How those five had the strength to walk to the penalty spot was beyond me. Batty had the craggy look that many fans have: in another deal of the cards, he could have been sitting in Marseilles with his shirt off and tattooed body, yet now he had to score to keep England in the World Cup. He was in a no-win situation and amongst the 30 million watching, you would have been hard-pressed to find a volunteer to take his place at that second. It wasn't badly struck but when Roa the keeper threw himself in the right direction as soon as the ball left Batty's boot, the dream died. Nobody leaving the stadium that evening blamed Batty because they didn't want that penalty. Beckham had let everybody down by being sent off for his petulance. Beckham would go back with his good looks to his multi-million pound deals and pop star fiancée while we would stagger back to real life like Frankenstein's monster.

Back in England, my nine-year-old son lay on his bed sobbing his heart out, as did millions of others, while the numb England fans left the stadium to a galaxy of camera crews and photographers waiting for one last violent attack. But that story was beyond old; it was ancient about three hours after the first surge in Marseilles, even if, in St Etienne, some local lads and England fans indulged in handbag skirmishes. Everybody just wanted to be somewhere other than France and the thought of fighting was somewhere else – in another world.

One more lonely trudge away from a foreign stadium. Tony Blair talked about how the country could be proud. If Lord Alfred Tennyson had lived today he would have written a piece of glorious poetry which summed up our thoughts because tonight there really was glory in the death of a dream.

'Once more into the valley of despair we go,
Half a pace, half a pace.
Riot police to the left,
Riot police to the right.
Into the depths of sorrow go the ten thousand.'

Harry was not impressed. In the land of Napoleon he'd wanted lucky footballers not gallant ones. 'Just once, just one time we'll get lucky, get a break like other teams,' shouted an upset fan at his mate in a pathetic attempt to make himself feel better.

One more defeat to put in the annals of injustice and for England fans, of course, one more TV camera to stare back at. Yet the TV camera didn't show angry faces, just a defeated, bedraggled army of dejected fans. Barry, Harry, Tids, Motty and the rest of the Worthing Mafia felt anger, however, at the injustice of it all: 2–1 up, we miss a gilt-edged chance, we concede a stupid goal, then Beckham lashes out unnecessarily. After a silent walk back to their van, they had a few beers and retired to bed. Other England fans shuffled around aimlessly for hours, unable to get into the soothing arena of restfulness and accept that their fate was never to see England win the World Cup.

This would go down as a wasted opportunity, especially if Argentina went all the way.

'Even with ten men they couldn't break us down,' remarked Harry ruefully. After the match in the England dressing-room, Adams walked in and told the lads that they couldn't have done any more. He walked over to Beckham and told him he loved him.

When Harry read that he exclaimed: 'I'd like to shake Beckham warmly by the throat.'

But you never see the game as other countries see it; or do you?

'This star is leaving us prematurely after a Titanic match. And who should you curse the most, the referee or fate? There would definitely be headline tears in the tabloid-reading villages of England in any case. Michael Owen is the extraordinary little blonde which England had up its sleeve – with good clean looks, he is the model of a well-behaved young man. He has everything to make his parents, coaches and country proud of him. And while we're at it, everything to restore England's image, which was becoming that of a simple factory of tattooed hooligans and alcoholics.' – *Le Monde*, France.

'This was a game people will remember watching from wherever they were. It was captivating from the very first minute . . . Argentina versus England was the first game of the World Cup that actually got the French excited.' – *The Washington Post*, USA.

'England went out again in the way that haunts them. They lost on penalties . . . after an outstanding game, both in its length and its emotions which were more intense than any other game . . . the players were so similar in skill and approach that the match was only ever going to be resolved by the tiniest of errors.' – *El País*, Spain.

'Argentina deserved to win, and within 90 minutes. Luck and Roa finally gave the win to the team that deserved it.' – *El Sitio*, Argentina.

'England slumped into tears. Argentina's tears were of joy in their luck. The ice-cold gauchos drove the ten, brave Englishmen to misery. This was the first great classic of this World Cup. And what a classic it was!' – *Bild*, Germany.

13

Final Moments

Without England, the World Cup meandered on like a river at the end of a waterfall, the foam still around from the force of what had gone previously yet nothing in it to excite you in the way the water crashing down in torrents does. I watched Italy play France with the French people from the Bookham bistro. To the England fans who'd been in Italia '90 and Rome in October '97 there is an enmity between them and the Italians which words cannot do justice to. When the Italian Di Baggio missed the penalty, the England fans cheered as loudly as the French. After the match, one of the French chefs walked around thanking the English for supporting their country. Why shouldn't I support his country? I had just been made an honoured guest by every French person I had met. Even the bar owners in Toulouse and Lens were up in arms and were threatening to sue because they had been denied, by legal decree, the right to English money and company.

After that win, the French suddenly came to life, surging into the streets and blocking the Champs Elysées as though they had just realised that there really was a World Cup going on. Later, I half-watched the Brazil v Denmark game. The reality was that I was in a state of denial the way I had been in '74, '78 and '94 when England hadn't been there. I just wanted it to end so that I could go back to my domestic football like every other fan and pretend I didn't care about the World Cup. The beautiful game had become just another televised match. The fans with their painted faces all looked the same now as did the sponsors' logos. Their frenetic, happy dancing was dismissed like another frivolous wedding, birdy dance. On the same day the UK corporate hospitality circus moved on to Henley. The same people who had sat in Les Echevins restaurant with us at the start of our adventure were probably drinking champagne by the River Thames, watching amateur athletes rowing their hearts out, my blonde friend no doubt telling stories about how he survived the maelstrom of Marseilles and passing good wine to another erstwhile companion.

Argentina played Holland in Marseilles on a hot Saturday afternoon. While the rest of England enjoyed the spectacle, those who had sampled the delights of travelling to France watched with an aching heart. And every one of them sat in front of the TV telling everybody who'd listen that we should have been there. Now, as Holland and Argentina strove to outdo the contest between England and Argentina to produce the best game of the tournament, the irony of the words of Marc Overmars struck home.

'We'd rather play a good Argentinian team than face England.' It made our exit harder to stomach, thinking that the Dutch would have gone out on that field fearing us.

In the second half with the score at 1–1, a Dutch player was sent off. Argentina then hit the woodwork twice and themselves had a player sent off before the match concluded with a sublime skill which befitted this French World Cup which had so far been lacking in true football drama, England excepted. A 50-yard pass went through to Dennis Bergkamp who controlled it in one movement, flicked it past the Argentinian defender then curled it with the outside of the boot into the top corner. I had seen the same goal scored by Dennis playing for Arsenal in the previous English season. Now, as then, the execution of it, under the noses of defenders considered so good they had been purchased by Italians – something similar to Bill Gates hiring a computer consultant – made me gasp and reaffirmed my faith in inspiration over perspiration. In a World Cup where athleticism had eclipsed skill to the point of exasperation, this touch of class was so refreshing, like seeing a Rembrandt in a room full of modern art, that you sighed with pleasure. The money men can have their slogans –

'It's our religion' – *Sky TV*;

'Eat football, sleep football' – *Coca Cola*

– because they know that what Dennis Bergkamp did was the reason why people do irrational things in an otherwise ordered world. It is the reason, too, why football will overtake the Olympic Games to become the world's greatest money-spinner. In the Olympic 100-metre final, the gun goes off and eight superbly conditioned athletes explode out of the blocks to run for nine to ten seconds and break a tape. You marvel at the speed but you know at the sound of the gun what will happen in ten seconds' time. In the World Cup, on the other hand, there may be nothing happening when suddenly Dennis plucks a ball from the air, recreating every drama and emotion in one second. They can't bottle it, so they do the next best thing and sell everything they can on the back of it.

The shock of the quarter-finals was Germany's humbling by Croatia to the tune of 3–0. My thoughts turned back to Nice station when an England fan, all statistics and Walkman, confidently told me that England would beat Germany in Lyons because the Germans were too old and no team had previously won the World Cup with such an old aggregate-age team. Not only that, but without the injured Sammer, they were flat-footed at the back. I have no doubt that I will bump into my friendly anorak again and he will have the exact reason for England's defeat but he was right about Germany. Maradona, who was not averse to the odd little cheat here and there, stated that the whole World Cup had been set up to enable France to get into the final. How he worked that out all by himself baffled me because when he played football he did or said nothing unless he was surrounded by more advisers than the Royal family. He was even fantasising about coming to work in England. There you have it: a perfect advert that too much cocaine sends you bonkers.

Maradona's sneaking *francodisgustia* came true as France beat Croatia to qualify for the final. In it, they would face Brazil who overcame Holland after another penalty shootout. The whole world was becoming one huge penalty shootout. Somewhere in the marketing stratum an American executive probably sat in his office, watched a penalty shootout then phoned FIFA and tried to sell the idea that the whole preceding two hours could be cancelled and the World Cup just become one huge advert surrounded by mass penalty shootouts. At least there was no way of cheating or conning the referee in this penalty finale; not like the rest of the matches. Poor referees were being conned by players going down as though they had been hit by a Lennox Lewis punch, then looking up and waving their hand at the referee to intimate that he should flourish a card. Seeing Bilic get pushed in the chest by Laurent Blanc and go down holding his face made you want to vomit, because while England fans might well be drunken hooligans, but at least we know that to feign attack is cowardly. When Dennis Bergkamp was quoted as saying that England would have a greater chance of winning the World Cup if we cheated more, something inside me said 'good'. I don't want to win anything unless it is fair and above board. The rest of the world looked at England with its quaint views on fair play like some loved antique, cherished for its past splendour yet non-functional in today's real world. Perhaps England will have to learn to cheat to get on to the podium because nobody remembers a good loser, after all, and cheats do prosper in the modern marketing world of brand winners.

Holland had suffered because of this. In the last minute against Brazil, Van Hooijdonk had gone through and been held back. He threw himself theatrically to the floor, for this was a blatant penalty. He was booked for his trouble and Brazil lived to win on the penalty shootout. Once more, Holland would be the nearly-men. Even from the comfort of my own front room, the injustice shone through. Glenn Hoddle was now picking up lucrative work as a commentator and he, too, spoke of the unfairness. Then we witnessed the tragedy of 10,000 people dressed in orange slipping quietly out of the tradesman's exit.

France and Brazil lined up in the World Cup final in the magnificent Stade de France which brought to mind the words of Charles de Gaulle: 'France cannot be France without grandeur.' In this Stade de France, which cost £330 million, France and Brazil would play out a final which would be lacking because England should have been there. I thought back to all those people with whom I'd laughed and cried over that glorious fortnight. What we wouldn't have given to be walking up those glamorous steps for our date with destiny. As I sat watching, I thought back to that day I longingly stood at the bottom of the steps. One day, one day. Please God, let it be England one day.

Then the Brazil team sheet came out on the screen. Quite what had happened nobody will ever know, but first Ronaldo was out then he was in. Harry, being truly cynical, stated that Nike demanded the inclusion of Ronaldo, especially as France were sponsored by Adidas. Some said that Brazil were half a team or a team demoralised. Later it was stated that Ronaldo had suffered a stress fit – I wonder if we will ever know the truth. The fact of the matter is that Holland had exposed Brazil, and now France, with their fluid midfield movement, controlled the tempo of the ball and therefore the match itself. Zidane scored twice before half-time (were France to have had Shearer in their team, they would have been over the horizon by then). Sitting in the VIP box next to an animated President Chirac was Michel Platini, wearing a French football shirt underneath his designer suit. I somehow couldn't imagine Sir Bobby Charlton doing the same.

In the second half France defended intensely as Brazil came back at them. Denilson – £21 million of touch, pace and more tricks than a circus monkey – even hit the woodwork. France were not to be denied, even if they made it difficult for themselves by having Desailly sent off with nearly 20 minutes to go. In the last minute, Petit slotted an inch-perfect pass into the corner of the net and France went berserk. The French President jumped up in rapture. As the French went to collect the cup, Michel Platini kissed every player and engaged in some deep conversations. Little Deschamps jumped onto the shelf-platform separating the corridor from the VIPs and everybody celebrated as one class – together as one, fan class. Brian Moore, commentating on his last match for ITV, made a barbed comment at the difference in celebrations between France and England, asking why England couldn't do it the French way. Little did he realise that this showed up the fact that French people had instigated a revolution against injustice from the upper classes, as well as revolutionising their training of young footballers, giving them a conveyor belt of talent, while England had committees and sub-committees which only produced an outline report on the best way to progress. As Arsene Wenger had said only a week ago, 'France will win the World Cup because their midfield is so strong and England are maybe ten to fifteen years behind in their development of young players.'

Nobody in England heard because we were still congratulating ourselves on being good losers in a penalty shootout, with Beckham as the villain of the piece. In Japan and South Korea in four years' time, England will be four years older. I doubt whether they'll be wiser because English football is littered with the corpses of honourable, well-intentioned fools. The phrase, 'Lions led by donkeys' was uttered over 70 years ago but it remains relevant today. Our repeated failures reflect our football administrators – and it is the bitter legacy we, the fans, are forced to carry with us.

The Brazilians trooped off, unable to believe they had been second best. The French, well, they were just the French. On a Paris pavement café, an English journalist was charged £5 for a small beer while pretty girls danced past him.

At the final whistle the French went out on to the streets for the biggest party since General de Gaulle walked triumphantly back into Paris after liberation from Germany. Looking at the faces of happiness amid the deafening sound of mass car horns, the true power of football came through. Here was a country with racial strife and division but the French team was only one colour, Les Bleues. The skin colours reflected the widest racial mix of any team ever to win the World Cup – Senegal, New Caledonia, Algeria – they came from all over the world yet because they had played football as a team, nobody saw colour or origin. That night, everybody was French and across France, everybody was just a celebrating football fan. From President Chirac to the lowliest beggar on the Left Bank, they were all equal. France: one nation, one colour, one love – all thanks to football.

14

Back to Blighty

When I watch the newsreels of the columns of refugees fleeing a front-line war zone, one thing always strikes me: there is never any conversation going on. All you see are sad empty faces travelling somewhere. That was what it was like for the England fans heading back to the Channel ports or airports. We had nothing to say, we'd given all we had to give and were leaving with nothing. Some half-wit said that in four years' time Owen would only be 22 and ready to take on the world properly. Harry summed it all up.

'In four years' time I could have four more children, Worthing could be a nuclear reprocessing site and we could be the same as we were in USA '94 after Italia '90 – non bloody qualifiers. Tuesday in St Etienne was our chance and we blew it, big time.'

The good people of fansville were even told, by the same tabloids that told us that James Shayler was a hooligan organiser, that the Queen had shouted her displeasure at the referee while watching the TV when he disallowed the Sol Campbell goal. It was obviously supposed to make us feel better that the Queen had suddenly become a depressed football fan – like one of us. Had England got to the final, would she have jumped up and done a Chirac and pumped the air with her fists? The only emotion we'd get from the Queen at any final is the 'We are the Champions' words to the song.

All the fans felt like it was a job half done, almost as if the English were destined to be glorious failures, as if failure hung well round English necks, unlike the Scots, who went to fail. England went to win yet fate had pre-determined failure. As the lads drove up the ramp for the ferry, the words 'If only' rattled around their brains. Like the mystery of the *Marie Celeste*, we would never know. A little bit of something died in every England fan when Batty missed that penalty. Some, like my boy, cried, while others went on to the streets of public house, big-screen Britannia and fought with their fists against other English people and the police. Great though the game was, it was only a game. The corporate Coupe du Monde looked at lost profit opportunities as unsold merchandising sat on the shelves, while those who really cared just felt the same as they'd felt so many times before.

On the Friday after the St Etienne match, a 42-year-old England fan was arrested after a fight in a hotel. He then confessed to the murder of a man on a train before the Argentina match. He stabbed him to death because the man had smiled at him and he mistook this smile to mean that the other man was Argentinian. I found it difficult to reconcile that report with the wonderful England fans I had just spent two weeks with yet when I thought back to the category N fan that Matty had tangled briefly with in Toulouse it all made sense, and for one brief moment the thought crossed my mind that it might be better if England didn't qualify if it would prevent tragedies like that.

Harry stood on the front of the Dover-bound ferry like Leonardo di Caprio in *Titanic* and looked up disconsolately from his beer as the White Cliffs loomed into sight – always a comforting sight in any other circumstances except when it means defeat for England at football. His thoughts were not on the white limestone, however, but the next World Cup in four years' time. Japan and South Korea would be against him financially then after that it would be politically correct for it to go to South Africa. It would be 12 years before it returned to Europe, probably to Germany. '2010: BLOODY HELL! I'll be middle-aged with a pot belly by then,' he thought.

'That's it now; never again,' he muttered.

'Shut up,' said Barry, 'You know you don't mean it.'

'No, I really mean it this time.'

'Harry, you said that in '82 after Spain, the Germany and Sweden Euros and again after we'd lost in Rotterdam when we were walking back across that field and you stepped in a cow pat. Give that man another beer to cheer him up and shut him up.'

One more beer, one more laugh, one more trip back to Blighty – to the country they love which sometimes disowns them. The boat steamed closer towards Dover. France disappeared into the distance as though dissolving into the clouds. Perhaps he would wake up and this would be a bad dream. England would still be in the World Cup.

Barry, proposing a toast, brought Harry back to reality.

'Here's to a great trip, great football, good company, good laughs and a poor ending.'

'Crap ending,' interrupted Tids.

Barry continued, 'Yeah, extremely crap ending, and . . . ,' he paused long enough to draw breath as they all raised their glasses:

'Never say "never" to an England fan.'